VERONICA

The Lost Years of Jesus

by

Jacelyn Eckman

Published June 2010

Visit the author at

www.JacelynEckman.com

Copyright 2010 Jacelyn Eckman

ISBN: 9781453608395

Printed in the USA

TABLE OF CONTENTS

PART THREE

PART FOUR

GRATITUDE

There have been many, many people along the way who contributed to the realization of this book. Only now am I coming to see the important role they played, often silently, from the background. Sometimes all it took was a small act of kindness, a nod of the head or smile to smooth out the rough parts, to encourage me to stay on the path, to light the way. To each of you, well-known or unnamed stranger, I will be forever grateful.

I would also like to thank those who were involved in bringing this book into print, contributing in varying combinations of inspiration, technical assistance and support: Wayne Wilson, Steve Doolittle, Wally Benson, Sharon Richards, Beth Edmonds, Tracy Edmonds, Patti Ellis, the group of 12, Aleah Fitzgerald, Jan Connell and the many others from 2,000 years ago who are back in my life today.

And, of course, these books would never have been written without the patient, loving and firm guidance of the one we know as Jesus, or Jeshua – my spiritual elder brother, and to the Others who continue to guide us all along the path to our greatness. We pay them back for their selfless service by holding out our hand to others.

* * *

This book is dedicated to all who seek to live by the Law of One, knowing we all come from and are returning to the same Source, called by many Names.

PROLOGUE

This is a true story, drawn from my memories as Veronica, a cousin to Jesus 2000 years ago. I know such a thing may seem hard or even impossible for some of you to believe ... but in many ways my memories of that lifetime are as vivid and real as those of my own childhood in this one. I would ask that you take a step back from your beliefs of what can or cannot be, and approach this story with an open mind and heart.

In the end, it doesn't matter to me personally if you believe this to be a true story or a work of fiction. It embodies my profound love and respect for the one we call Jesus, and all those who follow his teachings, whether Christian, Jewish, or any other, with or without spiritual or religious affiliation. He did, after all, study with the masters of his age, from India and Tibet to Persia and Egypt, bringing together the wisdom of all ages into a singular teaching of love, forgiveness, and recognition of our oneness. The story will speak for itself, challenging each of us to ascend the heights of our personal potential, as we seek to live the principles he offered us.

*

I have been a student of comparative religions and various esoteric traditions for 35 years. I don't recall when I first heard of reincarnation, probably because it seemed so right to me that I naturally integrated it into my mindset. It explained why I often knew certain things with no basis of study or personal experience. A life-long global traveler, I frequently knew what I would find around the next corner in a place I'd never been before, or had fragments or full memories of having lived somewhere I'd not yet visited.

My first unequivocal past-life memory was of a terrible death in my most recent incarnation. I wasn't eager to learn more about other lives and deaths after that, and tried to put it behind me. But memory of that lifetime eventually returned in growing detail, putting the death into a broader perspective which allowed me to learn a great deal about my family of the time, the historical context (World War II in France), and in turn much about myself now. I have never sought out these memories; they simply come to me. I believe that is the way our souls work. When we are ready to know, when we are ready to learn the lessons offered to us in remembering, our soul will bring them to us, either directly or through the assistance of regressionists, or others.

Such things are not for entertainment or vain ideas of *I was so and so* (whether we might be proud or ashamed of the association). Our memories have the potential to help us understand current challenges, providing us the opportunity to heal the past so we might live more fully in the present.

*

Memory of the Veronica lifetime came to me in a most roundabout way. Early in 2003 I began to feel a strong pull to visit the small Bosnian town of Medjugorje. Researching the place I learned that in 1981 "the Blessed Virgin Mary" began appearing to six young Croat children who lived there. Since then it has become a pilgrimage site for millions of Catholics who are devoted to Mary. Though I love travel, I initially resisted the impulse to go there because, frankly, there were *many* more places I'd rather have gone, especially as I had little sense of connection then to Mary, or anything church-related.

But as with anything intrinsic to my soul purpose, it was pointless to resist. Next thing I knew I had a ticket to Budapest, Hungary – a place I *did* want to go. From there I took a train to Rome, ultimately crossing the Adriatic by ferry to Bosnia (seeing lots of wonderful things en route).

I spent several days exploring the ancient sites of Rome, and set a day aside for Vatican City. While walking around the narrow gallery inside the cupola of the dome of St. Peter's

Basilica I fell into a peaceful reverie. And then, without warning, I felt something like a bolt of lightning hit the top of my head. I would have sworn my body had been split in two, leaving me inflamed and trembling. I was unable to understand what had happened, or for a time, even where I was. And when I started coming back to myself, I realized I was crying.

There were a few people standing nearby, but thankfully no one approached as I would have been incapable of speaking. They might have thought I was having some kind of religious experience (given where we were), if they noticed me at all. Eventually my surroundings came back into focus and the weeping stopped. The first thing my eyes lit upon was a small bronze plaque that had the name St. Veronica engraved on it.

I had no idea who Veronica was, but something inside me said I was she – that is, my soul had incarnated as this person called St. Veronica. I saw myself, *felt* myself as this person who I would learn was a contemporary of Jesus 2000 years before. I knew it without any doubt, though for some time I rebelled at the idea I had been *saint anybody*. I was raised a Lutheran and we just didn't go in for saints. In fact I had left the church in my teens, and felt no affinity with anything resembling the tradition I'd been born into. I loved the cathedrals in Europe and sometimes attended masses simply to sit in all that grandeur and beauty. But that was pretty much it.

I had been a psychic child, having many visions and premonitions of things to come. But I had no framework for understanding those things, and closed myself off to them as I approached my teens. My reawakening sense of spirituality began at age 25, focusing first on the Hindu tradition, eventually becoming a teacher of yoga. At 30 I made my first trip to India and spent nearly a year traveling and studying both Hinduism and Buddhism (including several months with the Dalai Lama's teachers in Dharamsala in northern India). My spiritual studies and practice broadened over the years to include Native American/shamanic practices and finally the

Ancient Wisdom teachings reinterpreted in the Theosophical tradition. I honored Jesus as one of many master teachers who have lived and taught in our world, but would not have called myself a Christian -- except in the broadest sense.

But throughout the years there were other forces at work that I didn't recognize until years later. In 1978 I stayed in a Monastery on the Island of Cyprus, spending many delightful hours talking with the Abbot about God. When I left he gave me a letter of introduction to the Patriarch of the Greek Orthodox Church in Jerusalem. (The Patriarch is the equivalent of a Roman Catholic Archbishop.) No doubt this added to the increasing pull I felt to travel to Jerusalem for Easter week, instead of going on to Egypt, for which I was already ticketed. But all flights and commercial ships from the island to Israel were booked until well after Easter.

So I went to the port in hopes of finding a cargo ship that could get me there. A British merchant marine captain cabled his home office seeking permission to take me on board, but the request was denied for insurance purposes. That had been my last hope.

As I left the ship, two crewmen approached suggesting I return that night just before they sailed and they would hide me in the ship owner's cabin (who was not on board at the time). They would wait until the ship was far enough out to sea that it would be uneconomical to return to port once their stowaway was "discovered." The whole thing seemed quite insane, even for a free-wheeling traveler. There were only a few hours remaining to make a decision, and I went off by myself to pray and meditate. I had two choices: to give up my plans to be in Israel for Easter, or to stow away. And so I took my chances. It was nearing midnight when I threw my pack on board and scrambled up the gangplank. I'm sure you can imagine the thoughts that went through my mind over the next couple hours, as I felt the thrust of the engines and the feel of the sea under us.

The crew woke the captain a couple hours later, as planned.

His curses could be heard down the hall, but when I was brought to him he burst out laughing. "Oh, it's *you*. I guess you really *did* want to get to Israel!" Despite the trouble I caused him (the many cables back and forth to the UK) he treated me wonderfully and ordered his crew to do the same. To solve the immigration issue in Israel he signed me on as a member of the ship's crew, librarian to their grand collection of fourteen books, mostly spy novels.

Jerusalem was packed with pilgrims, but I miraculously secured a bed in a convent right on the *Via Dolorosa,* the path Jesus took to carry his cross up to Golgotha. It was a powerful experience being in the middle of thousands of people singing songs of praise as they reenacted the Passion. The following day I took my letter of introduction to the Greek Orthodox Patriarch who invited me to join him Easter Morning at the Church of the Holy Sepulcher for their celebration of the resurrection. It's almost impossible to get anywhere near the church with the massive crowds, yet there I was standing next to the Patriarch just feet away from where many believe Jesus had been entombed after the crucifixion. Any misgivings I had about the religiosity of the event were transcended in the ecstasy of the moment.

I spent three months in Israel, visiting many of the ancient sites, Christian, Jewish and Muslim. I also met and traveled with a group of Old Testament Biblical scholars -- all Catholic monks and priests – into the Sinai Peninsula. Among other things, we climbed up the mountain known as Jebel Musa (Mt. Sinai) in the middle of the night, so that we might be there when the sun rose. (It is believed by many this is the spot where Moses received the Ten Commandments.) I later stayed at their Monastery in Ein Karem -- the town just outside Jerusalem where John the Baptist had lived -- joining them each morning as they gathered to sing the Psalms.

The Greek Patriarch in turn gave me a letter of introduction to the newly installed Pope, John Paul II. When eventually I made it back to Rome this letter secured for me an audience with him (along with a dozen others whom I did not know). When he entered the room he walked right over to me, and taking both my hands in his, spoke to me in English for some time about my spiritual path. There was never a flicker of judgment in his eyes or a shift in his behavior as it became apparent I was not Catholic or in the least mainstream in my beliefs.

There have been many other events that put me in the middle of the Christian (and usually Catholic) world, in the United States and in other countries. Yet the incident in St. Peter's in 2003 was the starting point for my memories of having been incarnated as Veronica: cousin, childhood friend and finally, disciple of Jesus.

Some time after the shock had worn off from this experience, and the actual memories of that lifetime began slowly to intrude upon my consciousness, Jesus came to me one day during a meditation. He asked me to write a book, saying that the writing would draw out many memories which had been hidden away deep in my consciousness. (It is said, and I believe, that we have stored within us memories of everything we have ever known, awareness of every incarnation we have lived, and that nothing is ever lost.) I had already been writing books on other subjects for the previous seven years, ever since leaving the U.S. Diplomatic Corps (where I served as Cultural Attaché). So the idea of writing a book was not foreign to me. But the idea of writing about *Jesus* was something I would have to get used to – since I had not yet reconciled my lack of affinity with the historical Jesus and my new and growing *experience* of him.

In the meantime I tried to learn what I could about Veronica. Research turned up little, and nothing substantive. There is the tradition of someone called Veronica wiping the face of Jesus with her veil as he carried the cross to his own crucifixion. This event is enshrined in the Catholic *Sixth Station of the Cross.* (Remember, this played directly in front of the convent where I stayed during Easter week in Israel.) It is said his image was permanently fixed on the cloth, which became one of the Church's most sacred relics. (The Church hierarchy is by no means in accord as to whether the cloth within St. Peter's is the authentic one, or whether it or even Veronica ever really existed.)

I realized that if I decided to write the book, it would have to be based exclusively on my personal memories, since there was no historical record of the so-called 'lost years' of Jesus. But would anyone believe me? I had no proof of anything, and did not enjoy the thought of being the target of ridicule. Jesus was always there when I came to meditate or felt a need to express my concerns, but he never pushed or pressured me, leaving me to come to my own decision. It was maybe two years later when I finally took up the project. After about a hundred pages he came to me again and said, "Well, that's all very good. But I want you to write *your* story, the story of Veronica and the other women in my life. Without you [the women] there would be no story to tell. Without you, I could never have done what I did. Your story has been lost, and the world has suffered for it. And *my* story is incomplete without that part. Go back, and start again."

I groaned. My first thought was no one would want to read my (Veronica's) story. *It was all about him.* But the more I thought about it, I realized he was right. It certainly wasn't about me personally, about Jacelyn, or even about Veronica. It was, in large part, about the women who comprised the other half of the story.

And so there are two narratives in this book that have been woven together in a single tapestry. It is the story of the women <u>and</u> the story of Jesus, the man, the teacher, the great one who came to show us the way – all told through the eyes of Jesus' cousin, Veronica. It is the story of Miriam* (known to us today as Mary Magdalene), of Veronica's mother Salome and her sister Mary, mother of Jesus. It's the story of our friends and families, of Jewish religion and culture, and the Roman occupation and its terrible consequences in our lives at that time. It is the story of the extraordinary travels Jesus undertook throughout much of the known world to study with the great masters of his time, and of a great and ancient Brotherhood, of which the Essenes were a part – all profoundly influencing the teachings of Jesus. And this, of course, has left its mark on the world we live in today – especially in the West – influencing our world view, from religion to politics to economics to how we care for our planet, even if we do not think of ourselves as Jews, Christians or Muslims.

This book is not channeled. Neither Jesus nor anyone else told me what to say. It is the story of a life remembered: I feel Veronica's feelings, see through her eyes and think her thoughts as clearly as my own. I *relive* what I am writing about, and Jesus is with me, coaxing me, guiding me, helping me to see those events where Veronica was not present, and on rare occasions pointing out inaccuracies.

Getting here has been a most circuitous road: from an ordinary childhood in Minnesota to the nomadic life of a seeker, into the U.S. Diplomatic Corps, and from there – finally – to following the soul impulse to return to my spiritual roots and to write about them. Even then, when I left the government to begin this latest task, I would never have dreamed that I would one day be writing a trilogy** that revolved around the life of Jesus the Nazarene -- Jesus, my beloved cousin and friend.

Jacelyn Rae Eckman

Thanksgiving 2009

* **Miriam of Magdala**, Veronica's dearest friend, is generally known today as Mary Magdalene. Some called her Mary back then, but I have honored her preference for Miriam in these books.

** See the **Afterwords** at the end of the book for more information on the trilogy.

PREFACE

His parents tried to give him a normal life. Everyone knew something of his unusual birth, even the other children. And while I often saw him do marvelous things, I never gave them much thought. He was smarter and more thoughtful than other boys his age, but he could also be just as mischievous.

Jesus was nearly three years older than I. He loved to play, and laughed often. His heart was light and joyful, but he was never frivolous or self-absorbed like the rest of us. I could tell him anything and he would listen thoughtfully. He was a part of every childhood memory, and it never occurred to me that would someday change.

One morning shortly after his thirteenth year he appeared next to me at the well. "You are the only person who can slip up behind me like that," I said, poking his shoulder playfully. But he did not smile, instead taking the pitcher from my hand he pulled me over to a bench to sit next to him.

"Veronica, light of my heart, I have come to say goodbye . . . for a time," he said, gently stroking my long hair, as if to soften the impact.

It was only later, when mother explained to me yet again why he had to leave, that I was able to recall those last words, "for a time." All I knew then was my best friend in the world was leaving me.

"I have to go, to prepare myself. There is much I have to learn now, while there is still time."

"Couldn't you study here?" I implored, having no idea what he was talking about.

"My brothers will watch over you," he said, ignoring my question. "Come, let's go for a walk." Jesus took my hand as we turned up the dusty path, walking beyond the great boulders that marked the edge of the village. He sat me down under the canopy of an ancient olive tree. Bells tinkled in distant hills where sheep grazed. The only other sound was the noxious flies buzzing around my tears.

"Cousin, when will you leave?" I whispered, avoiding his eyes. I was unready to face his scrutiny, embarrassed to be so completely exposed, shocked at the depths of my fear.

"Now. This morning." He reached over and turned my face to him. His eyes searched mine, moving deep inside me. I tried to turn away, but he would not let me. "No, Veronica, you must look at me. Do not close your heart. It was hard enough to say goodbye to mother and father, my brothers and sister, though they have given their blessings. You are sister of my heart, and I ask you also to release me. Then I can go in peace."

I felt my chin tremble in his hand, but still he held me. At last the fear began to subside and I straightened my shoulders. After all, I was ten years old, and would soon be a woman. It was not right for me to act like such a child. And besides, if his family could find it in their hearts to do such a thing, I could as well.

He smiled, and the sun returned to warm my heart.

"I..." My throat tightened and I closed my eyes, gathering my resolve. "You have my blessing as well. But where are you going, and why leave so suddenly?"

He squeezed my hand, and a river of strength filled me. "It is not sudden. I have known for a long time that I would leave, but I did not know when until last night." His eyes, though still looking at me, flickered as they lit upon an unseen thought. "The journey will be long," he sighed.

He enclosed my hands between his own. They were calloused from working the wood with his father, yet gentle as a healer's.

"I will come back to you now and then," he said earnestly, "and share what I have learned. You'll see. It will be as though you are traveling with me. You know how you suddenly know what I am thinking or doing, even though I am somewhere else?" I nodded. "Well, this will be the same. In our thoughts there is no distance."

"I am sure you are right, cousin. But I will miss you. I will think of you everyday until you return."

"Then let us think of each other as we look into the colors of the rising and setting sun. And if any should ask you where Jesus is, just point to the sky, and I will be there."

"Starting tonight?"

"Yes, starting tonight."

He placed my hands back into my own lap, and with a final smile turned and walked away. He walked west, with nothing more that I could see than a flask of water hanging from his shoulder.

I sat awhile in the shade, pondering what life would be like without my constant companion. Of course, I had other friends and family whom I loved, but none could replace him. On the walk home it seemed the flies were buzzing around my insides.

Mother met me at the door and led me to the table. Returning with a plate of my favorite sweet cakes and a cup of goat's milk, she sat down across from me. "Leave your chores," she said. "We will spend the day together, just the two of us. I have some things to tell you."

*

And so he left us for the first of his journeys out into the world. Now and then, with his help, I could actually *see* his surroundings and the events of his life, as if I shared a portion of his travels with him. At other times, he came to me in dreams or moved my heart so I would know how he fared.

To this day I look for him each sunrise, and often find him waiting.

PART ONE

Chapter 1

THE LIGHT EMERGES

Days passed slowly, stretching me until I thought I would break. The winds of loss howled through the empty places I now saw in my world.

"My going was as much for your benefit and that of others, as for my own necessity," Jesus told me later on one of his return visits. When I asked what he meant, he replied, "It is not good to forfeit yourself to another. It places too great a burden on them, and impedes your own growth. Unless people meet halfway, they lose integrity."

I wasn't sure what he meant at the time. I was yet young and my cousin often spoke to me of things beyond my years; understanding would come to me by degrees. It was one of the things I loved about him. He never talked down to me, even when I was very young. Now I think of it, he never really spoke as a child himself, but as one older and wiser than even our elders.

During those first days after his departure Mother stayed

nearby, knowing how deeply I would miss him. In time we

all came to understand the importance of his travels, and a quiet joy took the place of our sadness, sustaining us and, I hope, him.

I thought often about mother's words to me that first day. We set out in the opposite direction from that taken by my cousin, walking in silence. I began to wonder if she would speak at all. So deep was she within her thoughts that despite her usual grace, she stumbled twice, nearly falling.

At last she veered off the path and started up a hill. Near the top was a small cluster of date palms that offered us refuge from the sun. "Come," she said, "sit here beside me." Mother untied the scarf she had twined around her waist, and offered me the morning's bread, dried fruit and a piece of cheese. I passed her my goatskin, the water already warmed with the day's heat.

I had been drifting between pain and emptiness, like a ship listing from side to side. We ate in silence. She leaned forward then and took my hand, holding it to her heart. "My daughter, hearts do not really break. You will find that after the bruising heals, your heart will be as whole as ever it was. Having loved once only makes you better able to love again."

She let go my hand and leaned back, retreating back into her own thoughts. The squat trees huddled close together, and I leaned against another, directly across from her. I wondered how often mother's heart had been bruised, and if my cousin's departure had wounded her as well. And if it had, surely there were others among us who felt the loss. His own mother, Mary.... I hadn't even thought of her! My cheeks burned in silent shame.

"We will all miss him," mother said, as if reading my thoughts. "But there are things you do not know, that might help you understand."

And she fell back into the silence. It was usually easy for me to know what she was thinking, or feeling. But now she walked a road unknown to me, and I could only watch and wait from a distance.

At last she began her story.

"Many years ago – I might have been seven and Mary nine – my sister burst through the door, out of breath. 'Come!' was all she could manage to say. I had been sitting alone, just inside the open door out of the sun's hot reach. The spindle in my hand fell to the floor and rolled away, breaking the thread. Her pale face frightened me, like a bird that had just seen a falcon. 'Please,' she begged, dragging me outside."

Mother's eyes darted back and forth as she relived her past. "Mary took me to this very hill. She had been sitting here when your grandmother came with the news."

Mother cleared her throat, took another sip of water and continued. "You know about Judy's school?" It was more a statement than question. Judy was an old, though still comely woman with long silver braids and a soft smile. The school was in Carmel, overlooking the great sea. I recalled how once when we were preparing dinner mother looked up with a start, and said, 'I must go meet Judy. Finish dinner for me.' And then she was gone, returning after a time with Judy in tow. When I later asked how she had known Judy was on her way, she just waved the question away.

"Yes, I know of the school."

"Mary told me she had been chosen to go live there. Twelve girls were being brought together, for some kind of training. They would study the ancient teachings, in preparation that one among them might serve as an instrument for our Father's son to be born on earth."

I really had no idea what mother was talking about, but did not want to interrupt.

"My heart sank, certain I was being abandoned by my older

sister. I can only imagine the face I made, as she grabbed my arm, laughing. 'Sister, you are coming too!'

"And so we made ready to leave our parents. Once there we all worked hard, but Mary was the most steadfast among us. Some years passed and then one day, while ascending the stairs on the way to devotions, it happened. A brilliant light appeared out of nowhere."

Mother paused, and I waited for her to go on, more engrossed in watching her face than hearing the actual story. I had never seen her so … so … beautiful. She seemed almost to be glowing herself.

"Mary fell to her knees," she whispered, "disappearing into the light, lost to us. When the light faded away Judy and the other instructors moved in, ushering the rest of us back to our rooms. Mary and I shared a room. I feared she would never return, and fell into all the emotions I had worked so hard to bring under control. But at last she stood at the door, looking a little embarrassed.

"'An angel came,' she told me, her eyes glistening. I can still see her, Veronica, as though it were she sitting here with me in your place…." Mother's face held a faraway look as she absentmindedly chewed on a date. "I hardly recognized my sister, so radiant, so composed . . . and will never forget her words. She said 'The light blinded me and I fell to my knees. There was a buzzing sound and out of that words came, and I realized an angel was *speaking* to me. He told me I would conceive and bear a child. An older man had been chosen to share the blessing with me as my husband, a man with inner strength and purity of heart.'

"'I know, I know' Mary said, shaking her head, obviously flustered at the sound of her own words. 'This is why we have all been working so hard, but until now I don't think I really believed the strange prophecy, or that I would have any part in its fulfillment.'"

Mother looked at me. "I confess, Veronica, I was totally

bewildered by what she was saying. All I could think to ask was who she would marry. Her reply shocked me. Joseph. Joseph *was* old, maybe three times my sister's age. Well, they did marry, as you know, and it wasn't long before her rounded stomach began to press against her robes. Once I heard two women at the well talking about how unseemly it was they had not waited a decent time after their betrothal to wed, and wasn't the baby coming a little too quickly. When they realized I had heard them talking, they abruptly left. There was other talk like that, but such people do not warrant consideration. Besides, this was no ordinary wedding, daughter, and no ordinary child.

"I have also heard some say that Mary and Joseph did not lay together as man and wife until after Jesus' birth, that it was the emissary of God who planted the seed. It was not my business to ask Mary if this was true, but it seems to me this would diminish God's children as a whole, and Joseph in particular. He had undergone comparable training to prepare him for his part in this great event. We know that love between man and woman honors the Creator, that God reveals Himself through all acts undertaken in love, especially this most sacred union." Mother's eyes glowed as she said these things, and I saw in them the memory of her own years with my father before his death.

Mother spoke to me of the ancient prophecies then, of a king who would come to liberate us from bondage, a king of the Jews. She talked about the strange birth in a cave in Bethlehem, and how people came to see the infant who was destined to change the world. They came in groups, from nearby and from distant lands. Many had heard the story in their own prophecies, or seen it written in the stars. Some came for a blessing, others to bring gifts or share wisdom, while others were merely curious.

"That child is your cousin, Veronica. His mother, my sister Mary, was indicated by the angel on the stairs, ordained by the Council of Light which guides the great epochal events of human evolution."

Her words sent a shiver up my back. I had heard bits and pieces of this before, but never thought of it as anything but a strange tale that had no bearing on my own life, or my cousin's for that matter.

Mother continued, oblivious to my confusion. "When the wise men of the East came, they added what they knew of the old stories, each from their own land, details we had not heard before. They told us that when the child approached manhood, he would leave his home and family, traveling out into the world to study the ancient mystery teachings held sacred among many peoples. In time, out of fear and ignorance, people will sow chaos, hatred and separation in his name," she said. "But even that will never dilute his essential teaching, which is the brotherhood of mankind. We are here to learn to live together as children of the one Mother-Father God."

Mother and I picked at our lunch as I struggled to reconcile what I knew of my cousin, my friend, with his divine mission.

"Will we ever see him again?" I asked, almost afraid to hear the answer.

"Yes, of course. He will come back, though no one knows when. And then he will go out again, and again. He no longer belongs to us, my dear. His life has grown beyond his family here, beyond our village. He belongs to the world now." I wasn't sure if her words calmed my fears, or stoked them. Of course he never really belonged to us. But that he would never again make Nazareth his home was hard to hear.

Not everyone loved him as we did. Some were glad to see him leave. He showed disdain for those who concealed greed for power or money behind priestly robes or virtuous words. Some called him blasphemous, since his interpretation of Holy Writ often differed from theirs. But then, those of us connected to the Essenes were accustomed to such things, victims of intimidation and persecution ourselves, even by other Jews on occasion. An Essene seeks nothing of personal or political power. We do not want what belongs to others. We want only to be left alone to continue our search for union with God. It is not always easy, but we are taught the only correct response to attacks is to forgive.

My cousin and I frequently spoke of this on the stoop behind his workshop after he'd finished his chores, or on our long walks together. Of course we weren't always engaged in such serious discussion. We were children, after all, who loved playing games and making up stories about what had gone before and what might yet be. And now he was gone. How I would miss his laughter, his gentle voice, his spontaneity, the wild ways of play-acting, his unfathomable imagination....

That evening at sunset I told mother I wanted to take my meditations out under the sky. She nodded, and turned her attention back to my little sister Elizabeth and the family altar. Arriving at the very spot where I last saw my cousin I faced west. Where would he spend his first night out under the stars? I thought of him alone, sleeping on the ground, without blanket or anything to cradle his head, and shuddered. In that same instant I saw his face. And for a brief moment I was sure he saw me too, before his eyes turned away to a place I could not follow.

While I was often able to sense his gaze in the days and years to come, it would be some time before I was trained in the art of soul travel. And more time yet until I learned to move through the realms of light, when I would, in moments of grace, actually be with my cousin in his travels.

Chapter 2

THE GUARDIAN

Though tall as a man, the fine hair upon his face betrayed his youth. Jesus lay asleep on the rocky ground in the predawn chill. His hand brushed across his neck: the tickle shifted, and the hand unconsciously swatted his ear, startling him into wakefulness. Narrow black eyes looked back at him, breath hot on his face. The young man jumped up, not understanding what he saw until he and the creature were both on all fours, nose to nose.

The wild dog bared his teeth, growling, and Jesus whispered something under his breath. The dog's ears fell limp, its tail fanning the air frantically as he nuzzled the man's neck again with a soft whine. A passerby would have thought they were old friends.

He scratched behind the dog's ear and stood up, brushing dust and brambles from his robe. Pulling a cluster of dates out of his sleeve, he wished he had something to offer the poor animal to eat. But the scruffy black creature leaned against his leg, not seeming to mind.

The man relieved himself, and then walked over to a clearing. Slowly, he stretched this way and that, calling spirit back into his body. He drew slow circles with his torso as he had been taught, moving first one direction and then the other. Arms above his head, he arched his back, then coiling like a snake, folded himself in half with hands resting on the earth, nose pressed up against his knees, breathing deeply. After some moments he uncoiled with a soft groan.

He walked up a small rise, squatted, brushed some stones out of the way and sat back down on the ground. Gathering his robes about him, he closed his eyes, hands limp in his lap. The dog, now forgotten, walked a small circle and lay down not far away, keeping his eyes on the man.

"Father, I am here," Jesus said into the wind. "You have called me, and I am here. I have come with nothing to sustain me, and am completely in your hands. Your son has returned to you."

Mind stilled, he was as an infant, newly born. Alone with his God, a soft iridescent light rose up from him.

After a while he stirred, and the dog came over to nuzzle him. His eyes were still trained on some inner vision as he stroked the dog's head. Suddenly the creature yipped and turned as if to run away. Did I do something, he wondered absently? Maybe touched upon a hidden sore? The poor dog can't have fared well out in the desert on his own. But after a few steps, the creature stopped and ran back, yipping again. He repeated his odd behavior until Jesus got up to follow. The skinny creature ran circles around him, jumping into the air excitedly, herding him in a straight line from the meditation spot.

"Where are you taking me?" he asked, laughing at the strange display. Dog and man stepped over a pile of large stones surrounding some thorny shrubs. The dog's nose disappeared into the shrubs, then jerked his head back out, teeth bared. Again his nose disappeared and Jesus thought he heard slurping sounds.

"Water!" he exclaimed aloud. "Water. You have led me to water." He dropped to his knees and carefully parted the shrubs with his hands, cautious of the thorns, and wary of snakes or other small creatures that might be hiding in the shade. The dog paced back and forth, panting excitedly, his muzzle wet.

Jesus scooped a few hands full of the still cool liquid into his mouth. "Ahhhhh," he said savoring the treasure. "Won-der-ful." He pulled a withered skin out from under his robe and filled it, careful not to draw sand or vegetation into the bag. He then bent forward and put his whole face into the water, laughing aloud as he came up for air. The dog jumped back, startled, then lunged forward, tail wagging wildly. Moments later they were both splashing in the water, playing like two puppies in the wet sand, until they were completely soaked. The dog glistened darkly and the man's bronzed hair shone brilliantly in the sun, his arm draped over the dog's back as together they fell into silence.

"Thank you Father for this fine companion, and for the living waters that are always with me."

Nibbling a date, the man stood to resume his westward journey. The dog kept pace with him for a time, then turned off onto his own path.

Chapter 3

ELDER BROTHER

Mother had no sons, until I was much older. My only sister was less than three years old at the time Jesus left on his journey. Though he was my cousin, I considered him my brother. My thoughts often return to him and our lives together, now I am old and living far from all I knew and loved back then.

It seemed he had always been there. My first childhood memory was of waking up one night to find him kneeling over me in the darkness with his enormous eyes. There were earlier fragments of memory that contained snatches of sounds or smells, light or perhaps the outline of a face, but that was the first time I was *aware* of what I saw. His eyes awakened me into the world. I watched him watching me, so serious. And then he smiled, brushed my cheek with his fingertips, and walked away.

It might have been two or three years later when I remember the two of us sitting on the ground in the courtyard, off by ourselves in the cool morning light. I still recall the smells coming from the outdoor kitchen where someone was taking bread out of the large brick oven. Noises from my empty stomach vied with the buzzing flies.

"Father said it is time I begin to learn to work with the wood. I am to go to his shop after lessons tomorrow." He leaned closer to me and whispered. "I will not be so free to spend time with you after this, little sister." He always called me little sister, though it was our mothers who were sisters. Somehow I understood the door into the world of men was opening for him -- though he couldn't have been more than seven.

Just then we were called in to eat. After the blessing began a noisy discussion of how good the food was, how the days were lengthening and the planting was nearly complete, along with the exciting news of the coming visit of our cousin John, and his father, Zacharias. Everyone loved visitors.

Our community was small, perhaps a hundred souls spread among twenty or more households. As in all villages, the well was the center of our communal life. Women fetched water for the home and for washing, men and women alike carried water into nearby fields, and children built walls and houses and tiny people from the mud. And everyone paused in their labors now and then to refresh them selves, and to gossip. It was also the first place strangers stopped when they came among us.

Though it stood in the center, it was not the heart of the village. That would be a small group of buildings to the east. There we met on the Sabbath to honor our Father God, and to pay homage to the Divine Mother throughout the week. Of course, we were taught early on that Father and Mother are but two complementary aspects of the One, each manifesting uniquely in our daily lives, impacting men and women in different ways. Our own earthly fathers and mothers are loved equally by the one God, as are all children. No one is placed above another.

Here too was our school. Several adults served as teachers, each specializing in certain subjects, according to their interests and talents. Both Nathaniel and Martha taught the scriptures and life studies. That's what they called it, though I later learned its name was cosmology, wherein we learned the secrets of life and our world. Nathaniel usually taught the younger children and Martha the older ones when they began to ask their own questions. Jesus had recently been moved to Martha's class. I missed him terribly, and couldn't wait to rejoin him when I was old enough. "Be patient, little sister," he would say, "your time will come." On the days he was not expected at uncle Joseph's workshop, he would join me after class and share their lesson for that day. I didn't always understand, but he was always patient, explaining any questions I could think to ask.

At the time I was sure Jesus liked me best, of all our friends. But in truth he was kind to everyone and there were probably others who had the same high opinion of themselves.

He loved to play, as do all children. At a certain age he began to run off with the other boys, slingshot in hand. He often brought rabbits or the occasional bird to his own household, since it seemed there was always a new brother or sister to feed. But now and then, when he had been particularly successful, he'd bring something to Mother, a special treat for a family with no men to hunt for us.

"I do not like killing these creatures," he told me one day, as I watched him skin a rabbit. Our people depended upon the plant world for most of our food, but supplemented it with small amounts of meat and cheese and goat's milk. "Uncle told me I should go into my heart before I hunt, to ask if any creature would consent to make itself a mark for my stone. And it always seems to me that one or another comes slowly to my path, as if willingly." His father, Joseph, did not hunt. The man he called uncle was Peter, Joseph's foreman. To us all older men were our uncles and the older women our aunts.

Some of the boys said he was the best hunter among them, but he would say he was not really a hunter at all. It was the same when they went to the river to fish. He always came back with the biggest catch. But by the time he left on his first journey he would give up fishing and hunting altogether.

Around the age of ten he began spending more and more time in Joseph's shop. "Father said I should apprentice with each of his workers in turn, as they all have their specialty. He told me I could make my own choice about whom to study with, but I must complete an entire project with each one before going on to the next. I chose Simon first. The corners of his cabinets are joined almost seamlessly. "My project will be a surprise." He grinned, poking me in the ribs, knowing how I loved surprises.

Simon was Nathaniel's eldest son. He had been with Joseph for several years already, and everyone said he would make a fine finish carpenter one day. Joseph employed six men in our own village, and another dozen in his shop in Bethlehem. Only a few of the men in the Bethlehem shop called themselves Essenes. The rest were a mix of Jews whose interests were closer to those of the Pharisees, or the Romans. It was unusual for such men to work together and more so for them to become friends. But some had managed to cross those barriers into friendship, occasionally visiting our village.

Jesus loved the work, but confided once that he did not intend to take over his father's business as a carpenter. "But what will you do?" I asked. He didn't answer. He generally answered most of my questions readily, patiently. But whenever I saw a certain look on his face, I knew not to push. He had his own world, which admitted no one.

One day, I couldn't help myself and asked him, "Where do you go, when you leave me like that?"

His eyes were gentle, though he took some time to answer. "Veronica," he began. He almost never called me by name, and I knew at once he spoke to me from that inner place. "I go to my Father."

"Your father?" I asked, dumb. "But, your father.... "I stopped, realizing he did not mean Joseph, his earthly father. As time passed my cousin spoke more and more often of this Father.

In time his work would be revealed to him, and to the rest of us. As the years passed he shared the unfolding revelation of his sacred journey with those of us closest to him. Even he had to discover strength and understanding in stages, else courage and resolve might have eluded him along the way.

Chapter 4

THE SEPARATION

A blast of hot wind called in the day. On a rise just outside Alexandria a man stood silhouetted by the newly-risen sun. Staring down at the low buildings still shrouded in shadow, Jesus wondered what lay ahead.

Thoughts of home and family barely entered his thoughts these days, though they often stole into his dreams. Some mornings he awakened in a daze, not knowing where he was, or what his purpose might be. This had been one of those mornings, the last of his long journey alone.

His head ached, and he bore a large bruise on his right arm. A boulder had shifted underfoot as he descended a step ravine a day or two before, hurtling him and a flurry of rock into a dry riverbed. He had lost weight too, having eaten little on the long trek to Egypt. Even in the desert there had been game but he no longer had the heart to hunt. Even so, he seldom thought of food. Water seemed to find him, when he was most in need.

And now the journey was over. The woman Sarah, his teacher for the past several years, and Judy, who had recently visited his family from Carmel, each said they had nothing more to teach him. They said he now surpassed them in learning and in wisdom, and was ready for the next stage of his training.

But no one suggested where he should go, or who might guide him toward this goal that people were always hinting about. They would only say he must discover that for himself, when he was ready.

The riddles at turns confused, frustrated, and taunted him. But these people loved him, and would not withhold such information out of unkindness. Perhaps they didn't know, or maybe they were forbidden by the ancient teachings or sacred law to speak what must not be spoken. He knew only that nothing he could say or do elicited more information. And while the days crossing the desert had not increased his understanding, they at least had brought him a peaceful acceptance of the mystery.

A fortnight before his departure, at the full moon, a great light had come upon him during the monthly feasting. It had been some time since he'd experienced the light with such intensity. Slipping away from the others, he went to the place where he always went to commune alone with his Creator. The light increased: blinded, he fell to his knees. Though God does not require His children to approach on their knees, Jesus could not keep to his feet under such power and simply surrendered to it. The light surrounded, and then filled him until he lost sense of himself. It conveyed this message.

"My beloved son, your time approaches. Prepare yourself, for the new moon will illuminate the path laid out for you from the beginning." And then the light dissolved into a heavy darkness that lifted only with the dawn. He sat against the flat rock, tasting the loneliness to come. The vision had not said he must leave his home, but he knew it all the same.

Jesus said nothing of his vision, but began silently turning within, in hopes it would make his going easier to bear. Even as a child, though he played hard with the other children, he sometimes unexpectedly withdrew into a deep silence from which nothing could rouse him until he was ready to return. So no one gave much thought to the cloak of stillness that enveloped him now. Not even his father, Joseph. No one saw, except Mary. She saw, and knew his destiny had come for him, and there was nothing she could do to prevent it. Her maternal instincts would have her protect him with her life, if she could. But her own destiny had brought her to this same point.

So she stood silent vigil with him. And in so doing, the light wordlessly settled upon her as well. Like her son, she had been preparing for this time from her own youth. Judy had been her teacher too. Mary knew that she and her son had chosen their paths long before this little life.

She thought back to the time of preparation among the maidens, when none yet knew who would be the chosen vessel for the coming one. She had studied hard, and followed the strict regime as best she could. Some days she hoped she would be chosen, while other days she prayed it might be anyone but her. When the time came, and the light shown upon her, calling her name, elation and panic set upon her in the same instant. She felt herself still a child, with not only a woman's burden being laid upon her, but the *hope of the world* as well.

She was buoyed by the presence of the Great Ones, and the careful love of an older husband she hardly knew, but whom she grew to love as well. The next two years passed quickly, as in a dream. She bore the child effortlessly, it seemed, though circumstances had been grim. (She only realized when carrying her next two children how much she had truly walked in grace with her firstborn, and what other women endure in childbirth.)

Even the trip into Egypt with her infant son seemed blissful, despite the violence following in their wake. They moved at lightning speed, as if protected by the elements themselves. A cool breeze blew by day, warming at night. Their guides, born to the desert, called it uncanny.

Mary loved Egypt, and would have been happy to stay there if things had been different. However, she was bound not just to her husband, but to the ancient prophecies. While the

Egyptian Hierophants knew the prophecies and were as wise in the secret teachings as her own people, her son must return to be raised within the simmering cauldron of Romans, Greeks, Jews, and the Essenes who were keepers of the mysteries in that part of the world. It was this alchemical mixture that would shatter the outworn vessels, bringing a new world of greater freedom and understanding to all men and women.

As the new moon and the day of departure grew near, Mary's thoughts slipped back and forth between a thoughtful watch over her son's final days with her, and the years of his youth. *The years had gone by too fast*! she thought to herself. *He's too young for such a burden*! she silently shouted to God. But she knew if the decision were hers to make, she would never think him ready to leave. And she did not have the power, or the right to deny him his work.

The night before he planned to leave, Mary drew Jesus aside. He still had said nothing to anyone about what he must do. He especially dreaded leaving his mother, and stiffened at the hand on his shoulder. He knew she was the only one who truly understood what lay ahead. Even his father seemed to have forgotten, chastising him for lingering with the teachers in the temples to discuss holy writ. Joseph was also troubled at his son's angry outburst with the moneychangers, which he said threatened an already difficult association between Essenes and Pharisees. (His father was unaware that it was not Jesus who caused the commotion in the Temple courtyard, where he taken the blame for one of his younger brothers.) But maybe his father remembered the prophecies all too well, and simply hoped to avert the inevitable troubles he knew his son would encounter.

"Son," said Mary in a quiet voice, when they were well away from the house. "I know what you plan to do." The truth is she knew only that he must leave, and was trying hard to be brave when the pain of separation was already bearing down upon her. "I want you to know you have my blessing."

He looked at his mother, grateful for her understanding. For the first time he saw how young she was, hardly more than a maiden herself. He didn't think of his own youth, having only recently crossed the threshold into manhood. He felt old.

After a long moment he embraced her so she would not see his tears. Their shared secret seared their hearts, cauterizing the pain of his departure. He kissed his mother gently on the forehead and returned home, falling into a deep sleep.

*

Another hot blast of air brought Jesus out of his reverie and back to the present. The sun had crept high, illuminating the city below. A noisy tumult echoed up to where he stood, calling him down.

'I see you, standing up there on the cliff,' this strange new land seemed to call out to him. 'Come down to us. It is time.'

He sighed. Though no one had said where he was to go, he had always suspected it would be back to Egypt, the land that had offered him refuge as an infant. It would now offer him refuge of a different sort, as he took the first faltering steps into his new life.

He was ready.

Chapter 5

ALEXANDRIA

Heads turned to watch the man with unusual hair and eyes. Jesus' tattered robes were undecipherable, offering no hint as to his origins. They only knew he was not Egyptian. But strangers come from the sea, not the desert. They come in groups, with family or friends, not alone. Perhaps he was a criminal, who could not risk traveling by ordinary means. Men and women shrank from him while the children grabbed at his fluttering robes as he strode the dusty path, calling out to him in their strange dialect. He heard, understanding little.

His teacher Sarah had obviously known more about what was to come than she let on. Over the previous year she seemed to be encouraging Jesus to recall some of the language he had learned in Egypt as a child. Judy too, during her recent visit recounted memories of being a young novitiate in Alexandria, using entire phrases from the Egyptian in the telling. He thought it odd, since few present knew anything of the language. But they had lived among the educated in Egypt. Those around him now were poor, illiterate people, cast off to survive on the discards of the workers who build the great temples and cities.

Though Egypt had passed its zenith, Rome still sought its

support in military and political matters. The two countries had secretly divided things up between them, agreeing not to intrude upon the other's lands, nor threaten each one's holdings.

Philosophers and elites throughout the world still favored Greece and Egypt over Rome. Greece was thought to have a superior culture while Egypt appeared strong and vibrant, with great cities, awesome temples and pyramids, innumerable slaves and bondsmen. Rome was little more than an enormous garrison, preparing endlessly for war, a people given to excesses of every kind.

Most importantly, Egypt was one of the main caretakers of the ancient wisdom teachings. Acolytes came from every land to study, and the wisest of teachers and counselors traveled between Egypt, Persia and the Brahmanic lands, ensuring that the teachings would not be lost as the world moved toward an increasingly secular age.

In going there Jesus had already passed the first test. No one is told he or she is even a candidate for the higher teachings. They must discover this for themselves, and when they heed the call no one arrives to slap them on the back and congratulate them on their prescience. Instead they are turned out into the world to find their own way to their next teacher. Some falter or grow weak in resolve, reverting to a more mundane, safer life. But a few persevere and after considerable testing awaken a connection with the only Source of clear guidance and true wisdom, which lives within the cave of their own heart. Through consistent use, buoyed by faith, the connection to that Source strengthens. This is the pilgrim's path. No one is exempt from this fate, though it will come to some sooner than others.

Jesus was accustomed to seeking direction within the stillness, in prayer and meditation. The guidance he found there led him into the desert. Some are called to risk their very lives in the quest for wisdom, while the cost for others does not appear so grave. The stakes grow greater along with the capacity to respond. My young cousin was sent into the harshest of environments, challenged to fend for himself while not losing sight of the goal, however dimly perceived.

He had heard fragments of prophecies that some claimed referred to him. He did not know if they were right. He only knew he must follow the silent voice within, or he would not be able to live with himself. The creatures and elements saw to his needs on his trek through the desert, so he did not suffer. And angels came to him in dreams whispering consolation, offering hints about the path that lay ahead.

And now he had come to the great school of Alexandria. Standing on the hilltop Jesus recognized the vast structure below from Judy's description, and made his way directly there. He had not encountered or spoken with anyone since our conversation at the well during the last new moon. Slowing his walk, he noticed the children had disappeared and the road was now deserted. There was no sign, no indication it was a school at all. But he knew he had come to the right place.

Just outside the small gate, he stopped. Though he had seen only small pieces of the wood in his father's shop, he knew the door was made of ebony. His reflection shone back at him from its polished panels, and for a moment he wondered at the man staring back at him. Hardly recognizing himself, he felt far older than his years.

Two young men in sandals and short robes stood at the gate, as if waiting for him. They had watched his approach with even eyes, each one's right arm crossed over his chest in the familiar greeting of the Brotherhood. Jesus' eyes stung as he returned their gesture. One of them stepped forward and pushed the bolt aside, and the other leaned into the door to open it. It led into a courtyard, larger than he would have expected from the modest size of the door that contained it. Perhaps he had come to the back door, he thought absently.

A woman approached, and the two men returned to their post, closing the door behind them. "Welcome," she said, lowering her eyes as she turned and walked away. He followed her into a low building constructed of finely cut stones. A heavy curtain hung across the doorway. Wet with perspiration, he shivered in the cool air.

The woman picked up a pitcher from a low table, poured water into a cup, and handed it to him. The hand that held the cup was smooth, and white. He nodded his thanks, took the cup in both hands and drank it dry. He saw her eyes on his hands, and noticed for the first time his ragged nails, and the dried blood on one hand. He realized too he was dirty, very dirty. Men and women bathed daily and kept their nails clean in his village, no matter what kind of work they did. The reflection at the main gate had revealed tangled hair and disheveled clothes. He felt ashamed.

The woman went out, returning moments later with a clean robe and a plate of dates, laying them on the table. "A bath is being readied," she said, indicating the door she had just used, "and a light meal waits when you have finished." With that, she was gone.

Jesus poured himself another cup of water, drinking it more slowly than the first. His robe was torn in several places. As he pulled it over his head, he saw a cut across his thigh beneath one of the tears. Clouds of dust billowed up as it hit the floor. The cool air caressed his skin. He stood, naked, lost in thought. He had not been indoors for a whole turning of the moon. "How odd," he said aloud.

"What?" a voice replied, from an inner door, just opened. In the semi-shadows he felt suddenly disoriented. "Your bath is ready," the voice said softly, when he did not reply. And the person -- male or female, he did not know – slipped out the door, leaving it slightly ajar.

Jesus filled the cup again and drank his fill, then went out the door. Brilliant sun hit his eyes, and he telescoped his hands over them, looking for the tub. It sat in the center of the courtyard, a great stone creature with feet like an animal. As he approached, he saw the head of a lion had been carved on one end, and a tail curled back into the tub from the other. The stone was veined gold on pale cream, and it gleamed in the bright light, as if alive. He had never seen anything like it. "What perfect workmanship, what power of form" he muttered, not realizing he'd spoken out loud. He had become accustomed to talking to himself during his long days in isolation.

"You have a good eye," a voice came back. Startled, Jesus turned and saw the woman who had earlier visited his room standing on the other side of the tub. Suddenly self conscious, he quickly mounted the small step next the tub, and climbed in. She ducked into his room and brought out the robe she'd left earlier, placing it on a table next to the tub, then set a second cloth on top, "to dry your self before dressing," she said, then disappeared into another building across the way.

"Ahhhhhhhhh," he moaned, sinking into the scented water until it covered his head. Bubbles rose from his mouth, his sigh continuing underwater. Sitting up, he spied a small bowl on the table, filled with a creamy substance.

"It's a kind of soap, used to clean the body." A young man approached and handed him a small, rough but clean cloth.

"Put some on this and mix with the water. It will help clean the sores so there will be no infection."

"Thank you." This was luxury compared to the spare world of the Essenes. They too had a substance made from plants that grew in the mountainous areas for cleansing the hair and body. But it was not as fine as this.

"I have set lunch for you in your room. You have had a tiring journey, and will want to sleep afterward. Khu will come for you at sunset, and bring you to us. We can talk then. Enjoy your bath...there is no hurry." Before Jesus could respond, the young man was gone.

The cuts and sores throbbed in the water, and burned when he rubbed the soap into them. But he knew the man was right. They needed tending to forestall infection, though no doubt this place had unguents for such things. The bath was heavenly, and he dosed in the warm water. Rousing himself, he stepped out of the tub onto the tile floor. A gentle breeze wafted through the courtyard, lifting the fine hairs on his body. Sunlight brought out the fiery bronze that lay hidden within the hair that fell about his shoulders. The drying cloth proved unnecessary.

The sole thought occupying his mind was one of gratitude that he had rightly compassed the guiding hand that brought him to this place. He was filled with a peaceful acceptance, content in the moment.

A gust of hot air reminded him of the robe sitting on the table. Lifting it to the sun he saw it would shield the form beneath, though it weighed next to nothing. It seemed to float above his head before settling slowly to the ground.

Hunger now set upon him and returning to his room he ate the food that had been left there: fresh bread and honey, cheese and a sweet, dense fruit unknown to him. He did not even remember laying down on his cot before falling into a deep dreamless sleep.

Chapter 6

FIRST CONTACT

First light began to push back the darkness in the small room where I slept with my sister. My arms pushed out from the shawl that covered me, and a moan escaped my lips before I even knew it was there – regret at the loss of some sweet dream or other. But I gathered my will and pulled myself up so I could be outside before the sun rose. Slipping into my sandals, I brushed aside the cloth covering the doorway. A chill breeze struck my face as I ran down the path toward *our spot* on the little hill.

Bells tinkled in the distance; the sheep were already about, nibbling at the sparse grass. It would be another unseasonably hot day. Their matted coats begged shearing, but the shepherds hoped to put it off a little longer. There was always the possibility of a late winter storm and a newly-shorn sheep was especially vulnerable.

I stopped for a moment to relieve myself. A group of yearlings scrambled out of my way in the dawning light, bleating loudly. Snores drifted over from under a solitary tree. Peter, son of Reuben, still slept, despite all the noise. Running to the next hilltop, I arrived just as the sun began to move above the haze. My breath slowed, and I stilled my mind. I entertained no doubt our hearts would find a way to connect, no matter where he was.

Standing with eyes closed and hands stretched out in front, palms turned to the heavens, I saw his face before me. It seemed so *real* I had to open my eyes a little to see if hemight actually be there. But he wasn't, of course. Returning to my inner vision, I found him standing in a desolate landscape, with little vegetation and nothing to soothe the eye in any direction. He looked so *alone*, I wanted to weep. But in the next instant his eyes projected the peace of his heart into mine, crowding out my little sadness. The vision faded.

"Father," I said aloud, still facing the sunrise, "help me to accept his going, and to understand your purpose in taking my cherished cousin away from us. "Mother," I went on, breathing deep, "watch over your son. Protect him and see that he has food and water. Keep him warm at night and cool during the day, and help him to know how much he is loved." I didn't know what else to say, and returned to the prayers I had been taught, asking Creator to shed light and love upon all creation, expressing gratitude for the many blessings in my life.

I missed him terribly those first days, but soon grew to accept his absence. My loss was made easier to bear because I truly believed in our connection. Through his eyes I saw places and people I could not have imagined on my own, so different were they from anything I knew. It seemed a small part of me traveled with him.

No one asked where I went so early each morning. I had not spoken to anyone of our final conversation, or our agreement to remember each other at sunrise and sunset. As time went on, I let the sunsets go, as they coincided with our communal gatherings. But I remained faithful to the first light.

Not long after, when up on the hill one sunrise, a terrifying image stole into my thoughts and fear grabbed my heart. The barred teeth of a wild dog were a breath away from my cousin's throat where he lay sleeping. "Cousin!" I shouted into the still air, as if I could warn him. Almost instantly the image shifted, and I saw him playing with the creature as if it were a child of his own kind. He laughed as he scampered about, pretending to paw at the earth.

From that point on, apprehension turned to anticipation. If he could walk so fearlessly, well then, so could I. When later during one of my morning vigils I saw him fall down a steep ravine, I knew the angels cushioned his fall.

Then one night while asleep I dreamt of cool stone buildings that surrounded a quiet courtyard. The buildings shimmered under a new moon, the same sliver of a moon that came the first night my cousin left us. As the dream unfolded Jesus came out of one of the doors and walked toward me where I stood in the center of the courtyard, not far from a *lion*. Starlight reflected off the lion's mane, which I now saw was carved of stone. My cousin explained how the back of the lion could be removed, and the animal filled with warm water for baths.

I was happy for my cousin, realizing I had never before seen him truly content. He'd always had that distant look in his eyes, but in his new home he seemed of a piece, whole, happy.

The next morning I told mother what I had witnessed. She put a hand on each of my shoulders and nearly touching her forehead to mine, looked deeply into my eyes. A smile spread across her face and her eyes glistened. "Come," she said, "let us go to Mary. She will want to hear this."

We grabbed Elizabeth and ran to Mary's house. I loved mother more than ever for believing me, thrilled at our sharing. From that day onward, she treated me differently, almost as a woman, according me a respect and honor usually reserved for equals in age and temperament and training. Looking back, I can see that changed everything for me.

When we got to her house Mary pulled up two stools and we sat down directly across from each other, knee to knee, while I told her of my dream. She looked into my eyes the same way mother had, and I understood she was seeing *with* me. She beamed at the news of her son, of course, but also at what had been my initiation into a profound mystical practice. Such an exchange is possible only where trust exists between two or more people. Their open hearts create one mind, permitting a natural sharing of thought or experience across time and distance, down to the smallest detail.

The three of us laughed and danced around the room like schoolgirls, with Elizabeth looking on in wonderment. There was much to celebrate. Jesus had successfully completed his first trial, and was ready to begin his training as a man. And I had taken the first step in my own awakening. What a day that was!

From then on, my cousin's absence no longer saddened me. I still missed his presence, but there was no longer the deep sense of separation or loss that I'd felt before. In a way, we were closer than ever.

Chapter 7

MARY'S STORY

I am sure my aunt had her own way of knowing how her son fared, without any help from me. But our sharing created a bond among us, the seed of a growing sisterhood. I eventually learned that our deepening connection helped empower the feminine aspect of God to unite with the masculine, inaugurating the beginning of a profound shift in human understanding and way of living in our world.

Words are inadequate to express something like this, and the inner voice will be more eloquent than I. At that early stage none of us was aware of the enormity of the change or our role in it. But in years to come mother and I, and the other women with whom we were building a similar bond of trust, came to serve as support to Mary in difficult times, and friends to share the seasons of her joy.

The three of us continued our ritual of sharing throughout the years Jesus was away. In those early days, mother and I waited until Mary's children were in bed before going to her house. Now and then Joseph joined us while we described what we had seen. But as soon as we finished he would get up, kiss each of us on the forehead and go off to bed without a word. In fact I hardly ever heard him speak, and generally thought him distant though loving. He was much older than my aunt, and there were so many children that he probably took refuge in his alone time.

The three of us sat together sipping a strong, sweet tea one evening. I noticed my aunt and mother looking at each other during an especially long silence, after which mother nodded as if answering an unspoken question. Mary turned to me and asked "How old are you, Veronica?"

"Ten years." I sat up straight hoping to impress her with my maturity, though the truth was my body was still that of a young girl's.

"Ten," she repeated. Her eyes drifted from me to a place in the distance, and I thought she had forgotten me again.

Then: "I was not yet ten when my mother met me at the door one evening," Mary whispered into the silence. "I had been out helping the boys with the shearing and was eager to clean the musky smell out of my hair and clothes. We had recently come back from a trip to Carmel. Mother led me into her bedroom and sat down next to me on the bed." My aunt sighed at the memory. "Mother put her arm around my shoulders and told me it had been decided I was to move to Carmel to attend the new school they were building there, along with a number of other girls my age -- including Salome."

I leaned forward, excited to hear the story from Mary's own lips.

"I had seen the new building being raised behind the school, and while it seemed odd they would need yet another school in such a small town it hadn't occurred to me to ask about it. But before I could say anything about this surprising news, mother got up to start on dinner, saying we would talk later. I ran out the door to find Salome. I will never forget your face, sister," she said, smiling at mother. "You began to weep and would not be comforted, thinking I was going away without you."

Looking back to me, she continued. "Eventually she heard

what I had been trying to tell her, that she was coming too. But until we actually packed our bags and left, I do not think she quite believed me. And even after we arrived at the school, she would not let me out of her sight for a time. It was hard for me too, but she was my little sister and I knew I had to be brave for her.

"Before we left for the school I wondered aloud if we were being punished, and asked if we would ever be able to see our parents again. 'Oh my dear, of course,' our mother replied, rocking me on her lap like a child. 'Your father and I will see you each Sabbath, and you will still share some of your classes with the children in the village. You'll see. You will be happy.' But she sounded uncertain, and I was not comforted by her words. I realized later she really didn't know what would happen. No one did.

"You know Judy," Mary asked me, seeming to change the subject. I nodded. "Judy had just been named to head the school, though she was still young herself. So a council was formed to include her, a rabbi and two others who were considered prophets.

You see, it had been prophesied from ancient times that a great teacher would be born among us. An angel had come to the old rabbi in a dream to say the time had come, and the temple astrologer said the stars were in agreement. The prophets had said this teacher would be born to a maiden chosen of God, one pure of body, mind and heart. But no one knew how to discover the identity of the maiden. And so it was decided to gather together all Jewish girls of a certain age and temperament from Nazareth and a few other villages, and bring them into the temple school. There were twelve of us. We spent nearly five years there, leaving rarely. It became our whole world," she said, her voice trailing into silence.

I wondered what it must have been like for them, trying to imagine how it would feel to be taken from one's family so young, and separated from other children. At least the two sisters had each other.

"We studied the ancient religious texts," my aunt continued, and learned about the prophecies and other branches of learning from a succession of teachers who came to our Carmel from distant places. We became used to seeing people with strange dress and accents, never questioning why they would want to bother with us, a group of young girls. That which had been so strange in the beginning soon became the norm, and I began to imagine I was living an ordinary childhood."

Mother stopped her sister. "Dear child, it's alright," she said, taking my hand in hers. I had not noticed I was trembling. Though mother had told me some of this before, the implications of the story had finally begun to penetrate.

"Well," Mary continued quietly. "One day, as we were on our way to prayer, a brilliant light shone out over the stairs where we walked, and I fell to my knees. All the girls saw the light, but I alone heard the sound."

"What was this sound, auntie?"

"It was like thunder, and it filled me with fear. But then the light took on the form of an angel who led me to the altar at the top of the stairs. The other girls followed us, though none knew what had happened until Judy described the events to them later."

"Judy could see the angel?" I asked.

"Yes. Judy is a seer, and knows and sees many things. Without her, I do not know how I would have been able to ... to do all that was asked of me."

Suddenly everything made sense. I finally understood my cousin, and the occasional taunts he'd endured from some of the older children. And I thought of him now, so far away from everything he knew. I looked across at Mary, sitting there in her blue and white robes, perfectly straight, looking into her own dreams. Even with four children, and a fifth soon to come, she looked hardly older than a girl herself.

"Judy said once that I had been chosen from the beginning. Why, I asked, had the mystery been allowed to continue for so long then? She said there were two reasons. The most important being the development of a cadre of women who would support the revelation to humanity of a Son of God walking among them. This could not be the work of one or two people, but of a large group of men and women. These women, my girlhood friends," said Mary, looking at mother, "were there to lend their support and love in a task that would certainly have overwhelmed me alone. Judy was right. I do not think I could have undertaken the intensive studies and rituals by myself."

"And the other reason?" I asked.

"Well, nothing is ever forced upon us. Nothing. Even though this was God's will and surely that of my own soul self, another would be prepared to take my place should I have chosen to step aside."

"We have work to do at home, Veronica," said mother, giving me a little nudge. "Good night sister." She rose and kissed Mary on the cheek.

"Wait," I said, not wanting to leave just yet. "Does he know this? Does Jesus know of his destiny? Does he know what you did, and why?"

Mary looked at me for what seemed a long time. "Yes and no. I am sure he has heard some things about our special schooling, but we have never discussed it directly. His father and I decided long ago to wait until he came to us with questions which we would answer as forthrightly as we could. You see, even I do not understand or see it all."

"And did he?" I asked, meaning did he come with questions?

Mother sat back down, while I continued to stand, hardly breathing.

"The purpose of his journey is that the Holy Spirit may reveal this to him directly," she replied, not answering my question.

"Joseph and I provided the framework for his understanding, but it is for him to find his own way. We tried to give him a normal childhood, though he was anything but a normal child. You know this as well as anyone, Veronica," she added gently.

Tears welled up and I did not trust my voice to ask further questions, but gave my aunt a hug as we went out into the night.

Chapter 8

A DEATH IN NUBIA

The first light of dawn stole through the slats covering the window, laying down silver threads across his bed. His friend Hebeny purred softly in the darkness. Rather than keeping Jesus awake, the little sounds were a tonic, lulling him into sleep on those nights when too many thoughts crowded his mind.

The two men could not have been more different. Hebeny preferred to shave his head, revealing a broad brow and high forehead framing eyes that shone like obsidian above a flat nose and gleaming teeth. Up till now Jesus had seen few of the dark skinned men from the lands beyond Egypt. But there were many in Alexandria, mostly slaves brought there to help construct the great buildings. Some of these had since been freed, and now stayed on willingly. In Egypt there was work and food. Too many years of drought had brought starvation to their ancestral lands.

The father of his friend was no slave, however. He was chief among his people, and from the stories Hebeny told, a wise leader. His eldest son would succeed him when he died, already serving as his counselor. Hebeny was the second son, sent to Egypt to gain knowledge and acquire wisdom to stand beside his elder brother when he became chief. Two younger sons would inherit land and flocks, but they would never attain the status of the first two. Hebeny cared nothing for status. If he could, he would remain in Egypt's temples, leaving politics and worldly power to others. He loved it there, was happiest when learning the high teachings handed down from Thoth, at home in the temples, tending the gardens. He rarely left, unless Jesus coaxed him out into the streets.

My cousin understood his love of the temples, and disdain for the things that others held so dear. At the same time, Jesus felt drawn to the rivers of people who came through the city. It was sometimes hard for him to reconcile these two opposing forces. He tried not to think of the prophecies that others claimed were his personal destiny. Time would reveal the truth. For now, he focused upon his studies, his chores as an acolyte, and occasional forays into the city.

The two young men were close friends, often discussing their lessons in the darkness of night, when others were asleep. And they talked about their lives before coming to Alexandria.

One day a road-weary messenger arrived at the outer gate asking for Hebeny. His father was dying, the man said. He was needed. "Please come with me," he begged Jesus. "It is a tedious journey. But I would have you meet my family, and it may be awhile before I am again able to return to my homeland."

"I have long wished to see your lands, your people. But would I not be in the way now?" Jesus asked.

"No, you are also my brother. You will be welcomed. Besides, I could use a friend just now."

The next day they boarded a barge on the great river. It was filled with metals from the cold north, and would return laden with exotic woods. There were few passengers. A beaded canopy on the upper deck shaded padded chairs where they might find daytime refuge from the sun, and pads were laid out on deck at night under the stars, for sleeping. The current was against them, and the going slow. Slaves strained under the relentless sun, pulling the craft upriver, stopping only during the worst of the midday heat. Even the greediest captain knows he would lose more in the long run by demanding what could not be given. Tied up to the shore, the air hung heavy about them.

"What troubles you, my friend?" asked Hebeny. Though it was not unusual for Jesus to lapse into long silences, he seemed troubled.

"How can one man *own* another?" he replied in an anguished voice. "It is an abomination."

Hebeny had never considered a world without slavery. The two friends spent much of the rest of their voyage talking about what such a world might look like. "Imagine," whispered the black man, "since most slaves look like me, if there were no slavery, it would mean a fundamental shift in the relationship between dark and light peoples. Night and day would become equal, neither one more important than the other."

"We *are* different, you and I. But this is due to differences in our native lands, our traditions," replied Jesus, "I expect people would retain their unique qualities while meeting on level ground, just as we do in our school. It is true that most slaves in Egypt have black skin, but all alike are enslaved in other lands. To lose a battle results in slavery, as does the inability to repay a debt. Poverty is the biggest slaver of all."

Hebeny looked into the horizon. "Yes, I know. I am ashamed to say that my own people believe they have the right to own slaves, having no moral qualms about it." Brothers under the skin, the two men fell silent, imagining in their hearts a world that might be.

The following dawn Jesus awoke to find Hebeny standing at the ship's rail, a dark figure rimmed in rose and gold, robes billowing about him in the breeze. Muffled noises from the riverbank grew louder as they drew close to shore. What had looked like an encampment from afar burgeoned into a village.

Directly ahead of them, docks appeared out of the shadows and the men below began shouting orders to the slaves on board. The rowing ceased, oars were pulled in out of the way. Someone began throwing thick greasy ropes onto the docks, where they were quickly picked up by other faceless figures. With a sudden jerk, the barge came to a stop.

Covered bullock carts from Hebeny's village stood waiting. The two young men said goodbye to the other passengers, though there had been little opportunity to get to know them during the trip. They carried their few possessions off the barge themselves, there having been no time to procure the customary gifts a happier homecoming would have required. No close friends or family were among the party that met them. They had remained in the village, gathered around their chief. Hebeny was told his father still took breath when the small party had left the previous evening, though he no longer was conscious of his surroundings.

The two men bounced along on piles of ancient fabric covering thick pillows, the carts lurching down the dusty road. Bags of dates and nuts were tucked into the pillows and bladders filled with water had been stashed deep under the rugs to keep them cool in the stifling heat. Hebeny had withdrawn to a place where he held vigil with his father's spirit. As shadows lengthened and the sun neared setting the party approached a fire burning alongside the road. Two slaves approached with steaming pots of stew for the evening meal. They had stayed behind to better serve the son of their chief.

"Father does not like that I ride in the carts like a commoner," Hebeny said, dipping his hand into the bowl for another portion of the thick stew. "But I feel ridiculous being carried in a palanquin like an invalid or an old man."

After dinner they continued their journey. At sunset the two men got out of the cart and walked in the cool air, enjoying the night sounds. When night deepened they climbed back in, nestling down among the pillows to sleep. They arrived at dawn. It was too quiet for such a large village. Jesus glanced at Hebeny. His jaw was set. Silence meant his father yet lived; the ritual mourning had not begun.

A tall, slender but muscular man appeared in front of them. Despite the sad homecoming the two brothers grinned as they embraced, speaking quietly in a tongue unknown to Jesus. When Hebeny stepped back he took his brother's hand and placed it in friend's hand. "May you be as brothers to one another," he said, and they too embraced.

Jesus caught the subtle fragrance of some unknown spice in Arony's densely matted hair. He absently wondered if the scent came from the cooking fires, or something rubbed into the hair itself. The Nubian and the Nazarene stepped back from the embrace, holding each other at arms length in quiet appraisal. Arony flashed Jesus a quick smile, and turned his attention back to his brother.

They walked through the awakening village, Jesus flanked by the two brothers. He could feel people's eyes upon them from the shadows. They reached their destination just as the sun broke the horizon, flashing a golden beam of light across their faces. The rug across the door pulled back, as if on cue, revealing a silent darkness. The two brothers paused just a moment, then disappeared inside. Jesus followed. A long sigh reached across the void, followed by a rasping sound as the unseen form attempted to fill his lungs. He thrashed about, moaning at the effort. As Jesus' eyes adjusted to the sunless room the two brothers took form in front of him from out of the darkness.

Though he had not yet met their mother, his heart went out to her. Death may be a friend to one who suffers, and a gateway unto the higher realms, but it is painful for those left behind. To do nothing is the hardest thing of all. One can only stand with the departing soul as it takes its leave of the increasingly useless form. Chants can help him on his journey, and prayers sent out to summon guides to accompany him. But love is the only necessary component of the process. Love illuminates the darkness.

Jesus had been present at a number of deaths. Most had been family members. And Moeses, one of the elders at the monastery had made his journey into the light only days before they left Alexandria. Jesus didn't know why, but Moeses had asked for him to stand with him at his passing. Others had been there longer and seemed closer to him, but it is always an honor to be at the side of one who bridged the two worlds. This would be the first time, however, that he stood with one whom he had never met, indeed could not even see just then.

Another moan broke the silence, and a voice reached out. "Hebeny, is that you?" Labored breathing filled the air. "Have you come?" So much hope mixed with the pain.

"Yes father, I am here. Arony and I are here for you. We can begin now," he said.

Jesus had no idea what he meant by that, but the shadow that was Arony took his hand and guided him forward to stand with the two brothers at the dying man's side. He did not know the ways of these people or what might be expected of him. And so he turned his thoughts to that still place where all is known. The flame that yet burned in the dying man's heart flickered as if at a slight breeze, and then steadied when Jesus brought his attention to bear upon it. The flame continued to grow until it began to merge with the great light that surrounds and fills all living things – the light that is life itself.

Jesus *merged* with Hebeny's father, losing separate awareness. In that instant he knew him more intimately than one who had lived with him for scores of years. He knew all about him, his life as chief, his love of wife and children, his sense of honor and the weight of responsibility he had long carried. And then he watched it all drop away as the spirit gained ascendance over the man.

Jesus' attention shifted and he saw the two sons, one on either side of the diminishing form, each holding a hand of their beloved father, stroking, encouraging him in his passage with tender words of praise for his long life. And then the moment arrived. A flare went up from the old chief's heart; light surged up his spine to the center of his skull where it paused, pulsating. And then the two fires joined, consolidating the life force...which shot out through the top of his head, rejoining the overshadowing spirit.

He was home. The form lay lifeless, no more vital than a pile of old clothing, waiting to be put away. The light of day still lay beyond the heavy curtain and thick walls, yet Jesus saw it all as if the dark room had been illuminated by ten thousand candles.

At the moment of death, the two brothers fell silent. Arony's hand lay still upon his father's forehead, and Hebeny's rested upon his abdomen. Their chins dropped to their chests, standing in quiet observance of the great man who had been their father.

Then, without any signal that Jesus could see, each took the hand they held and placed it over their father's chest.

The elder brother closed the eyes, kissing each one. Hebeny followed suit. Then Hebeny turned and took Jesus' hand, leading him outside. The sunlight blinded his eyes, stunning his senses. He had so thoroughly immersed himself in the transcendent light of death that for a moment he seemed not to know where he was.

"Thank you," said his friend. "Thank you for your help."

"But I did nothing," Jesus insisted.

"Of course you did. You held the light steady when I began to waver. You brought me back to my purpose."

The three men walked over to a large building and entered an antechamber with two large windows that opened to a refreshing breeze. There the brothers left Jesus to wait while they went in to bring the news of their father's passing to their mother.

Moments later a mournful sound arose from the inner rooms, soon joined by others, men and women, throughout the village. No further messenger was required. All knew their beloved leader was gone, and that a new leader would ascend the throne on the third day.

"Why do they keen when they know that death comes as a friend," Jesus asked later.

"Yes, they know that my father's spirit endures, that his form had outlived its usefulness. But they loved him and will miss his presence. They cry for themselves, not for him. They will welcome my brother as their new leader. They already know and love him, but he will need to earn their respect. It is hard to follow a great chief," he added, almost to himself.

Chapter 9

THE HEAVY HAND OF ROME

Shouts reached them from across the water. Men were running in every direction. Hebeny jumped onto the dock while the barge still moved. Jesus followed slowly while scanning the horizon, detached from the convulsive movement.

They stopped a man running by who told them a ship with Roman soldiers had arrived in Alexandria some days earlier, and that some kind of power struggle was taking place between Augustus' men and one of the local governors. Hebeny and Jesus rarely used animal transport, but there was a taste of urgency in the air so they hired a chariot to carry them swiftly back to the school.

The crowds had thinned and shouts grew distant, but no one stood ready to open the gate at road's end. The horses were frantic from the commotion and the men thought for a moment they might actually crash into the gate, when the horses reared and stopped dead. Dust swirled, wrapping them in the sudden silence, save for the labored breathing of the mares.

Only then did they notice the two strangers standing in the shadows; eyes peering warily out from hooded robes. Several others lingered under the shade of a nearby tree watching them, whispering among themselves.

"It is too quiet," said Jesus. "Someone should have come to open the gate by now. Even if they are at prayers...."

Hebeny banged his fist on the ancient wood while keeping an eye on the strangers. "Open the gate," he shouted. No response. He called out a second time.

"Who is it?" someone whispered from the other side, barely audible.

"I am Hebeny and the Nazarene Jesus is with me. Let us in," he replied in a softer voice, not wishing to add to the fear he heard in that small voice.

Meanwhile Jesus paid the charioteer, who turned the horses and left. He seemed eager to be away. The two men waited anxiously for a response from the boy. Where were the village children who always greeted them with outstretched hands, hoping for a penny or a morsel of food?

Jesus noted the men watching them. Though the brothers of this cloistered community had always stood apart, there existed a reserved friendliness between the two worlds. But they had never seen these men, and that none of them lifted a hand in greeting was disturbing.

At last the metal bolt dropped with a loud clang, and the gate creaked slowly outward. A slightly-built boy stood in front of them, shaking from the effort of opening the door on his own. Or perhaps he trembled for another reason.

They had never seen him before. My cousin took a step forward, right hand on his heart and said, "I am Jesus, and this is Hebeny. We are brothers here, returning from a journey on the river." He wanted nothing more than to inquire as to the cause of all the confusion, and to know why this one small boy had been left to guard the gate. But he waited patiently for the boy to come around on his own.

Hebeny closed the gate, putting distance between themselves

and the outside world. When the boy neither moved nor spoke, Hebeny took his turn. "Please inform Zar we have arrived, and wish to speak with him." Zar was the school's patriarch and while no longer active as teacher or administrator, retained the love and respect of all who knew him. He had become like a father to the two young men.

Still the boy did not move, save for the quiver of his chin. His eyes seemed to be searching for an escape. Jesus knelt on one knee in front of him, taking his hand. "Look at me, son," he said. Though he was not so many years the elder, he was a head taller than the boy, and conveyed a calm wisdom beyond his years. The boy looked into his eyes and his trembling stopped. "Is Zar here? Would you take our message to him?"

Tears welled up in the boy's eyes, but he answered evenly: "Zar is gone, and I do not know if he lives. The older brothers have gone after him, and only the youngest of us remain. We have heard nothing, and it is almost three days now." He seemed to shrink as he spoke.

Jesus stood and looked at Hebeny for a long moment, then turned back to the boy. "What is your name, son?"

"Ishmael."

"Thank you for opening the door for us, Ishmael." The boy's eyes brightened, and he nodded. "Do you know who took Zar, or to where?"

The boy did not immediately speak, shaking his head from side to side. "I think the brothers did not want to worry us," he said finally. "They probably thought they would return that night. But they haven't," he finished, in a quiet voice.

Jesus led Ishmael to their room and sat him down on the edge of his bed, pulling up a chair so the two could sit face to face. Hebeny noticed a few heads at the window and walked over. The boys scattered. He spoke into the sunlight: "It's alright. You may come and hear what is said. There will be no secrets here." Three young boys appeared in the doorway. "My brother and I are weary after our journey. Would one of you bring us water and something to eat? I will make sure you miss nothing of what is said. Bring enough for all of us." He smiled as the smallest of them raised his hand, and disappeared. Though the two men were deeply concerned about what happened in their absence, they were careful not to add their worry to that already burdening the boys.

"Come and join us," Jesus called out in the direction of the window. Three girls and another boy came in and stood with the others just inside the door. He smiled at them and returned his attention to the first lad.

"Three days ago, you said." The boy nodded. "What happened three days ago? Tell us every detail."

The boy's face flushed and he stared at the floor. The other children looked at him, as if expecting to hear a new story. Droning flies circled monotonously. A clatter in the courtyard broke the silence and the small boy appeared in the doorway struggling with a large tray laden with a pitcher of water, two cups, a loaf of bread and bowl of honey. Jesus rushed to his side and took the tray from him, setting it on a nearby table. He turned to the young child and lifted his chin so their eyes would meet, and smiled his thanks. The boy reddened and backed slowly away from him, as if entranced.

My cousin filled a cup with water and handed it to Ishmael. The boy hesitated. Elder brothers did not serve those younger. "Here, drink," he insisted, and the boy took the cup. The simple act seemed to calm him. He finished the water and set the cup back on the tray.

"Three days ago," he began softly. Both men and children inched forward to hear his story. He cleared his voice and started again. "Three days ago in the early morning there was a loud noise outside the gate. One of the brothers called out that no one would be able to open the gate to visitors until after prayers, and to please be patient. His words seemed to anger the men, and they banged even louder, shouting that he would be sorry if he did not open immediately. The brother ignored them and went away."

Ishmael seemed to be thinking about what to say next. Hebeny rose and filled the two water cups, handing one to Jesus.

"We had just begun prayers in the chapel," he went on, "when we heard horses, then other voices and more banging. It was awful! I was afraid," he whispered. "Finally one of the older brothers got up and went to the gate. I could not see who had gotten up in the near darkness. I later learned it was Simon the elder. When the gate opened there was more shouting, the men demanding to see Zar. Most of the brothers argued he should not go, but the shouting just got louder. So a group of ten agreed to accompany the old man to the gate. Some of us," he gestured to the other children, "followed them out. It seemed to me there was only one side to the argument, as Zar's back was to us and we could hear nothing of what he said."

Tears began to run down Ishmael's face. "I do not know what happened next because Mordachai grabbed us and made us go into the kitchen, telling us to stay quiet. I tried to follow him back out, but then *fighting* broke out in the courtyard, and I ran back into the kitchen. I've never seen men fighting before! Well," he continued after a moment, "I don't think the *brothers* were really fighting, but the other men were."

One of the children could be heard sniffing back tears by the doorway, and Hebeny moved over, squatting among them to draw away their fears.

"And then what happened?" Jesus asked.

"It was over quickly. We heard the loud men running out the gate, get on their horses and ride away. Then Mordachai ran into the kitchen and told us the soldiers had taken Zar. He said they would go after them and that since I was the oldest of the younger boys, he was putting me in charge. *Me*!

We have no horses, only a single cart and bull. They brought the bull around and some of the older men got on the cart. The others took off on foot." Ishmael looked up at Jesus, with pleading eyes. "I didn't know what to do. How could I be in charge? I am only ten!"

"That's alright, Ishmael. You have done a fine job. Everyone is safe here. You know the eye of God is upon you, and you are protected. Are you keeping up with your prayers and your times of silence?" All the children nodded. "And your chores as well?"

"Yes," several answered.

"Good. Then you must trust that the Father is watching our brothers, and they will bring Zar safely back to us."

But Jesus was not so sure. Though he sensed no bloodshed, it had been too long since they all left. The children had no idea who the men were, but it seemed the brothers had been drawn into the power struggle between the Egyptians and Romans. The community had always sought to remain apart, especially in political matters. Their survival depended on it. Besides, the ways of the world were of little concern to them. Theirs was an inner path.

"Ishmael, it is time for meditation, is it not? Will you take the younger children?" asked Jesus. The boy nodded, and the children followed him out.

"What now, my friend?" asked Hebeny. "We must do something. The children should not remain alone. Stay here with them, and I will try to find out what has happened."

Dipping into the honey, they ate their bread in silent thoughtfulness. After they finished, Jesus said, "Let us first go into the cave of silence and see if we might learn something there."

They rose and crossed the courtyard, passing through a low door into a hallway that led left and right to the private rooms of the elder brothers. This area was off-limits to neophytes. The two men had only been given access recently. One of the few wood-paneled walls in the school faced them. Hebeny pressed his hand against the wall and slid a hidden door to the side. The two men entered a naturally domed room cut into the hillside, and closed the door behind them.

Without a word each went to his personal space. No one is ever assigned a particular spot, but is drawn there by his or her inner voice. The brothers (and this includes both men and women) only enter the cave when they feel called there, so there are rarely more than one or two inside at a time. The two men sat directly across from each other, Hebeny facing west and Jesus east. The silence held them motionless. After some time and at the precise same moment, they returned to physical awareness.

They rose and returned to their room. Visions are not discussed directly, as such are given to the seeker alone. Only the personal mentor assigned to each student is privy to their visions and dreams, who then points the way to their correct interpretation. Alexandria is known for this facet of its training, and schools and temples the world over recruit from among their students for this reason.

"The captors do not mean to harm Zar," began Hebeny

"Nor had they intended to hold him this long," agreed Jesus. "But someone is ill, dying. And they are biding their time. Our brothers wait with them, keeping vigil. There is honor, of sorts, among the captors. We too should wait."

Hebeny began to pace. "But how? I must do something."

"Go then," said Jesus. "Do as you must. I will remain with the children."

Hebeny went to the pantry, putting together a few things for his brothers and wrapped them in a shawl. He embraced his friend and left without another word.

Ishmael gathered the boys so Jesus could share with them what they had seen. Greatly relieved, they asked when everyone would return. "I do not know when," he answered. "But I know all will return safely."

Hebeny found the group that very night at one of the great

houses near the mouth of the river. When the guards found he had no weapons, they escorted him in to Zar right away. "They have treated me with respect," Zar said. "I am only a tool in their internal fights."

Hebeny and the old man sat and talked. Their captors even served refreshments for the new arrival, to which Hebeny added the food he had brought with him. They probably could even have managed to escape if they'd wanted to, as security was lax. But Zar hoped the whole event might ultimately improve relations between the local government and their community. And so they waited it out together.

"Mancor is the local prelate," explained Zar. "He recently took office from his father, who is old -- older even than I," he grinned, wrinkles spreading across his face. "His father had filled him full of tales about the soldiers coming by boat from Rome, convinced their captain intended to wrest power from him. Somehow Mancor learned that this captain, Arun, is from my own village, and he hoped I might talk him out of violence. I had never met Arun, but know something of his family. It was never Mancor's intention to kidnap me, but his men are mostly rough country people, who found it easier to take me by force rather than explain things. Of course, our brothers thought I was being threatened, and followed us. And now they refuse to leave me while I remain here. It might be funny if it were not so sad.

"These men would harm, even kill each other and many more besides, to protect their imagined honor. I have spoken with Mancor, his father, and also Arun now that his ship is in harbor. And just when I thought it might have been resolved, the old man fell ill and appears to be near death. At first Mancor feared poison, but now he is simply distraught and unable to see clearly to resolve this farce. So we must wait.

"I think they will allow you to leave though. You need to return to the children, and reassure them their world is not coming to an end," he chuckled. I am sorry you had to return to this. How was your trip south?" he asked, changing the subject. "Is your brother now enthroned? Are you content to have returned here instead of remaining to rule alongside your brother? And how is your mother?"

"My heart is glad to have witnessed father's last breath." Hebeny's eyes glistened. "He was ready to leave, though my family will miss him – especially mother. They had been joined at her first blood, and she barely remembers life without him. My brother is now chief. He will be a good one. By our law, mother might have taken the throne herself. But having stood next to father these many years, she is tired, and so has declined the honor." Hebeny's right hand reflexively went to his heart as he spoke, an unconscious gesture of honor and respect.

"I will be glad when my own home – the one here -- is restored to peace and quiet," he said, indirectly answering the old man's question.

Chapter 10

A VISITATION

It was the full moon of the Ram. Unable to sleep I got up and slipped out of the house and walked out into the hills. There was a chill in the air, and I wished I had grabbed a thicker shawl. A shadow moved among the boulders not far in front of me and I felt the hair on my neck stand up. Probably a feral dog, I thought, more afraid of me than I of it, remembering my cousin's encounter in the desert so many moons before.

An uneasy feeling had been stalking me since morning. "We may as well stop for today," Zebedee had said, long before we usually ended our lessons. "You are not here anyway," he added, grinning. "This will be your assignment for tonight. Find out what has captured your thoughts, and discover how to get them back again."

I thought it an odd thing for my old teacher to say. We had been talking about death the last several days, what it is and what it is not. I wondered if his great age helped him stand closer to the precipice of death, enhancing his understanding. He was renowned far beyond our little community for his insights into the matter. Some said he moved between the worlds as effortlessly as we walk through a doorway. I know that many in our world spend their whole lives in fear of what is one of the most natural, and inevitable parts of life. Though none welcome it out of time, my people are taught how to gently and naturally release ourselves from the hold of the physical form when our life purpose has been fulfilled.

I had been privileged to stand vigil with numerous people of our village as they took this step into greater awareness, or – as Zebedee would say – into greater life. It is part of the training of a healer, and thus my training, to accompany the pilgrim through to the final step when the last seed of light departs the physical, setting them free.

I wondered if there was something about these conversations that had disturbed me. Magrit, another of my teachers, said my natural ability to join with the thoughts and feelings of other people sometimes creates confusion in my own mind, when the boundaries between me and them become blurred. When others experience sadness or fear, I often feel it as if it were my own emotion. This is useful if I am attempting to help someone understand and move beyond their distress. But it can be harmful if I forget it isn't my problem to begin with.

"Hello Veronica." A voice rose from the shadows, interrupting my thoughts.

I froze, not from a sense of threat, but because the presence of another person out there in the middle of the night had been so unexpected.

"Who is it?" I asked.

The shadow took form, and I felt my heart leap. "Stay!" he said, as I tried to rush to him. "I am not here in the flesh, and physical contact would cause … *this* to dissipate."

I trembled at the effort to restrain myself. *Oh, my dear cousin…. It has been so long!* I shouted silently, unable to find my voice.

"Yes," he said, reading my thoughts. "The moon comes and goes, yet it retains its form. But we change with the seasons, do we not? You are no longer a child, but I sense the inner change to be the greater."

When he left our village Jesus said I would find him in the sunrises and sunsets, and I did look for him in the shifting colors of dawn and dusk. In the early days I thought I might actually see him on the horizon or in the sky, and I conjured up images of him walking toward me. When I learned that the interface between day and night creates a space for thought to travel unimpeded, that was when the real visions began in earnest.

But this time . . . he was here, *actually here*. A gust of wind blew against a tear that ran down my face, and I noticed I was cold. "Cousin..." and my voice stuck in my throat. He smiled, eyes older, shoulders broader than they had been when he left.

"Veronica, it is a joy to see you. Come, let us move to the rocks so you can sit and find shelter from the wind." He instinctively reached his hand out to me as we rounded a cluster of olive trees, but quickly pulled it back and shrugged.

I noticed a silvery glow around his form, like that of the moon, and looked down at my own hand and up to the hillside. The same shimmer rose from everything I saw. I opened my mouth to ask him about the phenomenon when he interrupted my thoughts.

"I am so glad you got my message."

"Message?"

"For the past two days I have been sending you thoughts to meet me here at the full moon, impressing it upon your inner mind." He grinned at my reaction. "Yes, I know the sending and receiving of telepathic messages is part of your training, but it is one thing to do so when you are expecting such transmissions to take place, and quite another to succeed when it is unexpected. Zebedee will be proud of you.

"What you see before you is my light body, projected through the power of mind from where my body sits in meditation in

Alexandria," he began. "You see, this body of light comes from the realm that bridges the world of form with the world of spirit. It is where our souls dwell. You have heard these things before, cousin, but now it is more than just words. I myself am only beginning to remember this ancient art of soul travel. We must eventually learn to -- not only project the light body – but be able to hold the form true so it can interact physically with others in the flesh." He paused. "Even now, not everyone would be able to see me. The shepherds on the next hill would see nothing at all, nor would they be able to hear my words. That you can is a result of your training with Zebedee."

"I have missed you so!" I blurted out, embarrassed at my childish emotions. He was little older than I, but right now he seemed a world apart, older than anyone I knew, even my old teacher.

Suddenly I felt myself grow very still, as if we were sitting at the center of an enormous, deep sea. I felt the power of the sea as though it was my power, felt stretched and compressed at the same time, heavy yet weightless. The shimmering light that surrounded us began to expand, and it grew until there was only light without shadow. Within the light each question that floated up from the layers of my mind was instantly answered – including questions I didn't even know I had. The light held the wisdom of the ages. And then . . . the questions themselves disappeared.

A bridge appeared that stretched from the Infinite back to the finite mind where my cousin and I sat among the rocks, and I understood that he had opened the door for me to where he lived, bringing me in to be with him. Even in the deepest of meditations I had never felt such peace.

The next time Jesus spoke it was in the language of the soul. "Now you *know*. This is the Father's realm. People like to speak of a place far off where the righteous go to be with their God, a place of privilege, reserved for a few. Some say entrance can be bought by tithing or good works. But that is not so. My Father, our Father holds the door open for all. It is the only place where we are reconciled with ourselves, with Him. It is our true home, the beginning and the end of reality. Leaving *here* is the illusion. It is where you and I meet in the sunrises and sunsets."

All my thoughts dissolved, questions disappeared, expectations, desires returned to their source and were no more. I was content. No, far more than that, I was filled with bliss and boundless joy.

How much time elapsed, I cannot say. But eventually I looked once again through my own eyes to see my cousin standing before me. "Come, let us walk," he said. I stood and followed, but it took awhile before I could actually feel my feet upon the path.

"I missed you too," he said, grinning in my direction. And there was my young cousin again, barely into manhood. "The Red Land has become home to me, and I have learned so much there. Of my lessons, I can say little, but they are not so different from your own. Eventually you will be guided through the same studies, the same path of initiation as I. In your own time," he trailed off.

I was to learn in future encounters that my cousin slipped in and out of this world that we all know so well, and call our physical home. His world was expanding rapidly, to encompass what the rest of us can barely imagine.

"You seem happy: will you remain there long?" I realized with a start that I too spoke with the inner voice, leaving the silence of the night undisturbed.

Ignoring my question, he said: "Ask Zebedee sometime if he would agree to walk with you into the past. The past is a forever time that exists within you, where your memories survive of days lived long ago. You, Zebedee and I, along with others we know, spent much time together in Egypt, learning the mysteries of life, walking the path of death with awareness, awakening the inner fire."

"Ah, so that explains my recent studies with Zebedee, my

disquietude, and your appearance just now!"

Jesus laughed. "You see, we meet often in the Father's house beyond our waking, and set up the circumstances of our lives that bring us to awareness of the whole of existence. *Life* is forever, without beginning or end, just as it moves into the above and below, bridging realms beyond what we can see or hear or feel. This world that you see is set into motion from this higher realm, and you are there taking part in the planning. But you are only now beginning to remember the part you played in its design!" He laughed as at a joke, carefree as a child.

And then a furrow appeared between his brows, something I had never seen before.

"Alexandria is no longer at peace," he said, his voice lowered. The muscles in his jaw tightened. "There are more of them all the time. They land at night, when few are about to see them, dispersing by morning's light."

"Who?" I ventured.

"Oh, sorry, the Romans."

I wondered at the tension in his face.

"There is no good reason for them to be in Alexandria in such numbers. It can only be a reflection of trouble in Rome. They have begun to see enemies everywhere, and are striking out before they can be struck. Anyway, that is how it seems to me. Egypt seems to have made its peace with their occupation. There is little hunger there, and opportunity abounds." He stopped and turned to me. "Just days ago they breached the gate to our school in the early morning hours, and spirited Zar away from his prayers."

I gasped. Even here we had heard of Zar. He was one of the most respected, most honored of men.

"I was away with my friend Hebeny when it happened, and upon our return we found only the youngest children had been left behind. The others had all gone in search of Zar. The governor had already called for reinforcements, certain the Romans were plotting his death. He then had Zar brought to him in hopes the old priest would somehow diffuse the threat – which really existed only in the governor's mind. But the implication of involving our community against their will is unsettling.

"No, there is a new and deadly pattern behind this fear. Not a week goes by without a man or two from the city disappearing into darkness, not to be seen again. People are afraid. Zar was returned to us unharmed," he added, "but the community was shaken. Especially the children."

I did not know what to think. There was an uneasy truce between our own people and the Romans, but I had never heard of them bothering one of the elders, let alone someone of Zar's stature.

"You know the men and women in the Brotherhood cannot and will not become involved, not in Egypt or anywhere else. This is the main reason Zar asked us to forget the incident when some of the younger brothers wanted to register a complaint with Pharaoh. It would only have brought further reprisals."

He stopped then, and turned to me. "I must leave soon."

"Can you not stay longer? It has been so long . . . ."

"No, that is not what I meant. I must leave Alexandria. It is rumored the soldiers are looking for two men from Judea. I am sure it is not I, but old Zar has been hinting for some time now that the next phase of my learning will be on different soil. I had hoped my path would bring me back through here, so I could see my family first." His throat tightened around his words, and for a moment the boy in him stood before me.

I did not like the sound of that. "Your mother . . . we all would have you spend some time with us." I felt myself flush, and was glad for the darkness of night.

"No. I will travel by ship to the far end of the sea, and from there go overland to Kushan." The light around him had begun to flicker. "I must go now."

"I know." Kushan – so far, I thought to myself. "Do you have a message for Mary? When will I see you again?"

"Tell her of our exchange. It will please her, though she knows of my comings and goings."

He had grown quiet and I thought he must have forgotten my other question. I waited, savoring our final moments together.

"I do not know when we will see each other again," he finally answered. "Only the Father knows such things. I am always there in the interlude between light and dark."

And then he was gone.

I sat awhile, alone under the moon. I still did not really understand my cousin's path, only that he had been called

to something extraordinary. The prophecies hinted of suffering, but it was primarily a path of healing and the power for good.

The wind gathered and I pulled the shawl over my head. The world had come back for me, and I turned toward home, thinking about what I would tell Zebedee in the morning.

Chapter 11

THE HALLS OF AMENTI

"No two people walk the same path, yet there is but one path."

Jesus had heard this said many times during his early years, and later heard Zar use the same words when welcoming new students. Such arcane-sounding statements are no mere word tricks to confuse neophytes, or to put them in awe of their elders. Words represent or transmit truths to the seeker, but only direct experience can bring the truth home. When statements seem contradictory, students are forced to probe more deeply into what their teachers are saying to them. Even when it appears obvious, there are often multiple layers of meaning.

For example, everyone knows that a sarcophagus is the final resting place of the body when the *ka*, or eternal spirit has passed on to new life. Because of this many people assume the granite sarcophagus inside the great pyramid at Giza is a tomb for the deceased – probably a Pharaoh or another in the royal family. Of course this is not true.

Unless a student evidences a probing mind that will not be satisfied with superficial answers, he or she will never arrive at the deeper truth. The teacher will thank the student for having completed a certain amount of time in his school, and send him home to pursue a life more suited to his capacities. Such a one would never find his way into the school at Alexandria, which admits only the most gifted.

Most of the teachers and philosophers who came through Nazareth during our youth were either coming from or going to Alexandria. They represented the epitome of learning in the world. The wisest among them understood their limitations, refrained from dogma and encouraged their students to challenge their teachings. And so it was that some of these came to my cousin -- though he was far their junior in years -- to stand within his light and learn from him.

Of course he still required counsel and guidance through the initiatory process that lay ahead. Every soul on earth is both student and teacher, serving in this dual capacity for most of their incarnations, finally making their way from ignorance to enlightenment.

As he prepared to leave Alexandria, Jesus knew yet another circle was coming to a close. Life moves thus, in circles without end. The completion of one round of experience signals the beginning of another, tracking the spiraling serpent through the worlds.

Experiences, lessons and learnings are like knots along the thread of life. Where the knots overlap there are moments of insight and leaps of perception, bringing growth. Along the way we begin to see we are both child and adult, wise and foolish, good and bad, everything rolled into one. In recognizing this, we are able to merge these contradictions within ourselves, and find that all conflict, confusion and yes, all paradox are resolved.

A man approached Jesus late one afternoon near the stone lion. My cousin had noticed the man inside the school walls several times before this, but they had never met. No one else was around at the time. "Night falls. Can the dawn be far off?" he asked.

Jesus looked into the dark eyes, overshadowed by thick white brows, but did not comment or try to answer the strange question. It was like a treasure hunt, where words provide but spare clues to the location and nature of the treasure. He had found in the past when met with other mysteries that his thinking mind was of little use. He had to move to the edges of thinking, where things not only appeared but *were* different in order to play the game.

This game is not for the simple-minded or lazy. To play it well and to the end requires intelligence, tenacity, an open heart and mind, and an inclination to joy, which taken together will bring the student to his highest vision. Demanding, yes, but the prize is a treasure beyond price, and none are excluded from gaining it.

My cousin and I spoke of this many times in the years to come, and when the circle around him began to widen, others joined in our discussions. Those would be my happiest memories. One night -- shortly before the event in the river with our cousin John -- Jesus, Miriam, James and I sat up talking through the night. Sensing the change to come, we savored the time we still had to ourselves. I recall a good deal of laughter as we took turns telling stories of childhood innocence, pleasant days with friends, embarrassing events in our travels (like the time the kings' soldiers unexpectedly rode by Miriam and me bathing nude in a river far from the nearest road), telling riddles and making feeble efforts at rhymes.

It was also the first night we dared speak of our dawning awareness of the new circumstances of our lives. The path we tread had shifted, and was taking on a force of its own. Jesus had little to contribute to the conversation that night, and I later wondered how much he actually knew then of what was to come. It seemed certain that events were leading us to some kind of crisis, and we wondered whether or not we were ready. We had been training our whole lives for it, though we still did not know what 'it' was.

When we finally fell into silence near dawn, Jesus shared the following story. It was the culmination of his stay in Egypt a dozen years before.

"On the morning of the first day," he began, "I rose before dawn to bathe in cold water. The air was chill, and I shivered under the fading night sky. By the time I returned to my room, a white garment had been laid out on the bed. Hebeny still slept, and I did not know who had put it there. I held it up in the graying light and saw it had no seams, woven of a single continuous round. By the time I slipped it over my head, Zar, who would be my guide, stood silently in the doorway. It seemed to me we glided across the stone flooring, and down to the river where we stepped into a skiff, just large enough for the two of us.

"I do not recall much of the trip, or even the means of propulsion. We traveled upriver, yet it required no effort on our part. After a time the pyramid came into view, continuing to grow to enormous heights until I was sure we must have arrived at its base ... and still we went on. I'd always thought my childhood memories of it had been exaggerated, but the great stone structure was even larger than I remembered.

"I know it seems impossible, but I do not think the sun moved in the sky during the entire journey from Alexandria to Giza. The air still felt cool to my skin, and my precious garment was as fresh as when I had put it on, though by rights it should have been late in the day and I drenched in sweat.

"The enormous limestone-covered structure seemed otherworldly, as if it had been dropped onto the sand by an alien race far advanced of our own. But Zar assured me that, while inspired by our Elder Brothers from outside our world, it was raised by men who understood themselves the higher laws. It could only be so, he said, else it could not have served as an initiatory chamber for humanity."

Miriam, James and I sat rapt, hardly daring to breathe or light a fresh candle, so as not to interrupt my cousin's narrative.

"A tall, angular man stood in the entrance, his brown skin

shining darkly against white robes. He gave a slight nod to Zar, and to me, then turned and disappeared inside. I stood aside for Zar to pass, as I always do, but he did not move. Thinking he might be daydreaming, I coughed lightly. But his eyes were focused upon me, and I realized with a shot of fear that I was to enter alone. It was silly of me to think otherwise. Of course he could not accompany me. It's just I hadn't thought of it beforehand. The old man's eyes softened, conveying encouragement, and I turned from him to enter the dimly-lit passageway.

"The guard, or guide had disappeared from view, and I was alone. The pyramid had been important in certain facets of our training, and I thought I knew what lay ahead. But the experience is altogether different than a mental image of something. It did not take long to arrive in the inner chamber, where lay the sarcophagus. There was nothing else in the room. I walked in and the outer door closed soundly behind me.

"I took a deep breath and slowly let it out, then crossed my arms over my chest and began slowly to circle the room, three times. By the time I completed this simple act, I had moved into a higher state of awareness. With arms crossed I managed to get into the sarcophagus, and sat down. I crossed my legs and stilled my breath, and began to lose touch with the world we know. At some point I was aware of lying down inside the cold stone, and only vaguely conscious of the great lid being closed over me. As no one was in the chamber with me, I do not know how the lid was closed; only that it was.

"This is the point of greatest danger for one who enters the tomb while still alive. Human conditioning reverts to its most basic belief – that we cannot survive long without a fresh supply of air. And while each initiate has already gone through extensive training, learning how to live in the airless state, there is always a risk the ancient fears will rise up and take over. Once that happens, it is almost impossible to resume control. Panic sets in, focus is lost, and the human self does indeed succumb to a terrifying death. One of our fellow students did not return from Giza and while no one spoke of it, we assumed this is what happened to him.

"The lid closed down upon me with the weight of ages of fear and unreason, that weight which has held humanity hostage since the beginning. I descended into boundless night, but did not waver. I knew ... I remembered that within the darkness is found the dormant seed of perfect light. One can only enter into that light, which is the real, through surrender to the darkness, the unreal. This is contrary to everything we think we know, yet this contradiction holds the key to our liberation."

Jesus paused and rubbed his eyes. We were all tired, but in no mood for sleep.

"After a time I heard a low groan coming from behind me, a deep sound like the earth awakening from a long slumber. I wanted to rise, to discover its cause, but could not. My body would not respond to my will to move. Through closed eyes I began to perceive a gentle glow, as from a candle that does not flicker. And then the groaning came again. This time my eyes opened, and a sharp breath filled my lungs. Had I been sleeping, I wondered?"

Jesus was speaking as if in a dream, words slightly slurred as he relived the experience.

"My paralysis had disappeared, and I turned to face the sounds, not considering or questioning how it came to be that I could suddenly move. I had forgotten the sarcophagus. I noticed a man standing in front of me, surrounded by a golden glow. Not a light really, just a glow, like that I had seen in my mind's eye moments before. His face was hidden in sapphire shadows, the color of his robe. I heard the word 'come' within my mind, which brought me to my feet. And then a second man stood at my other side. I began to walk. Shadows fell away, and the circle of light extended in front of us, illuminating a long corridor. We moved slowly and deliberately, in a manner not unlike my passage from the dock to the pyramid earlier. It seemed I had no weight or resistance, moving as a fish in water, or a feather lifted in a gentle breeze.

"At the end of the passageway my guides disappeared. And then the light flickered and went out, once again leaving me in darkness. I began to perceive a faint pinprick of a light, and focused my entire attention upon it, moving into it. Once inside the light, I took a slow, deep breath and repeated aloud the words I had been taught: *I am the Light. For me there are no barriers. Open, I command....*

"And then followed words of power I cannot now repeat. A massive door took form from the apparently solid stone wall, and began to creak open. As soon as the opening was wide enough I slipped through. As I did so I noticed a soft glow emanating from my own form, flowing into and joining the welcoming light from beyond the door. There on the other side stood the two companions who had brought me down the corridor and left me in darkness.

"'Well done,' said first one and then the other.

"Their hoods had been pushed back, revealing gentle smiles. I sensed from them the relief and joy that comes when a beloved child or student has learned the lessons offered him. Then they turned and continued down the passageway stretching out in front of us, and I followed between them. Ahead lay an open doorway, and when we had passed through, my companions fell away.

"There, in the center of the room, a solitary being stood on a slightly raised, round dais, arms crossed at the wrist over his chest. By then the light was so brilliant that I could not see what he held in his hands, though they were likely the objects of power common to such ceremonies in that land. He had the aura of a Pharaoh, though he was not dressed in kingly garb. His loose-fitting robe was cut rather like my own, but appeared to be spun of gold. Though of a serious mien, his blue-gray eyes sparkled beneath an elaborate headdress that towered above him. Beams of light radiated outward from the centers of power in his head, creating a constant spiraling motion which left me feeling dizzy.

"He bade me approach and as I did he reached up and removed the headdress, setting it on a small table. The swirling stopped, the light from those centers coalescing into a single powerful beam that either entered or went out of the top of his head (I do not know which) and through a small circular opening in the ceiling directly above him.

"In that moment I knew him, could see him weaving in and out of my life, my lifetimes, maybe even from the beginning. He had worn many faces, gracing my life as parent, teacher, cherished friend ... and now he stood as Thoth, the Hierophant, there to guide me through the portal of initiation. I remembered recent contacts with him during my nighttime travels in which he helped me recall my studies from throughout the ages, reviewing what would be required of me within the *Halls of Amenti* where we now stood.

"The moment I moved into position in front of the Initiator, each of twelve centers of power within our respective fields lit up, in sequence, sending forth a beam of concentrated energy into a place between us, where each point merged and exploded. I can say but little of what happened next. Each individual must earn the right to directly experience initiation himself through study, work and service.

"Out of the explosions of light a form, somewhat larger than my own, began to take shape. I struggled against the distractions of sight and sound, and focused my awareness into a single point when suddenly...that form *became me*. It was the marriage of light substance and physical matter."

Jesus lapsed into silence, his head hanging down as if in sleep or a swoon. We waited. Finally he lifted his head and looked at each of us in turn, saying, "The rest you must find within yourself. You too have been with the Hierophant during the hours of sleep, preparing for your own time. Each one's path will be unique, and I would not cloud your vision with preconceptions. When you enter into the chamber beneath the great lion (next to the pyramids), you must be centered in your power as are the Holy Ones, if you are to survive. The lion protects, or destroys, and it is wholly up to the Initiate, and not the Initiator, which one it will be.

"If successful, you will not leave from the sarcophagus by which you entered, as death has been conquered. You will leave from another passageway beneath the pyramid, a harbinger of life to the world. And then you will know without doubt that there *is only life*. Initiation ushers the disciple through increasing levels of awareness of this one fact of existence. Everything pulsates together in a single out-breath from Source, in forms apparently separate. Ultimately the breath returns to Source, and the myriad points of light that we are converge as one.

"'Descend from the mountain of Initiation and return to the valley of human endeavor. You must work and love among men for a time.' These were the Hierophant's last words to me. My path is with my brothers and sisters, drawing the light to them, where they are. One day the high and the low will be as one."

Chapter 12

THE ESSENES

We had not intended to start a group, but one seemed to be forming of its own accord. Whether groups develop around a philosophy, religion, a trade or shared activity, they tend to take on a unique identity and purpose. It makes sense, does it not? If my soul has a purpose for me (which I know to be the case), then when a group of souls come together with a shared goal or purpose, we begin to form an overriding intelligence, a sort of group soul that serves to guide us in realizing that purpose.

For us, the gathering had begun informally with mother, her sister Mary, and me. Our mutual love and concern for Jesus in his sojourn was the source of an ever-deepening well of intimacy. Each one of us developed a line of telepathic communication with Jesus, which eventually opened to envelop all three of us.

One day, perhaps a year after he had left, I heard mother calling out: "Veronica, help me!" Startled, I dropped the basket of wet clothes I was carrying, and ran around to the front of the house to see what was wrong. But she was nowhere in sight. Her voice came again, frantic: "Daughter, come now!" Tears burned my eyes. Where *was* she?

Just then Mary rounded the corner. "Your mother's in trouble," she said, gasping for breath. The look on her face frightened me more than mother's shouts had. She grabbed my hand and we began running away from the village, taking the road toward Sepphoris. While we ran I remembered mother telling me she was going there to deliver a small chest recently completed by one of Joseph's cabinetmakers. She had been looking for an excuse to visit their marketplace, hoping to find the dried insect that gave the blue dye she loved so much.

A startling vision broke through my awareness of mother backed up against a mud wall, with three men on horseback glaring down at her threateningly. One was shouting, but I could not hear his words. I only knew he meant her harm. There was no time to tell Mary what I saw. Once in the village, it did not take us long to find her. Sepphoris was close by Nazareth, and the compound where the drama was unfolding sat at the edge of town. Others had gathered to watch, holding back among the shadows. One did not willingly risk the wrath of Roman soldiers.

"You *know* where he is!" the man shouted, his face red with rage.

Mary and I ran into their midst, grabbed mother and tried to pull her away. One of the other men jumped off his horse and hit me across the face with the back of his hand. I lay on the ground only a moment before finding my feet again. We grabbed mother, broke through their ranks and ran into the village and behind another wall before the men recovered from their shock to come looking for us.

Only after they passed by did I notice the pain. But there was no blood, and my teeth seemed intact. Looking up to see how mother fared, I found three women standing behind her, eyes wide with shock and fear. "Come," one whispered, pulling us into her house, sitting mother and I on a bench next to each other, and Mary across form us.

"Salome, are you alright?" Mary asked her sister. "And you, Veronica?" she added, not waiting for mother's reply.

"Yes, yes, I'm fine. Mother, how did this happen?" The three women pulled up a bench for and sat down across from us to hear the story.

"They must have followed me from the market. I had noticed a few soldiers near the stalls, but paid no attention to them. Everyone, sellers and buyers alike seemed tense, reticent. I thought only to complete my business and go home. Thankfully I had already delivered the chest, but could not find the dye seller anywhere. I had given up and started back when those men rode up in a cloud of dust, shouting something I could not understand, forcing me against the wall where you saw me."

"What did they want?" asked one of the other women.

"I didn't know at first. They asked what I was doing in this village, though did not believe me when I told them. I do not think they singled me out because I am Jewish. Though Greeks are in the majority here, there *are* other Jewish women," she said to the women who nodded their agreement.

"And so I asked them what they wanted of me. My question angered them. 'You do not ask Rome its business!' the one shouted. So I fell silent and they began arguing among themselves in a strange mix of Greek, Latin and other words I did not understand. I thought they might have forgotten me, but when I tried to move away, they closed in tighter. Calling upon the unseen angels to protect me, I sought to calm myself.

"I believe the one soldier would have gladly killed me, but for the moderating influence of the other two. He moved in closer, his voice lowering with a hateful edge to it. I sensed he wanted nothing to do with me, this village or our land, but here he must stay until Rome tires of us and brings its men home. This was the source of his anger.

"He asked, 'You know where the Zealots hide. You are from Nazareth, which spawns the filthy creatures. I have seen you there. Your sons are among them. Where are they? Where is the one called Simon?'" Mother looked from Mary to me to the other women and said, "While I know there are some in our village who return the distaste the Romans have for us, I did not know they had begun to organize themselves to the extent these soldiers would know of them by name!"

Mary shuddered.

Mother lowered her voice and added: "I wondered if they might have confused you with me, thinking your sons mine. Do you think the Simon he spoke of could be Miriam's brother?" she asked her sister.

"I do not know. None of the men speak to me of these things. They fall into silence when I approach their heated discussions, knowing I disapprove. Their hatred threatens all of us more than it does Rome."

*

The incident was never mentioned again, as our attention turned to preparations for my coming of age rituals. These sacred practices prepare a young woman for marriage and motherhood, and help her assume her spiritual role in the community. Among my people preparing a woman for her communal responsibilities is the most important purpose for the rituals, setting us apart from the larger and more rigorously traditional Jewish community within which we lived.

We are called Essenes, among other names. Jewish ourselves, we are sometimes persecuted even by other Jews, and depending upon time and circumstance, have sometimes been obliged to go underground, meeting and carrying out our practices in secret. And even we Essenes have our differences. Our people are scattered throughout Palestine, many of us indistinguishable as we live shoulder to shoulder with others in cities and villages. But some choose to remain apart, in desert enclave or mountain refuge, living communally.

My own community believes that too many rules and laws dictate the lives of some of the other groups. The lists of prescribed and proscribed behaviors are in some cases even longer than among the Pharisees. And while the Sadducees have rejected many of the old laws and traditions, their willingness to compromise everything for the purpose of good relations with Rome seems often to have left them with no moral foundation whatever.

The Romans do not differentiate among us, generally confusing Essenes with the growing number of Zealots who are vocal in their desire to undermine and usurp their overlords. Many, though not all Zealots, are Essenes. They represent an extreme element, and are not generally supported by the rest of us, in part because of the sort of incident that involved mother at Sepphoris. Sadly, we were guilty by association with a group that was increasingly feared and hated by Rome.

I had begun to feel more of an affinity with our brothers from Egypt, Parthia or even Kushan, than with those who espoused violence as a means to solve our grievances. Of course, in all lands there is a tendency to dilute the teachings of the One in order to reach the many, yet we are told that at least within their schools and temples the pure teachings have been preserved. It is for this reason my cousin was sent out into the world, so he may discover the truths hidden away in those lands. Mother said his search will bring him to his destiny. And then he will return to us, spreading the light not just within our small group, but across the Jewish and Gentile world alike.

In the meantime, we women served as midwives of a new system for living. This was the purpose of our sacred ceremonies. Such traditions are deeply embedded in the fabric of our lives, and in accord with the principles of the ancient Brotherhood which claims the allegiance of all of us in our community, men and women alike. Preparations for the celebration of my first blood were entwined with our broader objectives.

In days past, each village had a special building set aside where women would withdraw during their moon cycle, and for childbirth. But the lives of women and men have become more integrated in my time, and we only go apart in this age to welcome a new sister into the covenant of womanhood.

A circle of women had gathered on the road in front of our house, among them Naomi and Miriam, my two dearest friends. They had gone through their own training just two years earlier, and would stand as my sponsors. I was thrilled to see them, as we rarely got to spend time together. Naomi was another cousin, eldest daughter of Joseph and Elizabeth. Miriam had just arrived the previous day from Magdala, on Galilee. It was rumored her parents drowned there when she was still a girl, though I never heard it from her. As close as we were, there was a part of her that seemed forever closed to me (and everyone else as well). It seemed she had basically raised herself. Her two brothers were not much older than she, and while they saw to her worldly needs, they knew little (and had little interest in) women's ways. Some called her Mary, her birth name, but she preferred to go by Miriam: there were already too many Marys, she told me once.

Mother went out to wait with them, leaving me some time to myself. She told me things would appear differently to me when I returned. I didn't know what she meant, but took a moment for one last look around at the home of my youth. Then I picked up the small bag I had packed and went out the door to join them.

Two carts waited, laden with pillows covered with fine fabrics, and a canopy coated with beeswax to shield us from the rains -- which were already threatening. The carts also held our bags, and packets of barley cakes, almonds, raisins, dried peaches and apricots, sweet dates, loaves of crusty bread and a huge round of soft goat cheese, along with several bottles of the best wine, and numerous water skins. It would be a feast for the Goddess herself.

Mother had also tucked a small bag underneath the pillows when she thought I wasn't watching. I guessed it held the robe I would wear for the ceremony.

Chapter 13

TRANSFORMATION

The journey to Carmel was filled with joy. We younger women would run off into the hills whenever the rains subsided, eventually returning to catch up to the lumbering carts. At other times the older women walked with us arm in arm, more like elder sisters than chaperones. The journey was long, and as the days passed I sensed the rising power of my womanhood.

Mary, neither nursing nor pregnant for the first time in a very long while, seemed as lighthearted as a girl. We teased her about Joseph, the two of them so obviously passionate after their many years together. She was an inspiration to us all. Married love would be part of my training in Carmel and I was eager to learn her secrets.

"There are no secrets," she would tell me. "Just keep an open heart in all realms, and not just the relationship with your beloved. If it begins to close elsewhere, it will only be a matter of time before the shadows steal into that area of your life as well. Honor both the human and the God within," she went on. "And"...a mischievous look came over her..."have fun. Life is serious enough without bringing the world's problems into your marriage bed."

My own father had been gone so long that I barely remembered how it had been between mother and him. I know she loved him deeply. She surpassed the required period of mourning, perhaps because his death had been so unexpected. It's not that she continued to wear black or to veil her face, but she was only then starting to look beyond the veil of sadness that had surrounded her. I sensed she was at last coming back to us, eager for the gifts of life.

"Mother," I asked, "is it possible for a woman to marry and not have children? I mean, if there is nothing wrong with her health? And is it possible to marry and yet have a vocation?" I wasn't really sure what I was asking, but felt with some certainty my own path would be different from that taken by women in my world.

We had arrived in Carmel. The house we stayed in belonged to Naomi's father Joseph, mother and auntie's uncle from Arimathea. He had it built as a retreat for the summer months when it often became unbearably hot in Palestine, which is where he had most of his businesses. It was an elegant place, yet modest in size, with beautiful gardens overhanging a steep cliff.

Mother stood a ways off, looking out over the sea, and I wondered if she had even heard me. But after a time she turned and held out her hands to me. "Come." A tear glistened in each eye. "All things are possible, and none is more right than the next. You will find your own way. These are not ordinary times, and you must not think of what others will say of your decisions."

Her eyes drifted away from me. "There is only life – remember that. We change forms, and nothing more. You know from your studies that what we see before us is the dream, and that which seems unreal is sometimes the greater truth. Search for your path in that unseen world, ask for guidance from the higher realms and know that you will find what you seek. You are far stronger than you realize, and I am afraid your strength will be tested many times over. Love to the best of your ability. That is all that is asked of you, now and for all your tomorrows."

I wasn't sure her words actually answered my questions, but my heart was comforted all the same. When we got back to the house we found the great room had been hung with garlands twined with different colored ribbons. A low round table had been placed in the center of the room, covered with finely embroidered linen. On its top sat a brass bowl partly filled with water, surrounded by bunches of grapes. I cannot imagine where they had found fresh grapes so late in the year, and it was all I could do to keep from helping myself before the evening ritual.

Naomi and Miriam took my hands and led me through a doorway into what would be my own room for the three days we were there. I noticed someone had placed my special robe on top of the bed. "But first you must bathe," said Naomi. "While you and Salome were out, we prepared ourselves so we may serve you in this ancient rite of sisterhood."

My heart beat hard and fast, not so much from excitement, but aroused by an inflow of light that I intuitively knew to be the Holy Spirit. Judy said this Spirit is the perfect living image that guides us all our earthly lives. God breathed it into us at birth, and Spirit serves as our lifeline back when our time here is finished. During sacred rituals, in moments of exalted awareness, or in times of great need, we can experience it in sometimes dramatic ways. It is the *mana* spoken of in the Torah.

The two women removed my sandals and robes, muddy from the journey, and unfastened the ribbon from my long hair. These they put into a crudely woven basket. Miriam said, "That which is old will be put into the fire, and returned to the earth."

A large tub sat in the middle of the room. Naomi and Miriam began to move back and forth between the doorway -- where mother and Mary handed them a succession of pots filled with hot water – and the tub, into which they emptied the water.

Streams of vapor began to fill the chill air.

Naomi (the elder of the two) picked up a sharp knife and cut my hair to just above the shoulders. "The maiden is no more" she said, letting it fall to the floor. It was the first time my hair had ever been cut. They held my hands steady as I climbed into the deep tub, and released me to sink down into the water. Essenes bathe frequently, and for most it is a daily ritual. But hot water is a luxury reserved for special occasions. I lay back against the warm metal, thoughts floating among the vapors.

When the water started to cool, I felt Miriam's strong hands on my head. I instinctively sat up as she began kneading a creamy soap into my hair. "Relax sister. Let us do this for you," she whispered. I closed my eyes and abandoned myself with a sigh.

"In reliving the ancient rituals, we are handmaids of the Goddess, who is being born anew in you," Naomi added. One of them poured cups of the scented water over my hair until it squeaked clean.

And then I was gently pushed forward into an upright position whereupon each lifted an arm and began scrubbing my skin with a rough, dried root valued for this purpose. After cleansing my upper body they reached deep into the water, lifted one foot, and both rubbed at it until the calluses softened. And then it was the other foot's turn.

"Stand up sister." I recognized Miriam's voice, and stood, eyes still closed, allowing myself to trust. They steadied me while washing my lower torso, between my legs, and down to my ankles.

Soft cotton towels enveloped me when I stood free of the tub. In the near darkness, my attendants could have been angel or human. It is a characteristic of such rituals that the human nature is transcended for both servers and those being served. We honor each other personally, but also stand in as archetypes, honoring and serving all women, all humanity, lifting them up until they too are transformed.

Soft chanting began to drift in to our room. Night was falling and candles had been lit. Still my eyes were closed. The two women led me to a table and helped me up onto it. The table was covered with more towels, lightly scented. And there, as shadows fell upon the darkness, they massaged oils into my body. Their hands were warm against my skin, working slowly, gently...and I felt alive as I had never felt before.

And then they were finished. Standing me on my feet in the candle-lit room they said: "It is time now to open your eyes, to behold your new life."

I heard myself gasp. I had never seen anything like it. There I stood, in front of a mirror that showed me to myself from head to foot. Few owned a mirror in our community, as the old way said it conveyed vanity to look upon oneself. The mirrors I had seen were small, held in the hand. But here...!

I glanced around, but my sisters had departed, leaving me alone. And so I looked at myself more closely, at my small breasts, the hair growing on the mound between my legs, and saw myself as my husband would see me. My face grew hot, but I was unashamed. There is beauty in the human form. After all, we are created in His image. Or in my case, *Her* image. I giggled.

"Sisters," I called out into the shadows, "is it time for me to put on the robe?" They reappeared, wordlessly lifting it over my head. And then they led me back to the mirror. I could hardly breathe. Never had I seen such exquisite workmanship. "The cloth..." I whispered to myself, wondering if it were of plant or animal origin. "And the embroidery!" Many sacred symbols had been stitched into the alabaster cloth: circles of different sizes, some with and some without designs inside, spirals and equal-armed crosses, as well as serpents and other signs of life and resurrection taken from the Essenes, the Egyptians and others. All merged into a single narrative of our common path, destined to carry us beyond our small selves.

"Salome wove the cloth herself," said Naomi, "and designed, then stitched the patterns too," added Miriam. They were proud of my mother and happy for me.

I was ready. My sisters led me into the room where the older women waited. While I had been at my bath, another twenty or so had entered in silence, forming a circle around the room. Mary and mother stood among them, with Mary facing east and mother, west. I waited in the doorway as my sponsors took up their positions in the north and south. The women all faced toward the center of the room, but with Miriam and Naomi now in place they turned as one to face outward. Having been prepared in advance, I knew I was to walk around the circle three times, stepping to the rhythm of my heartbeat. My timing slowed while I walked, moving evermore deeply into the center of my being – into my heart.

During the final revolution, I paused in front of each woman so she could place her hands upon me, and speak her blessing for my awakening. Each one did as she felt prompted, hands going where they would, speaking in her own words. By the time I arrived back at the beginning, I knew I was no longer the same person. The flower had opened. The girl was gone forever, and a woman born.

Two of the women stepped aside so I could enter into the circle, which closed behind me. As if on cue, the women turned back to face the center and began to sing. The song seemed familiar though I can't think of where I would have heard it before. Perhaps in my nighttime travels, where we are often given to know what is to come, but left with only hints or fragments of memory to guide us through the maze of waking life.

The women sang of toiling in our Father's vineyard, of how the wine of the new vine can be savored even before the cutting is taken from the old. They sang of our delight in watching the fruit ripen, and the joyful sharing when the whole community gathers for the pressing. And in the end everyone is blessed in the feast at the Holy of Holies. They sang of this, and other things, eyes shining like precious stones in the candlelight. They swayed as they sang and I felt myself cradled in their love, knowing they would always be there for me – and I for them.

At last, the singing fell off gently into the night, until there was silence. Then mother moved directly in front and stood, as if appraising me. Fragments of spoken words drifted not to my ears, but from her heart to mine, fashioning a bridge of light between us. I was unable to focus on them. All I knew then was love, and nothing else.

When I came to myself my aunt stood in mother's place, directly in front of me. My two sisters were to either side, and I sensed mother behind me. Mary lifted my robe over my head and I stood naked in the center of the circle. The women were humming now and the flames of the candles scattered around the room seemed to rise and fall with the rising and falling of their voices. My aunt whispered something into the air as she dipped a piece of cloth into the bowl at the center of the room, which she then raised over the crown of my head. Several drops of water fell onto my scalp, and I shivered. Her whispers changed tempo as she dipped the cloth again, this time dabbing it between my eyebrows, leaving behind a faint scent of myrrh. Her hand continued its measured movement back and forth, touching the cloth to my body in different places, connecting the points of physical and spiritual power until I began to answer her quiet chanting, and the women's humming, with my own inner song.

By the time she finished, my entire being was vibrating so intensely I was astonished I could still stand. The ritual was designed to ignite my power as a woman. Each woman must find a way to *be* in that power unaided, integrating it so she could, in times to come, be able to draw upon it at will. Each becomes a vehicle for the feminine power of God to manifest through her on earth, and as such, she becomes a healer.

And then it was over. The young women helped me on with my robe. The vibrating in my body subsided, candles began to sputter and burn out, the circle dissolved and the words of power and songs of support gave way to laughter and light talk. The bowl of water had been replaced by another, larger bowl that overflowed with fruit. Off to the side sat a table laden with food, and still another filled with the many gifts brought by the women. Among the gifts sat a beautiful box of hardwoods, stained a reddish color. The wood had been finely split and its grain gave the appearance of a softly defined butterfly.

"He made it for you." I turned to see Mary smiling. "Before he left he asked me to keep it for you until this day."

The surprise, I thought to myself, remembering Jesus' comment when he had first gone to work with Simon in Joseph's workshop. Though he had not said a surprise for whom, I hoped then whatever it was would be mine. And now, three years later, my dear cousin had managed to share this day with me through his exquisite gift.

But before I turned to the other gifts Mother came up and handed me a goblet of wine. At my first sip all the women lifted their own cups in my honor.

PART TWO

Chapter 14

THE BROTHERHOOD

The ship lurched violently, a toy in the hands of an angry child. Below deck a dozen cots were massed, pushed up against each other. Sleep was impossible. But those clinging to their cots were the fortunate ones. Another hundred men and women had only their mats on the filthy floor in between the cargo. Wave after wave slammed into the ship broadside. A sudden surge sent Jesus flying, landing him on top of a fellow traveler who lay next to him. The man muttered something, and shoved him back onto his own cot. Most crew and passengers were violently sick from the constant motion and nauseating smells.

In times past whole fleets plied the waters between Alexandria and Phoenicia, but these days an unnamed tension filled the air and those who could, stayed home. Dark whispers and uneasy glances were found at every turn, mirroring the foul weather.

The winds and rain dissipated before dawn. Not long afterward mou..   , broke through the misty horizon, signaling an end to their journey. But a fight had erupted on deck, and few noticed the sight. A bag filled with a man's only possessions had gone missing during the night. Amidst curses and shouts, fingers were pointed and accusations made -- born of fear and frustration, rather than reason. It was later found not far from where he had lain during the night. A man had nearly died for nothing.

The rain had been falling nonstop for an entire fortnight. In northern lands it would hardly be noticed, but in this dusty world such weather was rare. Moreover, the earth had been trembling intermittently for some days leading up to their departure, as if attempting to rid itself of something unclean.

While deep in meditation one evening, I saw my cousin standing on deck, apart from the raging men. His form was outlined by a slight shimmer. He alone saw the dawn as others struggled in the darkness.

Since that moon-filled night when he first came to me in his body of light, I have faithfully gone to the same small hill as sunrise. I seek him, not out of slavish devotion to my cousin and friend, but because when I succeed in finding him, I know I also discover my own highest good. And it is my hope that in some small way I might support him on his lonely path.

I was beginning to understand what our teachers hinted at. My cousin stands as a beacon of light, a way-shower to those who seek. Though my sight was limited, I knew he walked a path few have trod before him, clearing the way for the rest of us. The light of the Father shines *through* him. It is not a gift reserved for a favorite son, but the inheritance of all children alike when we have proven our worth and competency to wield the power that rises from the light.

Though the light has dawned over our world, much time will pass before the masses are ready to receive it. Men love the darkness and are unwilling to relinquish the safety they believe is found in shadows. Nor do they welcome the hard work of preparing themselves for the great transformation.

But, it will come, in time.

An arc of gold washed across his face. For a moment the magic of first light embraced the combatants behind him, and they stopped their fight to gaze into the sunrise, and for the first time saw the land that beckoned them. The moment passed and they returned to their blows, though the fire has gone out of the fight. It wasn't long before they dispersed to tend their wounds, to sleep or report for duty.

Still he stood, undisturbed. For a brief moment I saw through his eyes images of his life in Alexandria, parsing his past in preparation for the path ahead.

The vision faded suddenly, and with a jerk I felt myself pulled upward, hurtling into the sun. Its brilliance overwhelmed my brief struggle for control. But there was nothing to catch a hold of -- no thought, no form, nothing. And I was ... *lost to the light.*

*

Despite the fact he had not slept for days, Jesus sensed he must leave the port immediately to begin his journey overland. By nightfall he had attached himself to a caravan of traders bound for Persia. A few of his fellow travelers would eventually join other caravans, continuing along the Silk Road far to the east. But most of the men and their hangers-on, with whom he would be traveling, continually circled the lesser seas of the near east, carrying men and goods for trade. It sickened him to see men, women and even children herded like animals, often beaten, barely kept alive, only to be sold into equally awful conditions. The slave trade is one of the great evils of our world, and the flowering light will not bloom as long as it exists.

As they prepared for departure it seemed to the others the strange young man had fallen asleep among the camels. He cared nothing for the goings on in the port, desiring no conversation, hoping to blend in, to be forgotten. But he *was* different and no matter what he did he would always stand out.

The day after their departure, unbeknownst to the caravan, a brawl erupted back at the port, leaving many dead. The Roman soldiers surrounded and closed off access to the area for nearly a moon until the cause of the fight could be determined. Such disturbances would grow into great battles in years to come, spreading across the lands held by Rome.

"Where are you from?" asked a dark-skinned man riding a camel alongside the Nazarene. "Why do you walk, when a few coins would secure you a comfortable ride?" It was the second day into the journey, and up until then he had not spoken with anyone. A hooded robe and shaggy gray beard concealed the man's face. He spoke in Aramaic -- our native tongue -- though with an unfamiliar accent.

"Galilee," he said, hoping to discourage further conversation.

"But why do you come by way of the great sea, when another caravan could have brought you directly from your homeland?"

"I have been in Alexandria." Jesus was not used to talking with strangers, or even engaging in casual conversation with his friends.

"But why do you walk?" the man persisted. "Surely the *brothers* would not send you out onto the road without at least a pittance."

Brothers? Jesus thought to himself, stunned by the implications of the stranger's comment. But he said nothing, keeping stride with the camel and its rider. He had left his white robes behind, to shield his affiliation with the Brotherhood. And yet this man recognized him. How? The brothers had increasingly become targets of some who saw their cloistered life a challenge to the authorities. The brothers answered to none but God.

But finally he could not resist, and without looking at the man asked, "What do you know of the brothers?"

In turn his companion remained silent as they moved into late afternoon shadows.

"I once lived within those same walls that you have called home," he said at last, "some years ago, in my youth. But I am from Juggernaut."

In that instant Jesus knew he would visit this place, that it called to him. Indeed, he was certain it represented a key piece in the puzzle of his life. Unlike so many of us who try desperately to see into our future in hopes it will make sense of what's in front of us, he sought only to walk in the spotlight of eternity. Where is this place, Jug-ger-naut?" he repeated slowly, as if he could milk some meaning from its sound.

After another long pause the man answered. "Juggernaut lies far to the east of here. I will leave this caravan in Persia, and join another. It is a long journey, crossing the lands of many Rajas in their resplendent palaces. Though we skirt the highest mountains, we also pass through deep jungles and forests, where live elephants, great cats and" he sighed, "many other animals that I am sure you have never seen."

"And the people, the temples, the...?" Jesus pressed, showing rare impatience. He appreciated natural beauty more than most, yet it was the teachings and philosophy that drew him across the world.

His companion chuckled, giving him a quick glance. The man had baited him. His eyes twinkled out from under his hood. "Oh yes, the people. The temples and priests. The ancient manuscripts. Yes. They await you. "*We* have been waiting for you," he added, suddenly serious. My name is Krishna. I have been sent to accompany you, if you will consent to come to Juggernaut."

Jesus opened his mouth to reply, but Krishna went on, his voice barely a whisper. "We have waited a long time. There are some who would try to stop what you have begun, and the brothers thought it best you have some ... company on your journey."

"My brother," Jesus said, turning to Krishna after a long

silence, "I thank you from my heart. You honor me with your presence, and I will gladly go to Juggernaut with you. But I am expected in Persia, and first must spend a time there."

"As you wish," he replied, in a tone that seemed to say the subject was not yet closed.

In the ensuing silence new images mingled with others he had long suppressed. As a youth he had tried to live a normal life, focusing upon his studies and his family and friends. To fulfill his promise it was essential he be fully human in order to lift humanity up. While he experienced the entire range of feelings and thoughts we all do, my cousin *was* different and differences are not valued in our world, bringing unique challenges ... even dangers.

This journey represented a new phase of his mission, extending the message he carried beyond his own people to others. Prophecies of a great teacher had arisen in many lands, creating a sense of expectancy. Their anticipation, their desire is what drew him forward. Jesus also needed to broaden his own understanding, incorporating that larger universe into his world view. His time away would also offer him the time he needed to find peace with the weight of responsibility inherent in his calling.

He came to stir the pot of tradition, adding the exotic spices of many cultures and belief systems to the emerging philosophical blend destined to lift human understanding to a higher level. A new heaven and a new earth are being prepared, where separation is overcome and the two become one. Jesus and his followers sometimes imagined they would see the immediate fruit of his mission. But such a transformation is so absolute that it cannot be accomplished in an Age, let alone within the single lifetime of any man -- even one so evolved as he.

During the course of my own life I studied many of the same traditions as my cousin, and later learned directly from him. He explained that he was taking just one more step along a path walked by the one called Gautama Buddha, who in turn was continuing that begun by others before him.

The ancient prophecies tell us that the circle of followers that will form around him will one day expand to encompass the entire earth. The voices of the great teachers of all traditions and religions will be amplified through him. As he traveled, the saints and mystics of other lands would recognize this and invite Jesus into their world, sharing their most sacred and heretofore secret teachings with him.

That evening in camp the two men lay next to a small dung fire where together they prepared their evening meal. It was simple fare, gruel to which had been added dried dates and goat's milk. While they ate, a man approached from the shadows. "Ah, it is you, Pursa," said Krishna. He had mentioned nothing about a fellow traveler. Pursa sat down in a flurry of heavy robes between the two men, without waiting for an introduction.

"Here, I caught this trying to get into my tent," the newcomer grinned, showing even, white teeth. "Share it with me." It was a large snake, already skinned and roasted. Both men declined, neither one accustomed to eating meat. But at Pursa's insistence first one, then the other reluctantly took a piece and began to nibble from it. He seemed very pleased with himself.

Krishna introduced them. Pursa came from the land that worshiped Ahuramazda, representing the pure, eternal essence of the one God seen in the perpetual flames on their altars. It was the second time that day Jesus felt the thrill of recognition. When he was yet a child, a traveler from Persia had passed through Palestine on his way to Egypt. The man told all who would listen about the God of Fire, and Zoroaster, his prophet. Ever since that day he had longed to learn more.

"I am on my way there now," said Jesus.

But Pursa held up his hand saying, "Wait awhile longer, my brother. There are other things you must attend to first."

"You are surely mistaken. It cannot be coincidence we are

traveling the same road, in the same caravan," he said, looking from one to the other man.

But Jesus would learn soon enough the necessity of patience.

Chapter 15

AN UNEXPECTED RETURN

The following day Krishna removed his belongings from his pack camel, piling everything high upon a cart already loaded with goods, so that Jesus could ride between the two brothers. They swayed to the camels' peculiar rhythm, so suited to the monotonous desert terrain. The hypnotic gait supported their silence.

The caravan planned to stop at an oasis shimmering on the horizon, to wait out the heat of the day. As they approached, shouts erupted from somewhere in front of them. Jesus' stomach knotted. While he did not know the source of the disruption, he sensed it concerned him. Before long a sea of heads began to turn his way.

"There he is, the Nazarene," shouted someone, pointing him out. His heart stood still. Krishna and Pursa stiffened, right hands buried under their robes.

A man broke through the crowd and approached him, out of breath. "Jesus ben Joseph?" He nodded. "Thank the One I found you. They said you would be with the caravan ... I hope it's not too late!" Before he could say any more the poor man fell to the ground, exhausted.

Jesus did not ask who 'they' were, or how anyone had guessed where to find him out there, far from everything he knew. Without being told, he knew the message was about his father. He slipped off his camel next to the man and cradled his. "Here. Sip this. Slowly ..." he said, lifting his water skin to parched lips.

The man's chest stopped heaving and his eyes filled with tears. "You must return home. Your father is dying," he whispered.

"Tell me," Jesus asked, "how does my mother fare?" He worried about her once her husband was gone. She was the deep water of Joseph's lake, and he the blue of her sky. Each was strong and independent, and yet their souls were profoundly entwined.

The man's brow furrowed: "Your mother appears well, though tired. She is with him day and night. It was she who sent me to you"

My cousin knew that death, in its own time, is more to be celebrated than mourned, a release into light for one who has finished his work in the world. In his heart he was glad for Joseph. His father was no longer young, and had lived a happy and honorable life, true to his sacred Self. He would be welcomed into the Father's house. Jesus simply hoped he did not suffer. Joseph was well into middle age when he was born, so he never experienced the closeness some sons have with their fathers. But their bond was deep nonetheless, and he would have asked for nothing more, especially given the joy his mother had known with him.

"And so you were right," he said to his new friends. The caravan had found its way into the oasis and the other travelers had already forgotten the interruption as they settled into their afternoon nap. "Where shall we meet when I return this way? Am I to go to Kushan first then?"

The men knew their camels could not continue without a rest, and they lay back against the date palms while making their plans. "The caravan will arrive in Ur two days from now. I have business to take care of, and will wait for you there," said Pursa. "Ask for me at the temple of the eternal flame. They will know where to find me."

"But it may be some time," replied Jesus. "It might be better for you to return to Persia, and there wait."

"No. Find me in Ur."

Jesus turned to Krishna and knew before he spoke that his new friend would accompany him back to Nazareth.

"We should leave soon. We can cover much distance in the evening coolness," said Krishna.

Jesus tried to give the messenger a coin, but it was refused. "No, I was well-paid. But if I may, I would stay the night before returning. I have traveled as quickly as my horse would allow, and we must rest. Will you be alright? You know the southerly route, don't you?" he asked, looking from Jesus to Krishna.

"Yes, yes, of course. Stay here as long as you wish. We will find our way."

Pursa and Krishna hung back a moment, whispering, and then Pursa walked away into the crowd. "We will meet him at the new moon," said Krishna. "All we need for the journey to Kushan will be made ready. The timing is perfect. They could not have gone now, in any case."

Jesus wondered who 'they' were, but he didn't have time to think about it then. He stayed with the camels as they drank their fill, and Krishna went off in search of food.

That first night they slept only a few hours, following a little-used trade route as soon as it could be discerned in dawn's first light. Their camels seemed to sense the urgency as they raced across the desert. When they stopped at midday, sheltered in the shade of a crumbling mud wall, Jesus asked Krishna: "Why Ur? What business could he have in that ancient city? I did not know any commerce still took place there."

"I doubt his business is of the buying and selling kind" was all he would say.

They arrived in Jerusalem the following sunrise. A few pilgrims were already afoot on the outskirts of the city, and by the time they passed through the gate, a number of merchants were set up for business. They had trusted their animals to keep to the road during the last hours, while they dozed. But now the men were alert, and famished.

There is no city in the world like Jerusalem. In it beats the heart of myriad cultures, a seething caldron of human passions from the highest and noblest to the most debased. Standing at the intersection of several trade routes, it is blessed with nonstop commerce and a cross-pollination of ideas.

Our uncle Joseph had a home here, and the two travelers went directly to his house. He would have the latest news from Nazareth. Joseph was an astute businessman, and a great traveler himself, frequently visiting his business interests in many parts of the world. They were fortunate to find him at home. Some thought him stern, even foreboding, but that came from a fear of one who wields wealth and the power that goes with it. In fact, he was a kind and fair man, excruciatingly honest in his dealings

"My son," he exclaimed, jumping to his feet, fondly embracing Jesus. Joseph had just sat down to eat, and called out for more food for his guests. "Sit!" he insisted, pointing to two stools directly across the table from him. "And who is your friend?"

"Uncle, this is Krishna, a brother from Juggernaut, beyond Kushan."

Krishna stood and bowed to his host.

"A brother, eh? Then I am honored to meet you, Krishna. You have my gratitude for accompanying my nephew on this sad journey."

"It is *my* honor," he replied, bowing again.

"Your father is still alive, last I heard," Joseph said, pushing plates of fruit and cheese toward his guests. A young girl brought in steaming bread atop a polished piece of wood, setting it between them.

"It's Ruth, isn't it?" exclaimed Jesus, grabbing the girl's hand. "How wonderful to see you. You have grown so!" The girl blushed, pleased he recognized her after such a long time away.

"Welcome home. I'm so sorry....." she stopped, not knowing what else to say.

"Yes, thank you. But this is a part of living, Ruth. Death is only the beginning of a new life. And yet ... He will be missed. Jesus looked around. "Where is your family, uncle? It's too quiet here. I had hoped to see Josephus at least."

"He and the girls are with their mother in Carmel. She is with child again," he added, grinning.

"Congratulations uncle."

"Well, I must not keep you," said Joseph. "You will want to be there with your father, and with Mary. But still you must eat. Horses are being readied for you. You may return this way for your camels later on. I would have some time with you then, before you depart, for we will not see each other for a good while after that, and there are some things we must discuss. And you, Krishna, I am sorry there was no time for us to get to know each other. When you come back...."

By the time they finished eating, baths had been drawn for the two men and fresh clothes laid out. My cousin was impatient to be on the road, but the horses would speed the journey considerably, and it would not be seemly to attend his father in his current state. He had not had a proper bath since leaving Alexandria.

"I have never been on a horse," confided Krishna, "and do not wish to cause you delay."

"Come here and stand beside him," Jesus said. "Now place your hand gently on his neck, stroking him. Then walk slowly around to the front. Horses are intelligent creatures. He knows how a man feels about him, whether he approaches in fear, arrogance or respect. And he reflects back to us our own attitude. So put aside the first two, and look him in the eyes with the respect he deserves. His name is Herra.

"Good, now gently rub his nose . . . like this. Then do what comes naturally in getting to know him. When you are ready, I will show you how to mount, and the signals to which he will respond. You will find him a valuable partner, and friend."

They were soon on their way, arriving late in Nazareth, a quarter moon setting on the horizon.

Mary and I sat on a bench outside in the cooling air, waiting. We knew he would come. I trembled with anticipation, barely hearing anything my aunt had been saying. Mother had just gone home, having attended to Joseph throughout the day. She would be back in the morning.

The two men rode up and Jesus slid gracefully off his horse and embraced his mother. When he pulled back to look at her, there were tears in both their eyes, tears of joy at the reunion, and of sadness. But he also saw peace in his mother's eyes, and was glad.

"Cousin..." he said, turning to me. And I flew into his embrace like a child, tears streaming down my face. There were so many things I wanted to say to him, but the knot in my throat wouldn't let me speak. "I have missed you too," he whispered.

"We will have time later," I said, finally stepping back. I wanted nothing more than to have him to myself, but knew I must release him to care for his family. "Go to your father." I turned away so I would not weaken and grab his robe to keep him from going. Mother and son walked away, talking quietly.

"Veronica, would you take care of Krishna for me?" he called back over his shoulder. "I will see you both later."

"You are most welcome here," I said, turning to the stranger as I wiped the tears from my eyes. "Where are you from?"

"From Juggernaut, in India." I led Krishna around to a stable where he could find water and feed for the horses.

"I am Veronica. You can bed the horses here. And I will send someone to help you with your bath and show you your room. When you've finished, I will be eager to hear about your home, and how you came to know my cousin. I'll be back shortly."

I ran back to the house and found Mary and Jesus standing in the doorway of the room where Joseph lay. Mary went in to light a new candle, then stood back while Jesus approached his father alone. He paused a moment to look around the room, nodded to himself and knelt beside the bed. He took his father's hand and leaned in close to whisper in his ear. Then Mary went to Joseph's other side, and I left them alone.

In our world are no drawn-out mournful vigils, and no wailing when the final separation occurs. Whenever possible, one makes the transition with loved ones present and if requested, specially trained priests or priestesses come to speak the sacred words of transformation. The ancient rituals are intended to help the one who is dying keep focused upon their metamorphosis from the darkness of material existence into the realm of eternal light beyond the physical body. The passage of birth into light is emphasized, rather than death, or separation from the worn or diseased form. When the consciousness is thus concentrated, an opportunity is offered that only occurs at this juncture in a person's life.

Who can describe such a thing in worldly terms? It is enough to say that enormous spiritual growth can be experienced in this timeless moment; condensing epochs into a single instant.

Chapter 16

PASSING THROUGH THE VEIL

Mary sat at Joseph's left and Jesus to his right, holding steady the eternal flame between them. At his last breath, mother and son beheld the light emerge from its cave within the heart center. The eternal flame momentarily illuminated the room in which they sat, then compressed into a tiny pinprick of light and vanished from sight. The rite of passage we call death requires only a shift in awareness from separation to union. The prodigal son had returned home.

After a short silence they spoke his name aloud three times. When I heard his name, I knew it was finished.

"Gather the women," Mary said, standing in the doorway, "so we may prepare the body for burial."

It was traditional among our people for the community to go about its normal affairs for three days, holding love and gratitude in our hearts for having known the departed one, buoying him upon his journey. At the end of this period we come together to speak our memories of the departed, of Joseph. And then we must surrender our claim to him so he can continue on his journey unencumbered.

If anyone discovers they have unfinished business with the

deceased, it is imperative they go apart and remedy this through the process of forgiveness (of oneself or the one now departed – and usually both). The journey of a soul as advanced as Joseph would not be impeded if such a process were not completed by the one left behind. But that one would carry a shadow upon his own soul, until the work of forgiveness is done. This shadow *is not actually real,* of course, but such is the power of our minds.

Joseph's body was accorded a place of honor, in a tomb set high on the side of a hill, facing east. At his request, the tomb itself was modest, and the inscription gave only his name. People came from great distances, including four brothers from Egypt where Joseph too had once studied. He was beloved by many.

One of these brothers, a woman from Athens, would later become a close friend when I went to Alexandria for my own studies. She and Jesus were laughing about something as I approached them during the feast in Joseph's honor. "Veronica, this is Helen," he said, placing my hands in hers with a smile. Helen's hair was the color of ripened grain, but the Egyptian sun had turned her skin as brown as any in our village. She was beautiful.

"I feel like I already know you, though I imagined a girl rather than a young woman," said Helen, with what sounded like true affection.

"No, we have both left our childhood behind," Jesus said. "That world is gone." I felt a lump in my throat at the finality of his words. "Though it opens the door to new worlds for us to explore." He looked at me with a sad smile. "There are many roads we will walk together, my cousin, and I will always be grateful for your companionship."

His words unsettled me and I wasn't sure I was ready to know more just then. So I changed the subject and soon the two of them were back to sharing stories about Alexandria. My mind began to wander and after a time I realized they'd stopped talking and were looking at me.

"What?" I asked.

"You've been staring at Helen," chuckled Jesus.

"Oh, I'm sorry. It's just that every Greek I've ever seen until now was raven haired."

"That's easily explained. My grandfather's grandfather came to Athens from a land far to the north in search of answers to life's mysteries. Of course, such answers are not found in one place more than another, as they lie in here," she said with a laugh, placing her hand on my heart. "But the discovery can be made more enjoyable when the journey is taken with others who share the same goal." She looked back at my cousin and I could see he held a special place in her heart. He had always captivated people, even as a child. Thinking of that I felt a sudden pang of jealousy at those who had been close to him during his years apart from me. Unnerved by my feelings, I excused myself to talk with Mother and uncle Joseph.

"Joseph was a good businessman as well as the best carpenter around," Mary said of her husband. She was not bragging; everyone knew it to be true. "The children and I want for nothing." She paused. "I want to turn everything over to the workers who loyally served their master throughout the years." It was an unusual gesture, but we later realized she must already have known events to come would soon take her away from Nazareth.

"Oh Mary, that is wonderful," Joseph said. "I hope it means you will consider coming to live with us in Jerusalem." Responsibility for Mary's material support and the paternal care for her children would naturally fall to Joseph, as the brother of her father. He would be happy to offer both, though he sometimes worried he didn't fulfill his obligations even for his own family. "I know Elizabeth would love to have you and the children with her, especially now our family is expanding again. My long absences are hard on them all.

"And speaking of that, I must leave directly after we eat and travel to Petra," he went on. I hoped he would say more about his trip, but the conversation fell into a lull. Joseph was a man who loved words, using them with considerable eloquence. He often claimed he was no scholar, though he too had trained in the mystery schools of Egypt and Greece in his youth. And he was, after all, a member of the Sanhedrin.

When the plates had been cleared he remained seated and as he was the eldest among us, we all returned to the table to wait with him. He turned and winked at me. I had never seen him do such a thing before and my stomach erupted in butterflies. Uncle glanced at Miriam next, and then at mother, then picked up the theme of his conversation as if no time had elapsed.

"From Petra I will travel to the coast where I am meeting one of my ships carrying a load of hardwoods from Phoenicia. That ship is bound for Brittany, or wherever I can get the best price for its cargo. It has been a long time since I have visited my mines in that far country, and I plan to travel with the ship.

"Nephew," he turned to Jesus, interrupting his own narrative, "It is not your time yet, but one day I hope you will take this journey with me. There are other places to which you are called now, and I know you must resume your travels in the morning."

I noticed Mary stiffen at the mention of her son's imminent departure. It had been over three years since he left for Egypt. The boy was still very much in him then, while it was a man who now looked at her.

"But you, Veronica and you, Miriam, I would have the two of you travel with this old man to keep him company."

"Oh yes! May I, mother?" I grabbed Miriam's wrist across the table. For the moment I envied her, as she would need no one's permission to take such a trip. She would ask her brothers, but they could not deny their sister anything. Though they had no talent for parenting her, they loved her without bounds.

Mother didn't say anything right away. I could not even read her face. "Salome," Mary said to her sister in a low voice. "You remember what Judy told us long ago? Uncle," she turned to Joseph, "how did you know of this? Or did you?"

I had no idea what she was talking about, and neither did Miriam, judging by the furrow of her brow.

"I am aware of more than you know," he replied, enigmatically. "This concerns the three of you," he went on, looking at Miriam, Jesus and me in turn. "The seed of certain trees requires tremendous heat to break out of its shell in order to regenerate. Without fire the species would die out. Now some would say the fire is the enemy of this tree, because a few will perish when flames wash through the forest. But from a higher perspective we know the fire to be their preserver. It is little different for humanity. The time for regeneration approaches and we must be ready. We need your help."

Though he spoke to Miriam and me, he did not take his eyes off my cousin, who met his gaze unflinchingly. I did not understand how what he said pertained to us but in my excitement, I didn't really care.

Jesus got up then and hugged Joseph, and went out. Mary said goodnight, following him through the door. It would be their last evening together for a good while. Though both would have wished for more, they knew that higher forces were at work, and they would play their parts as best they could. My cousin told me later how difficult it was to be held to a different standard than other men, to always be asked to lay aside his own very human needs and desires. While it became a little easier to bear over time, there were moments when he wanted nothing more than to live a life like any other man.

Soon it was uncle's turn to say goodbye. We walked him out to his cart, where he took me aside. Looking at me with gentle brown eyes, he said, "Niece, after your father died I asked your mother to bring you and your sister to live with me. But she would not leave her Mary. And now it may be that Mary leaves her. Don't worry, child," he smiled at my sudden alarm.

"Both sisters and their children will be well taken care of, whether by me or another," he added with a mischievous grin. "And no matter what, you and I and our darling Miriam will have a grand time." He kissed me and left.

That evening mother told me I could go, and suggested Miriam stay with us until it was time to meet uncle in Carmel. The timing of our departure depended upon his business in Petra. In the meantime Joseph had already arranged for a messenger to travel to Magdala to meet with Miriam's brothers and obtain their permission for her to travel with us. It was more a courtesy than an actual request since her brothers were fond of Joseph and trusted him.

The following dawn Mary and Jesus joined us at the morning meal. Her handmaid, Sophia, stayed home with the younger children, so we could talk. "I will be saying goodbye too," said Mary. "When my Joseph's passing drew near Zebedee and his wife sent word, inviting us to stay awhile with them in Bethany."

While the others were talking I whispered to mother, "I cannot go with Joseph."

"And why not? There is more at stake here than you know."

"With Mary gone, you will be left alone," I protested.

"I will not be alone. I have Elizabeth, and there is family all around me. Besides, you will not be gone long." I couldn't imagine my little sister Elizabeth would be of real company for her, but despite her original hesitation about me going, mother would not change her mind.

I tried to talk with Miriam, but she didn't seem to understand my concerns. If fact she had seemed distracted the entire day and when I asked if something were bothering her, she grabbed her shawl and left without explanation.

A sudden noise outside reminded us Jesus would soon be leaving. It was too soon! There had been no time at all to talk, to hear the stories of his years in Alexandria, his travels afterward, not even how he met Krishna. No time to look into his eyes and see his soul. And now this morning, with uncle's news ... I too had been distracted, wasting the little time we had. But even if there had been time, his thoughts were on his father's passing, and his mother's welfare.

Mother called past me through the open door. "Just tie them up to the post, Krishna. Come in. Relax a little and have something to eat with us. I worried about you last night." She had tried to convince him to stay with us, but he would not have it. Another time, he replied, but not this night. "Where did you sleep?"

He grinned: "The shepherd Michael is my cousin Darius' uncle by marriage. I had long wanted to meet him. He told me tales of my cousin that had us both laughing into the early hours. I can tell you this: he is not the traditionalist he makes himself out to be!"

"What is your destination now?" mother asked Jesus.

"Krishna and I will go to Jerusalem to exchange our horses for the camels we left at uncle's, and then retrace our steps across the desert. A brother awaits us in Ur. From there we will travel to Kushan."

"...so far," she whispered, looking at her sister.

Mary's eyes were unfocused, as if seeing beyond the desert sands. I expected to see sorrow written on her face, but found instead a calm acceptance. I said a silent prayer then that I might know such serenity, and was surprised when Jesus took my hands in farewell that my eyes remained dry and my heart at peace.

"May our God watch over you, my dear cousin," he said

"And you. I am glad you are traveling with Krishna, glad you are not alone."

"I am too," said Jesus, smiling. "He is proof I am cared for...just as you are."

Sophia had come in with the children. Jesus rose and kissed his mother and siblings, from James on down, whispering something for each one's ears alone. The older children stood stoically, Martha and Jude giggled, while Ruth and Andrew hid their faces in their mother's robes.

He took my hand then, and glanced around the room as if he had forgotten something. With a sigh, he quickly kissed my cheek, and mother's forehead. Turning his attention to Mary, the two gazed into each other's eyes. Then, without another word he mounted his horse and the two men rode away.

Chapter 17

JOURNEY TO BRITTANY

It had been nearly two years since we last traveled the road to Carmel. The late autumn hills had been green with rain on the way to my first woman's rites. But now, coming on to midsummer, the same hills were parched brown. Even the purple vines were covered with a fine dust. The trees were heavy with fruit; grain was ready for threshing, while the olive harvest had already begun. Children played on the hillsides where shepherds tended their fattening flocks. The roads were filled with travelers.

It may be that little had changed along the way, yet everything seemed different. I thought about my life, and sought to name the changes I felt inside. My body was now that of a woman and according to Jewish tradition I should be preparing myself for marriage. I was, after all, nearly fifteen. But I was fortunate. In my community women generally choose their husbands. Relatives, friends of one's parents might make suggestions and offer introductions, but they let the young take it from there. I had not yet met a man with whom I could imagine spending my life, and was not in a hurry.

"Miriam, have you thought about marriage?" I asked my

friend. She looked at me, startled. We had walked in silence most of the day. "How old are you now?"

"At the next moon I will be seventeen. You are the first person to ask me this question, though I imagine others have wondered."

Mother walked behind the cart, out of earshot. She had seemed distracted since my cousin left, and I sometimes worried about her. At least Mary decided not to go to Bethany until we returned from our journey with uncle Joseph.

Amos, a neighbor of ours, had offered to accompany us to Carmel, so mother would not have to return alone. He was a man of few words, and hard of hearing, so I knew from where he sat atop the cart, he would not be able to hear our conversation.

"I have not thought much of the subject," Miriam said at last. I had come to know her well in recent years, and thought her voice belied her words.

"Not much means some," I prodded, needling her arm with my elbow

"There is no one … who interests me." Again, the hesitation.

"No one?" But she would say no more. I jumped off the cart and joined mother, who squeezed my hand in greeting.

"I never really thanked you for the beautiful robe you made for the ceremonies in Carmel." I had packed it away afterward, saving it for the day I married. To tell the truth it had passed from my thoughts until I came across it in preparing for this trip. "It truly is the most beautiful thing I have every seen. It must have been a year in the making."

"It was made from love, dear daughter. The time spent in the making was a like a second gestation, preparation for your birth into womanhood. I felt myself privileged to be present at both births."

I went to brush the unexpected tears away before mother

could see them, then noticed a tear on her cheek as well: a reflection, it seems, of the bond that had grown between us as mother and daughter, and as two women journeying through life together.

Joseph's house seemed cavernous without all the women who had been with us on my last visit. I hardly remembered the expansive view of the sea, and went out alone to sit on the great stones that guard the cliff. The hills outside Nazareth always seemed to me a kind of container for the world I lived in, while these hills formed a basin that opened to the sea beyond.

There on the cliff my mind traveled out into infinity. My eyes might have seen only blue sea, but my mind's eye could see forever, all the lands and all the people of the world – everywhere. Because my vision was unrestricted I felt limitless myself. And for the first time, I caught a glimpse of the magnitude of my being. The things I had been taught in philosophy, the sacred teachings, had all been taken into my heart, but in that moment they came alive. My soul encompassed all I could see and all I could imagine. My spirit was all that and more. I knew I am not separate from anything I perceive. And in that awareness I knew also I am forever one with God.

"Veronica." At first I did not recognize the sound of my name as having anything to do with *me.* "Veronica," it called again. And even as the name penetrated my consciousness, I resisted it. I wanted to shout, leave me alone! Do not make me return to the small world, when I am all *this.* But at the third call I gave in, and stood uncertainly to walk toward the voice. Elois, who served at the temple in Carmel, had spoken of the pain that follows such an experience of oneness. I now understood what she meant.

"What is wrong, daughter?" asked mother, when she saw me.

"Oh mother, it was so beautiful," was all I could manage. She looked at me, and nodded her understanding. The following day I asked Miriam to walk with me out on the rocks. There I tried to explain my experience to her.

"Yes, I know," she said, when my own words failed me.

The pain of separation followed me for days, and I vowed never to ascend the heights again if this was what came of it. But then I remembered something else. Elois had said, that the going and coming would get easier with time. We would learn to expand our awareness to encompass the *All* in our everyday lives. Our limits and boundaries would begin to thin, one day disappearing altogether. Her words gave me the courage to remain open. I would learn that for the heart to expand to encompass the light, the ancient lies that had defined it as small and limited had first to be shattered, and surrendered to that very light. It is not unlike the liberating passage of childbirth which is also experienced by us as pain.

On the morning of the fourth day a messenger came to say that Joseph would arrive that evening, and we should make ready to leave the following morning. There was little for us to do, as our bags had sat packed at the door since our arrival. Still the news set us fluttering about like birds. More than once I caught mother grinning at us, vicariously enjoying our excitement.

"I am so happy for you both," she said. "This will be a wonderful journey of discovery, of inner and outer worlds. When you open your heart each sunrise, my daughter, turn toward Nazareth as well, and send your thoughts to me."

"I will, mother. I will."

"Oh, this is going to be so much fun, Miriam," I said, twirling her around the room." She laughed, spinning me in turn.

"This will be my first time to travel so far from Palestine. But it will not be my last. I have seen some things . . ." she said, letting her words trail off.

I shivered. Her words triggered vague memories of dreams where a small band of people huddled closely, tightly holding hands. We knew that as long as we didn't let go, we would survive. It always seemed that even in the darkest hours, at least one of us held a torch that could not be extinguished.

"Yes, I know," though I could never have explained what it was I thought I knew. Somewhere inside of us we both knew what this strange future held, and also that we would be there for each other when the time came.

That night I dreamt of my cousin. His trip across the desert had gone well. He and Krishna were in Ur, having found the person they sought. I shared the dream with mother, asking her to tell Mary when she got back. She promised.

A horse-drawn cart waited for us outside to take us to Tyre, where the ship lay at anchor. Mother kissed first me and then Miriam on each cheek. "This is a renewal of the ancient bond of sisterhood. I am happy you two are traveling together." She turned then and walked back into the house. For a brief moment, I felt the child in me rise up and wanted to run after her. But the feeling passed, and I climbed up into the cart with Miriam and Joseph.

The driver snapped his whip over the horses' backs, and we were off at a trot. I was not used to traveling at such speed. The wind lifted my hair and it flew behind me like the horses' tails. The summer heat was upon us and I closed my eyes, savoring the cool breeze.

We arrived at Tyre in the early evening and spent our first night aboard-ship still tied up at the dock. The constant movement of the ship disoriented me and I ate little, afraid I might be sick. But the unpleasant sensation passed by the time we went to bed. My sister and I – for that is how I thought of Miriam – shared a cabin with separate cots. We had our own window that looked out over the lights of the city, a luxury aboard the small vessel. There were shouts and loud noises throughout the night as the cargo was loaded and stowed under deck.

A knock on the door woke us for breakfast. We dressed and joined uncle at a heavy table bolted to the floor, and sat on a sturdy bench equally well fixed. Though neither Miriam nor I felt like eating uncle insisted we try a little bread and honey along with a tea made from some kind of herbal infusion, all of which seemed to help. When we went on deck a little later we were straight away mesmerized by the deep blue sea. Except for sleeping and eating we would spend our entire voyage out there. My mind emptied of all thoughts, leaving me clear-sighted.

Uncle had planned to go the whole distance to Brittany by sea, which is the quickest way. But even in the best of times it can be very rough and so he decided we would sail to Marseilles, continuing the journey overland. In so doing, he'd be able to drop in on several trading partners along the way whom he had not seen in some time. It did not matter to us since everything was new and equally wonderful.

Even from a distance Marseilles was overwhelming, larger than anything I had ever seen or imagined. We disembarked into a crush of people and carts and animals. The people were of every color and manner of dress and their many languages all merged into something quite unintelligible. Uncle laughed and said we were better off not being able to understand what they said. The noise was intense, as were the smells, even as we moved from the docks into the city. Miriam wrapped her shawl around her head and face, muttering something about how they seemed not to hold cleanliness in high regard.

We were driven to a hotel at the other end of the city where uncle left us to rest and readjust to land. There were some past-due accounts to collect, he said. Joseph had a reputation of being a fair and honest businessman, and expected others to fulfill their obligations as he did his own. Only a foolish man would take advantage of his kindness.

A woman named Marie was left in charge of us. She spoke a few words of Greek, the only language we had in common. She was a bit dour, but won us over with food, starting with exotic nuts and cheese, and fish eggs on flat bread! I wasn't eager to try the eggs, but Miriam obviously enjoyed them, so I did. They were wonderful, like little salty bubbles that popped in my mouth when I bit into them. The wine was stronger, and more bitter than our own. And the sweets! I thought they must have come from heaven itself. "Can you imagine all the other wonders that are to come?" asked Miriam.

The following morning we left at dawn. Marie had put together food for the day, as we did not expect to find a place to eat before late afternoon. The shifting scenery captivated us, far greener than Nazareth, even in spring. Our road passed through dense woods that sometimes crowded out the sun altogether. The air was sweet smelling. It seemed Joseph knew the names of everything: the trees and crops in the fields, flowers unlike any I had ever seen. There were villages filled with houses made entirely of wood; only their foundations were of stone. And it seemed everyone had horses.

The land appeared tranquil and prosperous, but uncle said Rome held this area in as tight a grip as it did our own land. We were stopped frequently by Roman garrisons and made to pay road taxes. Not all were in uniform, and I wondered if they were true tax collectors or mere thieves. Uncle said they were much the same, and so it did not really matter. It was the one reason he preferred to travel by sea. Other than that, the days passed pleasantly. Most of the time we had the evening meal delivered to our room, since drinking often turned to fights in the public areas. It would quiet down by morning, and we'd break our fast in the common rooms before continuing on our way.

We arrived in Brittany early one evening, and took rooms in an inn where uncle was known. Over dinner Miriam said, "I wish Naomi was here with us."

"Yes, uncle, why did she not come? You know she is like a sister to us and being your daughter, she would not have had to ask anyone's permission," I joked.

"She was not happy to see you two go without her," he said, with a troubled look in his eyes. "She may not speak to me for a good long while. But it was not her journey to make."

"But why" Miriam persisted. "I miss her."

"She will join you in your next great adventure, I promise" was all he would say.

By the time we had eaten it was too dark to go out and see the town, so we retired to our rooms. "Quiet," said Miriam, putting a stop to my chattering in the flickering candlelight. In the silence I heard a dull roar off in the distance.

"What is that?"

"The sea. I have heard the waters in this area are wild, battering the land year-round. And that people are as tough as the sea is strong, so they might withstand the winter storms. But it is also said the people's roots go deep, like the great oaks that we have seen growing along the way. The country people may be as silent as these trees, but that silence contains wisdom that cannot be spoken with mere words."

I wondered where Miriam had heard such things. When her parents died, she was sent from family to family to live until her brothers were old enough to care for her. Her upbringing must have exposed her to many things I knew nothing about.

"I love water no matter where it is found, or the form it takes," I murmured. "But I sense it holds a special power here. What you have said just confirms this."

I slept well that night, dreaming of peace and power held together in one hand.

Joseph greeted us the following morning with these words: "The purpose of your journey is about to unfold."

Chapter 18

MIDSUMMER

"Who are these people?" Miriam whispered.

I had no idea, and the look on uncle's face ruled out any questions. We had walked to the edge of the village where we spent the night, and entered a wood. Plunged into shadow from bright daylight, all I saw were the forms of perhaps a dozen people gathered in front of us.

"Welcome." It was a male voice, speaking in Latin. The forms gathered around us in a circle and my skin prickled.

"This is Veronica, and this, Miriam," uncle said, putting his hands on our shoulders in turn. "I leave them to you now, and will return here before sunset."

"Leave us, uncle? What do you mean, leave us? Where are you going? Who are these people? Can you not stay with us?" I spoke softly, not wanting to sound rude. Miriam stood close, assessing the strangers silently. She grabbed Joseph's sleeve, enjoining him with her eyes to answer.

With a sigh he indicated the one who had spoken: "This one is Marcus. They are all our brothers. Each has visited our land, either at Carmel or with me in Jerusalem, one or two at a time so as not to draw attention to them. I know them well, and you will be safe here. They have offered to share something of their teachings and practices. I would ask that you be as open and trusting of them as they are of you." At that he turned and walked back out into the sunlight.

Miriam and I stood shoulder-to-shoulder facing the strangers. "Brother Marcus," I ventured, "might we know the others' names, and what our purpose is with you this day?" Though I had studied Latin, I was not accustomed to using it in everyday conversation and hoped they would not be offended by my rough speech.

"Today is midsummer," he began, "the most sacred day of the year for us. It signals an end to the cycle of expansion, giving us pause before the sun begins its retreat. In the stillness a fissure is revealed, through which we can penetrate through shadows into the realm of light, truth, wisdom. We will divulge our names if you wish, but it is our custom to disregard our personal identities from sunrise to sunset this day. Joseph spoke my name to set you at ease."

Miriam and I responded in one voice: "We have no need of names."

Four women approached, two standing on either side to usher us along a path through the trees. We entered into a large clearing and there beheld the first of many such sights to greet us in this new land. Just within the perimeter stood a circle of giant stones, facing a cluster of even larger stones in their center. Each stone seemed to have been cut to approximately the same proportions, and somehow stood on end. The one closest to us was at least twice my height, and those at the center were half again as big. I reached out my hands to touch it, and felt a thrill run through me.

Seeing the standing stones in their precise configuration seemed completely natural. Moreover, they appeared *alive* in some sense, intelligent even. To this day I cannot rid myself of the idea that they had somehow carved and transported themselves. A fantasy certainly, but I have no doubt that those who created the circle were in league with the stone itself.

The women took our hands and led us inside the circle, standing Miriam and me in front of specific stones facing the center. The others took their own places, male alternating with female in front of the other stones, a human circle within the stone circle. The similarity between our women's circle at my coming of age ceremony was striking, though here were both men and women. There was something else. The whole thing felt familiar, as if I had taken part in a ceremony such as this before. Miriam's eyes glistened from across the circle, and I wondered if she felt it too.

But there was no time to think. A current began to rise from deep within my chest, and my mouth opened to give it release, emerging as sound. Not singing in the ordinary sense, but song of another order. I later wondered whether we had served as the voice of the stones, of the consciousness that lay within them or if it were more fundamental than that -- *life itself* using our voices to harmonize with the celestial architecture of the stone circle in an act of creation. As our voices wove together I lost awareness not only of the other people in the circle, but of my own individual self. As the resonance continued, a strange glow began to emanate from that center, eventually forming into a large globe of pulsating golden light. The globe expanded until it encompassed the stone circle and the clearing behind it, swallowing the sunlight, now pale in comparison.

The next thing I recall was a vaguely familiar and insistent sound. It took an enormous effort to bring my attention to bear on it, until I finally recognized uncle's voice alternately calling Miriam's and my names. It hurt to open my eyes and when I did, I saw we were in our room at the inn. A hand touched my arm; it was Miriam's, her luminous eyes smiling at me. Joseph had moved across the room to a large chair in front of a sunlit window, beaming his joy back to us. I lay on the bed awhile longer, in no hurry to dispel the aura of deep peace that filled me. In the back of my mind I feared that should I move I might never know such ecstasy again.

And then my stomach made a most unseemly noise, and we all broke into laughter, shattering the spell. A whole day had passed, and a night – and I was ravenous with hunger.

Some time remained to us before boarding our ship at Morlais, so after our meal Miriam and I set out to explore the shoreline. The tide was out, and the roaring waves from the previous day had given way to a gentle swish. It was more like our Galilee, which satisfied a hidden longing for the familiar to balance the constant change and newness of our journey. We walked along the shore, picking up a stone here and a shell there, examining it in silence. And then, as if called by a silent voice, we turned away from our explorations and walked back to the ship. From that day on we would often act as with one mind, beyond need for words.

In days to come others would benefit from our intuitive rapport, in a time when speaking one's intentions aloud carried great risk.

Chapter 19

THE HOLY ISLE

We left Brittany, embarking upon a rough sea. The wind had come up suddenly, just as we lifted anchor. Joseph said it would be safer inside our cabin, but I do not think I could have managed being within four walls. It took all my strength to keep hold of the rail as the ship heaved from side to side, putting all my attention on each new breath of fresh air and my efforts to keep from being thrown overboard. The waves did not calm until we came within sight of a spit of land jutting into the sea, a place called Penzance.

The ship's captain, though Phoenician, was a distant relative of Joseph's. My uncle refused to sail with anyone else. "See," he said, "another might have lost the ship and our good lives in a storm such as the one we just passed through."

The captain apologized, as if he were responsible for the winds and rough seas. We assured him we were fine (though we were not). When our feet finally touched land, my legs were so wobbly I nearly fell to the ground. I did not think I would ever eat again, though by midday we were gathered around a table tasting the fruits of yet another land.

I asked uncle about our experience in Brittany. Words would serve no purpose, he said, advising us to let it gestate within us. One cannot force understanding, or artificially bestow it on another.

A few days later his business was completed. The squares of tin were being brought in from the mines, and stacked on the docks. It would take some days for everything to be loaded for the return voyage. In the meantime uncle said he had another excursion planned for us. Again, my skin prickled.

Neither Miriam nor I spoke as the cart raced along the fine Roman road. I was shocked to realize the Romans had pressed so far to the north, and wondered if they engulfed the entire world. The road ended abruptly at the edge of a lake. At first glance it seemed desolate, with boggy land around the edges and mists rising up where land and water met. All the same, the place had a peculiar beauty, with hanging vines and moss-covered trees all around. It was unearthly still.

Uncle pointed into the mists: "Look up there," he said. At first I couldn't see anything, till a sharp hill suddenly pierced the vaporous shadows.

Miriam gasped. "I have seen that hill in my dreams."

"I do not know if I have traveled here in my dreams," I replied, "but there is an eerie familiarity to it. I half expect someone I know to appear round that bend."

Uncle's face had the look that said 'you know better than to ask any questions.' He was up to something. He had the innkeeper prepare a basket of foods that morning, promising us surprises. We pulled the basket out of the cart, and spread a cloth on the ground not far from the water. There was a sound in the distance that came and went, but since no one else seemed to notice, I said nothing.

Miriam let out a yelp and I jumped to my feet, scattering food everywhere. A stag had bolted out of the trees not a stone's throw away, startling us. We laughed nervously as we tidied up the mess.

We had just sat back down when uncle cleared his throat. "The surprise I promised will not be found in what you are eating, but in what you are seeing."

Scanning our surroundings I noticed some birds, including several hawks of a kind I had never seen before. A hedge next to the water appeared to have been groomed, which meant someone lived nearby. There was nothing else out of the ordinary that I could see, but our meal had lost its appeal as I became intrigued with our new game.

We waited for the next clue. The wait would not be long. Again I heard the odd noise, now a rhythmic *swoosh...swoosh...swoosh*. I got to my feet and started toward the water, not noticing that Miriam and uncle followed. Suddenly a boat broke through the mist, nearly plowing into me. It stopped so suddenly when it hit land the boatman just about fell into the water. He probably had not realized he'd been so close to shore.

The man regained his composure. "I am sorry to have frightened you," he said to me, trying to sound serious while his eyes continued to laugh. "My thoughts were traveling among the mists, when suddenly there you were. I thought you were the fairy of the lake!"

"What is this place?" I asked, in between giggles. "What is the magic I sense here?"

The man looked at uncle, with a pinched brow, and I wondered if he were lost and did not know the answer to my questions.

"I have not told them yet," he said, suddenly serious. Then, to us he said, "Gawain is here to ferry us to Glastonia."

Gawain spit into the water. "That is a Roman name!" Though he spoke Latin with us, he obviously did not care for the occupation. "It is the Holy Isle, the *Holy Isle*."

I detected a note of awe in his voice as he said the name. We had climbed in and were huddled on a low bench that stretched across the boat, only a few fingers above the strands of slimy weeds floating in its hull. It seemed to me we sat dangerously low in the water, and I wondered how deep it was and whether I still knew how to swim though I had not done so since childhood.

His words echoed in my mind, and the water was forgotten. *The Holy Isle.* I had heard the name, but knew nothing about it, imagining a place where the ancient brotherhood might have established itself in this strange land, just as they had in our own, in Egypt and elsewhere.

"You are right," said Gawain, looking directly at me. "We are kin, all of us brothers, Sons of the Sun." I quivered. This stranger saw through me, as if I were nothing more substantial than the wind. He began to sing a quiet song, in words I could not understand. But I knew he sang of the wind and sky and sea. It made me long for something I had forgotten. Miriam's eyes filled with tears, and uncle's face turned away from us to the far shore. Something in that song tugged at our hearts, drawing us together as a family who pines for a lost loved one, sensing hope in our shared loss.

The mist dissipated, and the far shore grew larger. We were soon walking on solid land, a small path leading away from the water's edge. We followed Gawain, trying to keep up with his long strides. He was a handsome man, tall and finely built. His reddish gold hair was tied back, leaving soft wisps to curl around his ears, dancing in the slightest breeze. I found myself wondering what he would look like with the tie released, hair falling over his shoulders...and heat seared my face.

I turned my attention to my feet and became so intent upon where I stepped that I nearly collided again with our guide when he stopped short. He turned slowly and slipped into my eyes. Except for mother, and Jesus, no one had touched my soul before this … and surely no stranger. We swayed in a current beyond anything I had known to exist. Then I heard a snap and there he stood, looking every bit as startled as I felt. It must have lasted only an instant, as neither Miriam nor Joseph appeared to have noticed. I was glad. That moment out of time had been for the two of us alone.

When we resumed our walk, I felt dizzy. I knew my heart had been cracked open, and yet I felt no pain. I simply felt … larger … more.

We rounded a bend and found ourselves in front of a small stone structure. Its roof was woven of dried reeds that ended in a fringe cut like the hair of some young girls we had seen in our travels. A wooden door stood ajar, and Gawain gestured for us to stay back as he stooped to go inside.

Mists still surrounded the island, yet the sun shone brightly where we stood. The heat bore down on us, and I noticed my thirst, thinking of the basket we had left behind filled with drink and food. Just then Gawain and three others came out of the hut. The strangers were of Joseph's age, their graying hair framing serene eyes. They bowed in greeting, and led us around the side of the house to a small, circular platform at the base of a low hill. A stream tumbled down the embankment, gathering into a small pool in the center of the platform before it emptied into a well at the other end.

We sat here and there on benches around the water, gratefully accepting the cups of cold water offered us by one of the women. I had not noticed her carrying anything when she came out of the house, and must have looked surprised when she handed me the cup. She laughed: "Whatever you require, it is the Mother's good pleasure to provide for you." She had sat down next to me, her voice barely indistinguishable from the tinkling water falling at our feet.

"Who are you, mother?" I asked.

"I am only the Mother's handmaid. She…" and the woman gestured to our surroundings "is with us everywhere, and knows of our needs at all times, even before we are aware of them ourselves." Her smiling eyes reflected the blue sky.

She rose to her feet and we instinctively stood with her. I noticed absently that we alternated male, female, male and so on. The woman stretched her arms out to both sides, joining hands with Joseph and one of her companions. The others did the same until we formed a circle around the pool. Everyone closed their eyes, except me. Events in Brittany had taught me to notice everything, so as not to miss the underlying meaning.

Even as I watched with eyes open, my thoughts turned within to where I noticed a sound, almost a whisper, like wind in the trees. Intuitively I knew it was *our* sound, arising from our joining. As the sound grew in intensity it engaged the waters at our feet to spin around like a whirlpool. As the churning increased it lifted the water upward, swirling, a circle within our circle, rising, rising, until it reached the tops of our heads. It sprayed droplets of light rather than moisture, saturating us with its luminosity. Then suddenly it was over; the water settled back to where it had been and everyone opened their eyes at the same moment.

"What is wrong, my dear?" uncle asked.

"Well...there is nothing wrong. But...."

"But what? You look frightened. And you're trembling," he said, taking my hand.

"But uncle, Miriam..." She looked as bewildered as he. "Did you not see? But of course, your eyes were closed," I whispered, not sure if I had done something wrong.

"I do not know what you are talking about," he said. "I only know that we were called here. Long ago our brothers told me I would bring two young women, two virgins from among us," he said, almost to himself, ". . . who were destined to bear a portion of the burden to come. We were to join with you here," he gestured to our new friends, "to prepare the soil, seeding the new world of grace from our Father-Mother."

"And now the seed has been planted," said the woman. "In its time it will bring the gift of greater life to all mankind. Some will claim this boon for himself alone, or only for family, his people. But denying others only means denying oneself. Even so, an Age and more will pass before all will accept this essential truth."

She descended from the platform then and walked toward the cottage, disappearing inside. There were so many questions I would have asked, but my heart told me the answers themselves were not yet known.

Gawain led us back to the water and our boat slipped silently into the mists. No one had said a word. Now lost in thought, I barely noticed our oarsman. But when he took my hand to say goodbye I understood that whatever had happened between us earlier had somehow prepared the ground for the seeding.

Chapter 20

FROM UR TO THE KIBER PASS

Jesus wondered why Pursa wanted them to meet him in Ur. According to legend, it had once been a grand city, larger, richer and more beautiful than Jerusalem or maybe even Rome. But it had long since fallen into ruin, replaced by Babylon to the northwest.

"We will reach Ur by nightfall," said Krishna.

"Have you been there? Do you know where to find Pursa?" asked Jesus.

"No, I took the main route through Babylon to reach the great sea," he replied.

The two men had seen few travelers on the road from Jerusalem, and no caravans. They had been warned of thieves, but their journey had been pleasant if slow, free from danger. "Pursa will have people watching for us," Krishna said when they set out.

The day's heat had begun to subside and their shadows stretched out in front of them, when they spied the outline of a city rising up from the sands. On approach they found a ghost of a city. Portions of domes could be seen in the evening shadows. A wild dog howled in the distance, and scuffling sounds could be heard on every side as the night creatures came into their own.

"Perhaps we should stay the night out here," suggested Krishna. Jesus started to agree when a form separated from the darkness, man and camel joined as one, moving in their direction. The travelers instinctively stiffened.

"Why have you come? Who do you seek?" it said.

"We seek our brother," replied Krishna, "called Pursa."

"Come," he said, turning back under the stone archway that joined what remained of the walls. As darkness closed around them they wove through narrow alleys, the cobbles beneath their feet still largely in place. But few walls and no buildings stood intact until, that is, they arrived at what seemed a solid structure, limned in light. The man slid off his camel and led the animals away, leaving Jesus and Krishna alone on the doorstep. They expected the man to return, but after a time Jesus stepped up and knocked at the door. They heard footsteps, stopping just the other side. The large wooden door creaked open. Krishna whispered they had the advantage, should anything be amiss, but there stood Pursa himself, frowning into the darkness.

The two men quickly moved into the light and he broke into a wide smile, embracing both at once. "Ah, my brothers, you have come! The journey?"

"It was a lonely road, but one without difficulties," answered Krishna.

"Your father?" Pursa asked Jesus, guiding them into the room. He took their cloaks and offered chairs. "Or would you prefer to wash first?"

"Later, thank you. My father has journeyed home, and all is well," he replied. "I am content that mother and her children will be well cared for. Her uncle Joseph will see to that."

Krishna thought it odd his friend spoke of his mother's children rather than referring to them as his own brothers and sisters.

And it was *her* uncle, not his own. He had clearly been fond of his siblings, as well as Joseph, and so it was not from a lack of caring that he distanced himself from them. Indeed there were many strange things about this man with whom he had been traveling. He was unlike anyone he had ever known, from any land.

"Yes, he is home now, isn't he," replied Pursa. "My people would say the beam of light has returned to the sun, the flame to the fire."

The three men were silent as Pursa prepared a light meal for his brothers. There were no servants, and it appeared Pursa lived alone. No one was in a hurry to talk about that which was largely unknown to them anyway. All would be revealed in time. After they had their fill, Pursa brought out a small box out from under the table. It was covered with a fine cloth, as soft as a newborn kid, and as blue as midnight.

"Would you like to learn a new game?" he asked his guests

"I must seek guidance from the stars this night," said Krishna." Besides, only two can play, and I believe our friend will enjoy this new pastime."

The door opened and closed quietly behind them as Pursa pulled out a board the length of a man's forearm and the width of his hand. Jesus leaned in to see, his fingers drawn irresistibly to the lapis lazuli, shell and gold inlaid in the dark wood. An odd rosette pattern lay in certain areas, but otherwise the design seemed abstract. "I have seen something like this in Egypt, but nothing quite so fine, even though it was in a royal household." He picked up some small pieces carved of the same wood. They were of two similar shapes, half concave and half convex. "In Egypt they used pieces shaped like pyramids and . . . a cat-like creature representing the goddess Bast."

"In other lands, seeds or small pellets are used." Pursa's toothy grin gleamed in the light of the oil lamp. "In each place materials, design and strategy vary, but I have never found a single city where there was not an interest in gaming,"

They played until Krishna returned from his walk when the board was stowed and the men retired to their alcoves to sleep. Here the travelers found an unexpected luxury: mattresses thickly padded with sheep's wool. When such could be found in public inns, they were filled with noxious biting things, but Pursa assured them the herbs tucked in with the wool kept them away. "Besides, the wool is replaced at least twice a year, so it is always fresh smelling."

The next morning their host took them around what remained of the once magnificent city. "What happened here?" asked Jesus. "Why did it fall?"

"Greed, wars, unresolved hatred passed down from fathers to sons; the same things that still fester in the hearts of men. We have not come so far."

"And why are you here? Do you actually live among the ruins?" asked Krishna.

"It is the place from which Abraham came, to lay the foundation for a great people. Its isolation and neglect suits us. There remain points of great power within the old walls and nearby, but one must know where they are -- and few do. Wise men of old drew down arcs of light through their sacred practices, grounding it within the earthly realms. My brothers and I serve as caretakers. It is not my *home*, though it was an ancient home of my people when Persia took its turn as ruler of these lands. Ur is ignored today, and thus is a haven for the Brotherhood.

"This house belongs to any who have need of it. When I leave, I will do what I can to restock the cupboards and fill the cistern so no one who arrives empty-handed will suffer. There are six separate residences scattered among the ruins, each open to anyone who has need of shelter, no matter who they are. We ask only that all weapons be left outside the city walls."

Pursa looked directly at Jesus then. "You have made your way here largely unseen. Had you traveled the main road, all would know of the passage of the Nazarene."

Jesus shuddered, though he did not know why.

He went on. "And only those whom we trust will know when we leave, and for where. The danger will be left behind on the far side of Persia."

Neither Jesus nor Krishna asked the nature of the danger. It did not serve to name it. Glad for the respite, they were suddenly eager to be on their way. Before leaving, they met two other brothers, one from Tibet and another from Egypt. The latter asked for news of his homeland.

"More than a moon has passed since I left Alexandria. But I can tell you that Rome has overstayed its welcome there, if indeed it ever had it." Jesus spoke of Zar's kidnapping, and then of other more pleasant things. "I have heard the name Tibet," he said to the other man, "but know nothing about it. Shortly after I arrived in Alexandria, Zar told me I would one day travel there. What can you tell me about your land?"

Jingu narrowed his eyes as he silently probed the young Essene. He had known of his coming, and looked within the youth for the master that would one day emerge. It is said that all we are to become is even now within us. The purpose of our worldly existence is to awaken and reveal this to ourselves. Jingu did not have to look far for the divine spark.

In turn Jesus watched the old man. Eyes seemed to disappear into a weathered face; his skin was reddish brown, leathery and deeply lined. The thinning hair was pulled back under an odd flat hat, the color of blood. His worn and dusty robe had been dyed orange – or perhaps it had once matched the hat and simply faded. He was altogether a striking figure

Jingu pushed back from the table where they sat across from each other and smiled. His yellowed teeth framed a black hole right in front where one had been lost. Despite this, he looked like a child as he reached out to take the Nazarene's hands in his.

"Yes, you will come to us in Tibet. Soon, very soon. You will find it unlike any other place, so high in the mountains that your nose will bleed." And for some reason, this made him laugh. "But it is good for us. The air is too heavy here, and I feel short."

"Short?" asked Jesus.

"Short. In Tibet the air is light, and I am lifted up to the heavens. Here the earth pulls me down to her, compressing me." And he laughed again.

Jesus would learn that the people of Tibet laughed easily. He would also learn that their periodic wars with neighboring chiefdoms were no laughing matter.

"What did you mean when you said I would visit Tibet very soon?" asked Jesus, taking another tack.

"Ah, I am on my way there now, and you and your friends will accompany me."

"Now? We are on our way to Juggernaut now. Maybe I can go to Tibet after that."

"Oh no, it is now you will come to Tibet. From there you can go to Juggernaut, or anywhere else you wish to go."

Jesus looked to his companions for help, but neither would meet his eyes. Later they explained that it was impossible to argue with the old man. He was known throughout the East, and highly respected. His word was rarely challenged.

And so on the second day after the new moon they departed Ur and began the long journey to the high mountains. At times they rode four abreast, debating many subjects, from the creation of life to the nature of fire spirits to whether wine or beer was the better drink for one's health. At other times they rode in single file listening to the silence and probing the depths of their own minds.

At times firewood and dung were plentiful, while in certain areas there was no fuel of any kind to be found for their nighttime fires -- whether for cooking, warmth or the camaraderie of looking into the flames together. And even though the route they took was little used, they came across water at decent intervals. During their one serious windstorm they tied dampened cloth over the camels' faces and drew them into a circle, creating a windbreak for the men. The creatures wailed and moaned throughout the night, but all made it through. They were sturdy beasts, and greatly appreciated.

Eventually their path merged with the main trade route, which went directly through Persia. Pursa discovered a relative of his among one of the caravans heading in the other direction toward his home, and the man offered to take a message to his wife for him. Until that moment his companions had not even known he was married.

He laughed. "I tried to talk her out of marrying me, telling her I would be gone more than at home, but she said she preferred it that way. She was serious too! Still, we have managed to have two sons and a daughter, though they are different people altogether each time I do manage to get back." His laughter turned to wistfulness.

The brothers fell silent. Theirs was a strange path indeed, one that few men or women would willingly choose. While they rarely had what others took for granted, there were no regrets. They did not seek the riches of the world, but the treasures beyond.

Later my cousin told me how hard it was to pass straight through the land that had long held such fascination for him, but he knew he would eventually find his way back there. The goal now was Tibet.

At last Jingu began to speak of his homeland. "This is nothing," he said. They were passing through a chain of mountains at the time, and the younger men struggled for air. "Visitors often have trouble breathing in Tibet. The mountains there are many times as high as these, and people have been known to die on the spot, often in extreme pain. You will see." Such a prospect was hardly enticing.

They traveled a great distance; temperatures and weather conditions were often extreme. Fortunately for Jesus, his companions had brought heavy cloaks for everyone. A fur-lined hood fell down over his forehead. Krishna said it came from a wolverine. Jesus did not like killing animals for meat, and now he wore one on his back. And soon even heavier cloaks would be required, provided by a ponderous creature called a yak which lives in the highest mountains of Tibet.

At night, when weather permitted, they brought out their game boards and played around the campfires. One of the boards in particular intrigued him. It wasn't as beautiful as the one in Ur, but embodied a deeper symbolism. It was made of two woods, one dark and one light, which alternated three squares across and ten squares long. All boards were made with indentations to catch the playing pieces that were tossed out during the course of the game. Players must concentrate on their strategy, and this particular board was designed to draw them into a deeper awareness of the intrinsic nature of the seen life, which is dualism. The pairs of opposites that comprise our world are in constant interaction, such as dark and light, night and day, female and male, one hand and the other. The path of the markers across the board in the process of play mirrors our path through lives in which these opposites weave an endless pattern, alternately breathing in and breathing out, attracting, then repelling.

The men did not gamble, as most do. And their play did not interfere with their contemplative practices or the philosophical discussions that were more often responsible for keeping them awake long after the fires had sputtered out. They were, after all, men accustomed to turning aside from the world to go within. But these were also men who enjoyed life; laughter would alert others to their presence long before they could be seen.

At long last they approached the Kiber Pass, a high shoulder connecting the middle lands with those of the East, and there they rested.

"It is time," said Pursa, "for me to make the return journey to Persepolis."

"But you have come this far with us, my brother. Do not turn aside now," implored Krishna. He had long tried to get his friend to go with him to the sacred river and the great sea of his homeland.

"It will soon be time for our high council to come together and cast the stones for the next great cycle," insisted Pursa.

"Cast the stones?" asked Jesus. "I thought you were followers of the stars."

"And so we are, perhaps more learned than any other in interpreting our celestial brethren. But each twelve turns around the sun, we return our gaze to the wisdom lying dormant in the planet that sustains our earthly bodies. And there we find among the stones a deeper message of the stars reflected back to us. When we see the message written twice over, we know we have interpreted correctly. Only four moons remain before the council convenes. Besides," he added, his voice grown softer, "I miss my family. My father is old, and I would see him one more time. You understand," he added in my cousin's direction.

"If that is your true reason for leaving us, I understand, of course," said Krishna. "But if it is for the council, you have yet a while longer."

Pursa laughed. "A short time could not satisfy my longing to see Tibet or Kashgar, or the mother Ganga, or your Juggernaut. No, that will have to wait for another day. The men we met this morning are waiting for a caravan. They will go to Persepolis, and I with them," he said with finality.

The brothers spent three days there together, enjoying the clear air and each other's company. It was a rare interlude where nothing distracted from the simple joys of life. Besides, Jingu had needed the rest.

"This will be my last journey out of Tibet. I will not leave my beloved mountains again with this body." He slapped his knee and his face broke into a thousand little valleys. The men laughed with him, and even the birds croaked and cawed, looking down on the party below.

The following morning the three men prepared to depart. They would soon leave the main trade route, and follow a harsher path. A somber tone settled down around them. It came not from fear or dread of what lay ahead, but a blade-sharp focus, requisite for such a small band to survive in the harsh wilderness. The caravan had not yet arrived, and they left Pursa with the other men to wait. It was critical they cross the highest mountains before early winter storms descended upon them, and they dared not wait any longer.

"Will you stay in Persepolis?" asked Jesus. "I should like to know you will be there when I return, though I could not say in what season or year that may be."

"When the time approaches, send a message, and I will arrange to return if I have gone away. When I was but a boy the Elders chose me to serve as your guide when you come there."

The men embraced, and the small band turned toward the east. Riding into a strong wind the Nazarene wondered at the way of things, that the Elders of the star people had chosen his guide before he had even been born to this earth.

Chapter 21

ABODE OF THE GODS

An invisible curtain separated two worlds; the one side held traces of the life he had left behind, but the other ... Jesus had never seen anything like it, except in some half forgotten dream. Beyond the high pass all colors seemed changed, softening into pale grays and blues. Had he known it, even the color of his eyes had transformed to reflect this strange new sky. The air burned his lungs and he struggled at every step.

The three men had traded their camels for yaks, beasts more suited to the terrain and temperamental weather. Great hairy creatures, stolid, rooted to the earth, they offered reassurance in a land devoid of comforts. The female provided strong tasting milk to which Jingu added salt and rancid butter for added nourishment. There was little else to eat than dried barley cakes and the few remaining dates they'd carried with them from the desert.

The men spoke little. Winds howled, stealing their thoughts away from them.

The first day after leaving Pursa they met the caravan he planned to join, and purchased two sturdy yak-hair tents from one of the traders. Most nights thereafter they made camp before the sun set, eating their meals inside. The heavy fabric shuddered thunderously with each blast of air, counterpoint to the still calm within. These men, so far from home, were neither lost nor alone.

His first night in the tent Jesus easily shifted awareness into the intersection between life of the body and the life of spirit, a point somewhere between earth and heaven. In this point he found the *All*, life not contained in form. Within the absolute darkness he found the source of light and knew it as himself.

They broke camp in the icy stillness. The beasts were loaded with supplies for their journey, and goods they were taking to Jingu's temple complex, where lived a hundred monks. His monastery sat at the center of the Bon tradition, the largest such complex in that vast land. Jingu had told the two men that though Bon contained elements of the Brahman and other traditions to the south, it had many unique elements. Jesus was eager to learn more but each time he asked a question the old priest would hold up his hand, signaling patience.

Some days later the party began its slow descent. The town of Leh sprawled below them in a high valley, the last town of any size before entering into Tibet. The mid-morning sun burned through the chill and the yaks lifted their heads, nostrils flaring in the sweet air. The men felt lighter; their breathing not so labored.

"Leh is also a Bonpo haven," said Jingu. "We will see the first of the great monasteries here." As if on cue a small party of monks approached, dressed in the same manner as he. They bowed low to the old priest, the youngest among them prostrating themselves on the ground at his feet. But when they rose they laughed and patted him on the back, chattering away in their own tongue. Jesus was glad to see that Jingu did not take his position too seriously.

"Hurry," the old man said to his friends, "they have gathered monks from throughout the valley to meet you. There will be a feast!" He laughed and danced ahead of them like a child, happy to be with his brothers again.

Krishna and Jesus were left to prod the yaks, and quickly fell behind. Not long after two of the younger monks returned and with a few words and choice kicks on the yak's enormous backsides, got them running. They turned up a small path off the main road just before entering town, and there passed through a gate barely wide enough for the animals. When he later described the scene to me, Jesus said the yaks had to be wider than five men standing hip to hip, if such could be imagined.

Leh was comprised of small clusters of buildings, each surrounded by tracts of open land spread across a flat valley nestled among high mountains. The town had no center and no wall to define its boundaries. The monastery itself ascended a steep cliff and spread out over the rock face like a blanket of lichen. One level grew out of the next, added on as the complex had grown.

The two outsiders were led to a cell they were expected to share. Though the day had warmed considerably, a damp chill accosted them inside. It was small and nearly dark, with two rotting mats on the floor in front of what looked like a tiny stone altar. On the stone sat a gourd rattle and a butter lamp with a new wick. There were no blankets or skins on the mats, and the men were glad they had brought their own.

A chorus of bells sent them scurrying back down the narrow stairwell to the courtyard below where the monks were gathering. "Come over here," shouted Jingu. "Stand by me. They do this each time I come through here, bringing everyone in from their prayers. It's quite unnecessary, but they insist." He shrugged his shoulders, like an indulgent parent, grinning out over the assemblage.

Two elderly men entered the courtyard, and the grin disappeared. Their robes matched his, while the younger men formed a swath of peach. The men came and stood on either side of Jingu and the ritual prostration began again. Jesus watched the old men's faces for their reactions to the display. The two resident priests appeared alternately bored and smug, while Jingu shifted about uncomfortably.

"There is nothing to be done about it," he said, when they spoke of it later at his own monastery.

"But you are the Abbott," protested Jesus. "You can put a stop to it here."

"You do not understand. My position is both political and spiritual, and there are those who wield more power than I. They would not hesitate to remove me and put another in my place, one who would be more pliant."

"But why?"

"If the hierarchical order were to break down within our walls, then chaos could spread across the countryside. For order and discipline to be maintained outside, it must begin with the monks and priests, since we are the heart and soul of the people. Do not doubt the importance of this. You are here during a time of peace. Rebellions arise from out of nowhere among our people, and invasions by those who surround us. We must be able to mobilize the line of command at a moment's notice – or we are lost. I do not believe I am any better than those around me, and I try to be a kind and fair father to these, my children. But I dare not challenge the system that keeps our lands safe." And so the subject was closed.

After the ritual greeting in the courtyard the monks returned to their prayers or studies, and some to the kitchen to prepare the evening's feast. Unlike their neighbors to the south, these people ate meat. Jesus complained to Krishna that he had lost his appetite after seeing the bloody carcass of some unknown animal dragged across the courtyard. "Animal flesh helps us keep our strength," said Jingu when Krishna asked him about it later. "It is more difficult to maintain stamina so high in the mountains."

Everyone gathered inside the temple at dusk, where hundreds of butter lamps burned. Jesus felt claustrophobic. There were too many men in too small a space, made worse with the strong oily smell and cloying smoke. He could see the walls had once been painted, though a greasy film obliterated most of the color. The monks chanted and prayed until it was well dark. Then rising off the damp floor, they filed noisily into a room with four long wooden tables, lined with benches from end to end.

The visitors were seated between the two priests in the place of honor, with Jingu across from them to translate. "It is our custom to eat in silence, and then not after sunset," said one of the priests. "Some monasteries do not allow eating after midday, but we are more liberal here. The monks are like monkeys let out of their cage tonight," he said, condescendingly. "They will chatter like this until they return to their cells, and even then they will be difficult to shut up."

I know this man is my brother, Jesus thought to himself, but I do not like him. He was immediately ashamed at his thoughts, and then realized that the act of judging himself was only compounding the problem. But as he pondered these things something made him look up to find Jingu looking at him quizzically.

"Come, walk with me before we sleep," the old man said, pulling on his sleeve.

The two men walked away from the compound. Jesus asked, "How can it be: it is the dark of the moon yet it is nearly as bright as day?"

"We are closer to the heavens here," said Jingu. "You will find it brighter still in my home. Some people say Tibet is the *roof of the world*. But I think the better name is the *abode of the Gods*."

They walked awhile in silent camaraderie. Jesus had grown fond of his older companion, and looked to him as teacher and mentor. "The blessing goes both ways, you know," said Jingu, in response to his unspoken thought.

"A story has been passed down from Abbott to Abbott within our monastery, for many generations. When I took up my position, it was given me to hold in my heart. Now, when I pass the story on before leaving for the spirit world, it will for the first time be changed." The men walked on, and Jesus waited patiently to hear the story.

"It speaks of a young man who will come to us from somewhere to the west," he began, "far beyond the world which was known to our people when the story was first told. This man is fair skinned, and his eyes reflect the changeable heavens above. This was strange enough, but when my predecessor told me his hair would be the color of my skin, burnished as the morning sky, I laughed and thought it a fairy tale. It was foretold that the Abbott at the time of his coming would go out and meet him halfway on his journey to us, and bring him back so he would know he was welcome. He would come to us as a bridegroom comes to his bride. You see ...." The old man had stopped and turned to face Jesus, "... there is to be a marriage, a marriage of two great traditions, two ways two approach the holy of holies.

"You my son are that traveler, the one prophesied to weave the multicolored threads into a single rope. You were born with the words of Abraham on your breath, since adding to that the secrets of the Pharaohs. Have you heard the name Gautama?"

"Yes, but I know little...."

"You will learn more, much more of him. My people are not ready for the pure land teachings, but eventually they will tire of wars and then the Dharma will come to our land. Bon prepares us for that day. In the meantime I will share our teachings with you, and you will learn of Gautama and Brahmanism when you leave here. In turn you must teach all of us, shining a new light upon old doctrines. Before you are through all the ancient wisdom will be distilled in your blood, and a higher truth will emerge.

"You will encounter resistance both as to what you say and who you are, even among your own people. Remember that your purpose is to speak the truth as it is given you to know, and nothing more. Stand within the light of this truth, and do not concern yourself with how it will be received."

Jesus shivered, knowing this was only a part of the story. But it was enough, more than enough for him to hear now. He did not remember going to sleep that night, only that he opened his eyes to Krishna standing over him the next morning.

"We will leave after prayers," he said. "Even now our supplies are being replenished. Come." And he went out, leaving Jesus alone with his thoughts.

"Father," he said. "I am only a man, and cannot bear this burden alone. Send me your helpers, of flesh and spirit. I know there can be no separation from you, that we are one, just as all those I meet in this world are a part of you, manifestations of your love."

Later, on the road, Jingu said, "Let them think I am an old man who has forgotten his manners. It was the only way we could have gotten out of there before they began the Epics."

"The Epics?" asked Krishna, knowing well what he was talking about.

"Oh yes, the Epics. Once begun, the dramas and ceremonies would have had to play themselves out, from the creation through the interminable wars fought against their noble people, to their ultimate liberation from all oppressors," he said, exasperated. "I love the Epics as entertainment, but they fall short of the higher teachings. And besides, I will feel relief when I see my own home again. These old bones are tired, and seek rest."

It would be another week before they reached Shigatse. They encountered few travelers on the road, which was worrisome. And those few they met were disinclined to talk with strangers. Whether presaging war or bad weather, the three brothers knew only that difficulties were brewing on some level, so they pressed forward.

"I am concerned about Jingu," said Krishna one morning. "He weakens with each day." They had tried to get him to ride one of the yaks, but he refused.

"They smell," he said. "It is bad enough walking alongside them, and sleeping within tents carried on their backs." He made such an awful face his companions had to laugh.

"Alright father," said Jesus, "at least let us take care of the camp each night." The old man had insisted on sharing the chores, rushing about in search of something for the fire each night. Finally, in his exhaustion, he agreed.

The night before they arrived in Shigatse they set their tents in fresh snow. Krishna went behind a rock to relieve himself. A moment later he ran back, robes flying.

"What did you see? What is it?" the two men asked in unison.

"I am not sure, as I barely caught a glimpse of it as it ran away." There was fear in his voice. "But from the prints, it was a large cat of some kind."

Jesus went to see, and returned. "You are right, my friend. It was a big cat." He stole a look at the tents. "I do not know whether it would be capable of tearing through such strong fabric. But there is no firewood here, which leaves us two choices. We can all three sleep together in one tent, and hope for the best. Or you and I can take turns standing guard," he said to Krishna.

"Three can take turns," insisted Jingu.

They reluctantly agreed. But there were no new prints in the morning. Jesus was secretly disappointed, as he had hoped for a glimpse of the creature, having heard tales of their beauty.

Jingu's monastery was but a short day's walk beyond Shigatse. The town was a Bon stronghold, surrounded by scores of temples, large and small. But they decided to spend the night at an inn, sparing them the social obligations of a temple stay. There would be enough of that when they reached the monastery. They were entertained that night with stories from fellow travelers of imminent battles, frightful attacks by wild animals, a winter storm brewing to their south, and other dramas, truth or fiction.

Chapter 22

BODY OF LIGHT

Cool evening air brought relief from the heat of the day. It was nearing the end of autumn. Early rains threatened and the whole community had come together to get the barley seed in the ground.

"I do not think my hands will ever come clean," Miriam mused, picking at her nails.

"They will, when enough clothes have been washed."

She laughed. "But I cannot think about doing anything else today. Not even cook."

We walked to the top of my favorite hill and sat on the rocks, taking turns massaging our stiff shoulders. "It's curious," she said, reflecting my own thoughts, "how hard work often leaves me with a sense of peace."

"When we are one with our labors, there is no inner conflict, no battles between opposing forces." I paused before completing my thought. "It is unselfish, even if it is done for our own comfort ultimately. And it is honest, and thus there is nothing that needs be forgiven or brought to balance. It is therefore liberating."

Darkness settled around us, like a blanket in the night. I had been drifting in and out of awareness when I noticed a glistening of the air around us. Not light exactly, but a shimmer as when something catches light and reflects it back to the observer. At first I thought I imagined the faint outline of my cousin's face. It flickered faintly, nearly fading away, then sharpened and expanded into full view. Like us, Jesus sat among boulders, but next to a fast-moving river that ran at the foot of a steep cliff. Around him stretched out fields of green, dotted with tiny clustered flowers of a kind I had never seen. Their petals had a waxy appearance, veined purple and yellow.

When the scene did not disappear my heart began to beat rapidly, knowing I saw truly. In the distance behind him stood a large stone complex surrounded by high walls. And there were thin poles stuck here and there into the ground with ropes connecting them and on the ropes were tied countless flags, flapping ceaselessly in the wind. Many were white or near white, but a few were purple, blue, red and other strong colors.

I had on occasion been able to see through my cousin's eyes the very scene he was observing (even though he was far from me). But this was different: I could shift my focus at will to different parts of the scene, as if I were sitting there with him. I do not know if my eyes were open or whether I had lapsed into a meditation where I was seeing with my inner vision.

The sun was either rising or setting there, the shadows long. Its light paled compared to that emanating from him where he sat with eyes closed. This light encircled his form, growing slowly larger as he delved deeper and yet deeper within. I wondered at the back of my mind if the light which ensconced Miriam and me had somehow been projected to where we sat from his thought of us. Or maybe it arose from our own hearts, so strongly connected to each other and to him.

When eventually the light dissipated back into the night, we returned home, filled with a sweet grace. I knew from Miriam's face she too had seen him.

*

Jesus looked forward to staying in one place awhile. To be always with others was wearing, to be always on the move, disruptive. Change is of course the nature of worldly existence, but a solid spiritual practice requires some consistency.

While the younger monks in Jingu's monastery were unloading the yaks, he walked out beyond the walls alone. After the harsh and often desolate expanses of the high mountains, the valley was a salve to the senses. They had seen no trees since leaving Leh. But this place contained a vast array, some few of which were yet green. The old priest had said there were many kinds of fruit trees, though he doubted he would stay long enough to see them bear.

He needed to get away from the noise and excitement surrounding the return of their beloved Abbott. The river ran directly outside the walls. Walking upstream he was astonished to see so many birds even as winter approached. His breathing told him they were still in the high mountains. The valley must hold some kind of magic, he thought to himself, as it was nearly as lush as the land that bordered on the great seas.

Jesus chose a large flat rock next to the river and sat down, kicking off his sandals. He plunged his feet into the water, and the icy cold sent a shock through his whole body. He had already forgotten the year-round snow just above them. His feet had only been in the water a few seconds, but they throbbed with an unpleasant ache. This would be his first winter in a cold land.

He tucked his feet in under his robes to warm them, and turned his vision within. As his breath stilled, the swirling energy which had been so chaotic at first, began to slow as it gained in power. This energy is a living force, aiding us in our personal growth at the same time it radiates out into the world *from* us, like the beam of light projected from the lighthouse on the cliffs near Carmel. Its light shines upon all travelers in this world, no matter who they are, helping them upon their way.

After a time his consciousness returned to worldly things. He thought of his mother and the land of his youth, of his cousins, brothers and sisters, and of Miriam. How far away it all seemed, not so much in leagues, or even the years passed since he left home. Though it would not always be so, in that moment he felt content, without loss or longing.

That evening he sat through another feast, arranged for Jingu and his guests. Jesus did not know that the priests and monks had been eagerly anticipating his own arrival. Jingu had spoken of the prophecies related to him, but he did not know they were common knowledge. The teachings and esoteric knowledge that awaited him there, combined with all that he had already learned would send a thrill throughout the entire Brotherhood. Everyone would be lifted up, including him.

After the feasting came performances of many kinds. There were dragon dances, and war dances. And there were simulated battles with hungry ghosts who attach themselves to people, living off their life force. Horns and drums of many sizes and descriptions accompanied each event, unlike anything Jesus had heard or seen before. Throughout the evening a fire burned at the edge of the courtyard. Now and then someone threw incense into the flames, producing a small burst of smoke and releasing a pungent aroma over the assembly.

The ceremonial area was cleared then and a hush fell over the crowd. Villagers could be seen atop the walls and in trees, the better to see; they too fell silent. The shaman stood alone, wearing a headdress half his height sprouting long multicolored streamers flowing down around him to the ground. He did not move for what seemed a very long time, then staggered across the courtyard to the fire. Stopping at its edge, he pulled a substance out of a pouch hung round his neck, and sprinkled it into the flames. Leaning precariously forward into the smoke, he inhaled deeply. Then he began to circle the fire, exaggerating each movement, moving faster and faster, the circles growing ever larger, frequently returning to inhale the smoke. At last he spun off in a wide arc. The music was by then loud and urgent, and the audience swayed hypnotically to its rhythm.

Moments later the man and music stopped, and the audience gasped as if surprised. Then the shaman turned and slowly began to retrace his steps, now moving in smaller and smaller circles. The music once again accompanied him, but muted, unobtrusive. He began to spin in place not far from the flames, streamers flying out in every direction, one foot quite still while the other propelled him round and round. From a distance and in the eerie light he looked like a top spun by some maniacal child.

Finally he collapsed onto the ground, and the music stopped. No one moved and not a sound could be heard until he raised himself. A single high-pitched note sounded from the smallest of the horns as two of the older priests approached him with a tray held between them. The guests could not see what was on the tray, only that the shaman began moving items around, giving rise to a fevered discussion among the three of them. When that too stopped the priests left and several monks appeared to help the shaman back through the temple door.

And then everyone stood as one, and began filing out of the plaza. The two guests were guided to their rooms and left. There had been no explanation as to what just happened, though Jesus guessed it was a ceremony of divination for some purpose.

The rooms were next to each other, and thankfully more comfortable than those at Leh. The pads were thicker and clean. A shelf the height of Jesus' ankle ran around two sides of the room. Someone had placed his personal things on one side, next to a small lamp. The free shelf might serve as a bench, he thought absently. Most importantly, the room had a small window that looked out onto the courtyard and the night sky. The evening the air was tinged with smoke.

"What was the shaman doing?" Krishna asked Jingu the next day.

"He is called twice a year fourteen nights in succession between the full and dark of the moon, to prophesy for the community. It was auspicious that we arrived for the first night. We will have to wait to discover the meaning of what he saw, since he often is given but a portion of the visions at a time. Even last night was divided: one side showed a great light being enshrined over our monastery. This he attributed to your arrival among us. And the other was a shadow covering the light at your departure. The important thing is that the light is not extinguished, but only covered over," added the old man to himself. After the first night only the senior priests attend the shaman to complete the fourteen days of ritual.

A group of traders arrived several days later, carrying rumors of preparations for war brewing to their north. This was the source of the shadow.

"I am afraid we bring this upon ourselves," said Jingu.

"Many of our people love nothing better than the passion of battle. And if one is too long in the coming, they go out in search of it, attacking first if necessary. Of course there can always be found an excuse -- someone's grand uncle was said to have been killed by a man from a neighboring village; a child was mauled by one of the great cats in the mountains, which had surely been agitated by spells; the poor hunt was caused by another village over-hunting the year before. And since we call our Gods by different names, we can always blame their God for a stillbirth or a crumbling wall or...." And he walked away, muttering to himself.

Jesus had learned only a few words of the local language from Jingu, who had preferred to speak with his young friends in Greek or Latin. My cousin was eager to learn about the Bon religious tradition, but had to rely on the old abbot (who often could not be found) or Krishna (who knew only a little more than he) to translate the daily lessons.

And then he discovered a young monk who, while far from fluent, seemed to know a good deal of Greek. It seemed Mongol invaders had kidnapped his grandmother from her father's house in one of the Greek subject lands, carrying her east when they returned home. But when Jingu's people later invaded the Mongol lands, they slew her new husband and brought her here.

"And she taught you Greek?" asked Jesus, incredulous.

"Yes, though by the time I was born, she was already beginning to forget her native tongue. She gave me my name, Homer," he said, somewhat embarrassed. "She said he was a great and wise man among her people, though not a god. Grandmother now walks the spirit worlds, and I worry that her gods will not recognize her."

"You need not be troubled about that. The one God knows all His children, no matter what name they use for Him," Jesus assured him, "and calls each one home when they are finished here."

"One God? But there are many gods, are there not, more than can be counted. We have our own, and Krishna's people have many gods, and you have yet more. Grandmother spoke of the Greek gods, and I hear the people under the Pharaoh speak to their own. And...."

Jesus interrupted his accounts. "There *are* many names, and many aspects, but only One from whom all the peoples of the world emerged. It does not matter which name we use, or upon which aspect we place our attention. What matters is the condition of our heart when we make contact. What matters is how we treat each other every day of our lives, and whether we are thinking about our God or instead forget him. In the end it matters only that we look for the presence of God within other people, no matter who they are. God indeed lives within each of us." He had placed his left hand over his own heart and his right hand upon Homer's heart as he spoke these final words.

It was natural that this young man, a product of many cultures, should be the bridge for my cousin in this ancient land. Homer came to his room often, and in time began to bring other, mostly younger monks with him. Some of the older priests shunned Jesus, perhaps out of jealousy, or maybe because they felt awkward at their differences. But one of the priests, nearly as old as Jingu, opened his door and his heart to the strange young man from the west. His name was Norbu, and he would become both mentor and trusted friend to the Nazarene.

The prophecies would come to pass, that the light was spread over the monastery and the land. Jesus stood in the middle, learning of the Bonpo teachings and traditions from Norbu, sharing in turn his own wisdom with Homer and the other young men. He refused to be bound by that which binds other men, and took his teachings out into the community as well, offering them to male and female. In the beginning this disturbed even Jingu.

"That cannot be done," he said.

"And why not?

"Because we monks take a vow of celibacy, and are forbidden from interacting with women, and because the teachings were given to men, and men alone, and because women can not understand the subtleties of our teachings, and..."

"Nonsense," said Jesus. "I am surprised you would repeat such things. If your monastery requires celibacy and the young men entering here renounce worldly ways voluntarily, that is good. But I know that many or perhaps most of the young men are not here by choice. Their families leave them on the doorstep as infants, either because they cannot afford to feed them or because they have been told they will benefit in some way from having one of their sons in the service of the honorable Jingu. And by the time they grow to an age where other young people are making important decisions on their own, they can no longer imagine a life other than this, making no other decision possible."

When he stopped speaking, Jesus flushed at his indiscretion. But Jingu surprised him. "You are right. And there is another reason they come, that you overlooked. To avoid fighting in the many wars that take place during a man's lifetime.

But it is the way of this land." He sighed. "One day it will not be so. Men, and women, will enter into the service of God voluntarily, eager to learn and be of assistance not just to this God, but to each other and the world outside. And while some here will continue to look down on what you do, you have my blessing."

Jesus studied the teachings of Bonpo, learning about the ocean of misery and suffering in which all people are immersed, and the means to rise above it. The monks were taught a vast array of rituals relating to their own enlightenment and to guiding villagers through the rites of passage of birth, death, marriage, and so on. He learned their approach to astrology and prognostication and exorcism. He was taught the ten principles of right activity and the gateway practices to enlightenment.

In turn he shared his own view of Bon *tantric* traditions, in which purification of the body could take place with right thought and use, rather than renunciation. He had been taught in his homeland and further in Egypt how to balance the five elements, thereby transforming the body into radiant energy, which is light. This, he discovered was analogous to the *way of great completion* in their tradition, in which the light body vanishes like a rainbow in the sky. For each of these traditions the ultimate goal is reunion with the God Source.

Even as he studied and taught, winter raged along the mountain peaks surrounding their peaceful valley. Cold crept into their rooms, and the temple was warmed only with the bodies of everyone gathered there twice a day for prayers. This was the greatest incentive for not missing devotions. Baths were rare, as ice on the river was broken through only to draw water for drinking, cooking and for rituals. Firewood was a luxury, even in that verdant valley, burned only to brew tea and prepare their meals.

Jesus was accustomed to daily cleanliness, and found the body odors in crowded rooms most offensive. At times he could bear it no more and broke the ice on his own to bring a pot of frigid water back to his room where he quickly washed himself. Once he encountered Krishna on his way back from the river, carrying his own pot of water.

"One cannot approach the temple, especially in certain rites, without first bathing and fasting," said his friend. And so it was in the Brahman tradition.

The two men grew close during those months, and Jesus looked forward to their journey south when mountain passes reopened in spring.

Chapter 23

SPRING FESTIVAL

Jesus had little interest in the arts of divination. He once told me, "All that needs be known can be found within the self. We are better off getting to know the real source instead of digging through entrails or inhaling toxic fumes." Still, he had enjoyed the Bon shaman's performances.

The spring festival was the year's largest and most important. "Where do they all come from?" Jesus asked Norbu. The mountains had seemed sparsely populated when they crossed the mountains the previous autumn, yet visitors continued to flood in.

"There are encampments throughout the mountains. With up to twenty people to a tent, it is easier to keep warm." Norbu laughed. "And some of these people are coming up from the valleys. In the winter they cluster in villages where they are more secure, resuming a nomadic life when the passes open."

People brought their yaks and sheep, scarcely giving the new grass a chance to find its way to sunlight before it was gone. But at least the dung collected provided fuel, so fewer trees were needed to feed evening campfires.

Jesus missed his quiet meditations next to the frozen river. During the winter he had carried a heavy yak skin with him down to the rocks. It was large enough to provide both a rug to sit upon and a wrap to shield him from the winds.

The bitter cold air tempered the smell. Paradoxically, now that warming temperatures called him outside, he felt more and more confined to his little room.

"You might as well get used to crowds, and being stared at," Krishna said to his friend. "Juggernaut is a large city, with a constant flow of pilgrims. Peace you might find, but quiet, hardly ever." He grinned at the thought of going home.

It is just that I do not know when my own homecoming will be, Jesus thought to himself, with a touch of homesickness. I keep going further and further away. But, he reminded himself, my family constantly grows, not diminishes. "You are right," he said to Krishna, "we will be on the move soon enough.

The two men planned to leave at the new moon, five days hence. Once the day was set, he realized he had become very fond of his temporary home, and especially of Norbu and Homer. Their guide and friend, Jingu, had become increasingly reclusive since the autumn.

"He does not seem unwell," said Krishna.

"He is just old," replied Norbu, when they asked after him.

"But, forgive me, you are older than he – are you not?" asked Jesus.

He nodded. "Some flesh bodies are more durable than others, and some energy bodies more elastic. There are many variables. *And* there are internal timetables set by the gods themselves that must be honored. It is not for us to know or understand."

"So he is not sick then?" Krishna persisted.

"No, he is not sick in a way that requires healing," said the old man with finality.

Festivities began that very evening. Copious amounts of spirits had been drunk throughout the day, and by nightfall the welcoming speeches and prayers were drowned out by raucous laughter and the occasional fistfight. And when the dancers and musicians took the stage people shouted and clapped, banging on anything they could find as accompaniment. Sadly, few possessed a sense of rhythm. The monks and priests too had their share of the barley malt, and a few were inebriated. Krishna and Jesus were persuaded to join them in a cup of the sharp, bitter tasting brew.

"I miss the grapes," Jesus whispered to Krishna. "Wine is more suited to food."

"That's just a matter of taste," argued Krishna. Neither beer nor wine was served in his home. "You will rediscover many of your favorite things as we travel south. At least there will be more variety than here. And I am not a priest, so you will once again know the hospitality of women!"

The men laughed. Though Jesus offered his teachings to women as well as men, few dared attend his talks. Those who did were met with ridicule, and worse. And the only two women allowed into the monastery itself were as old as the mountains, and as weathered. They actually lived outside the walls, going in and out to pick up the robes that needed mending, or bringing new ones in to the monks, fashioned by other women whom the men never saw. These two along with one of their middle-aged sons also delivered foods and other supplies, as needed.

In fact the residents of the monastery did little for themselves, except for basic gardening and emergency maintenance in the compound. "The villagers take care of our material needs, and we take care of their spiritual needs," said Norbu. "The arrangement suits everyone."

Jesus did not believe it was an even exchange. The belief we need intermediaries to God undermines the spiritual quest, whether it take the form of priests or sacrifices or rigid rituals. He was grateful for the wise and loving counsel given him by his many teachers; every one had affirmed his direct connection to Source. Temples provide a place for seekers to gather, for priests to offer guidance, and altars to focus one's gaze, but true union can be found only within the heart. At the same time he understood that few are ready to assume responsibility for their own atonement, much less prepared to cast their inner eye on the great Light. They are yet dependent upon the altar, the priest, the temple as garments of the Divine, outer representations of the inner essence. Such people as Norbu, Jingu and young Homer brought honor to their roles as shepherd to their flocks, until such time as they became ready to enter the inner sanctuary alone.

A sudden noise brought Jesus out of his reverie. "Come!" shouted Homer, grabbing his sleeve. "It's starting, and we must find our places!"

"Where is Krishna?" Jesus asked.

"He is already there, saving your spot."

Krishna waved them over. He sat on a long bench on top of a raised platform, reserved for the priests and a few visiting dignitaries. Jesus climbed up and sitting down, turned to Homer. "Where are you going?" The young man was already moving through the crowd. "There's room here," he added, patting the bench next to him.

"I will sit here. It is better," he shouted back, finding a place on the ground some distance off. He preferred sitting directly in front of the night's entertainment, and the platform was near the back of the arena. Protocol required only that those of higher status sit in elevated though not necessarily better positions!

Jesus was glad to be on the periphery, especially with that night's crowds. Drink was already being served by the newly-consecrated acolytes, even before the priests had all taken their seats. Except for alcohol, feasts were spare that time of year; there would be little else than a winter-hard goat cheese and unleavened bread. He got up and left the stand to relieve himself, and immediately found himself surrounded by a group of boys.

*

Some of them had become deeply attached to him, spending as much time with him as he would allow. When they learned their beloved teacher would soon be leaving they hardly left his side, not wanting to miss a single glance or word from him. As expected he found these boys standing apart from the older men. He took the hand of the youngest, a boy named Yeshe, and started walking towards the gate. When they tried to follow he held his hand up to the others, saying "Don't worry; we will talk again before I leave."

Jesus sat Yeshe down under a tree and asked "How old are you?" When he did not answer the man took a different approach. "Do you know how long you have been in the monastery?"

The boy whispered, "I was born here."

He might as well have been. He had known no other home, nor his parents. A few parents did visit their sons once a year, but that was rare. The older priests paid little attention to their young charges and unless one of the other monks reached out to them, they were left to raise themselves. The little social life that existed evolved with rank and privilege. No wonder he had become so attached to the foreigner.

"Yeshe, I am happy we met here." The boy's eyes filled with tears. "You have been a special joy to me." He paused, looking up to the mountains. "You know I am going away tomorrow."

"Will I ever see you again?" the boy pleaded, tears now streaming down his face.

Jesus raised his chin and looked in his eyes. "Yes, I think so, though I cannot promise you. But it does not matter because you will always be here in my heart, and I will always be in your heart. All you have to do is look inside, and you will find me. Do you believe that?"

He bobbed his head and said, "Yes, I believe." But the tears did not stop.

"You call me teacher, and I am glad to share what I know with you and the other boys. But you too will one day be a teacher, a very wise teacher. Remember this," he said, still holding the boy's face to his, "the teacher, the priest is here to serve others. No one is better than anyone else, not even the Abbott. You are here to serve your brothers and the community. To God those who serve and those who are served are the same, every one of them his children. Neither are we less than God."

The boy stared at him, eyes huge with disbelief. Everything he had ever heard before argued against what he was now being told. After all, he was a boy without family and without status in the only home he knew.

"You do not have to believe me now," said Jesus. "Just remember what I say, especially the part about being of service. That is what's important to know."

Some of the priests were secretly glad the two men were leaving. Those who loved position and authority did not like to see it undermined, even by one who did not seek it for himself. They tolerated Jesus only because they knew his time among them was growing short.

*

Returning to the stand, Jesus confided to Krishna that he was in no mood for another night of revelry, longing for quiet their last evening there "I agree," said his friend. "But many of these people have suffered greatly this winter. It was mild here, but in your absence I have been hearing tales about the bitter cold and hunger endured. They are celebrating just having survived, honoring God the only way they know how. The priests are beholden to their support, and indulge them in their excesses like children. We will have our silence soon enough." Jesus nodded and sat down.

The men were up early the next morning, ready to leave. The yaks had been loaded with enough provisions to get them over the highest mountains which stood between them and their destination. Weather remained precarious this time of year. The children and some of the monks had gathered around. Jingu and Norbu embraced the two men, and then Jingu pulled Jesus aside.

"I am sometimes given my own visions, in the quiet of night," he said, not having spoken of this before. "You will return one day. I will no longer be here, and so this will be my farewell to you, father to son."

He shook his head, to ward off any comments. "When you return, you will not stay long. Have no regrets at your sudden departure," he said enigmatically. "There is something you must do at the full moon of the bull then." His old friend went on to tell him of a sacred valley several days' walk from where they stood, offering few hints about its location. "I was called there myself when I was about your age. A very old man told me then that I would, in my last years, meet someone of your description. I was instructed to tell you it is your destiny to travel there to take part in a ceremony unlike any other that you have seen." Jingu would say nothing about the ceremony itself, telling Jesus he must learn the rest on his own.

When they returned to the others Norbu said "You two have the blessing of the Great One, as you have mine.

Jesus turned to say goodbye to Homer, when Norbu interrupted. "We thought he might like to see some of the world, and have given him permission to accompany you as far as the foothills."

"They wanted it to be a surprise," said Homer, excitedly. "The only way I could keep from telling you, was to stay away. I hope you did not think I was angry these last days, or that I did not care."

"That is good news. Oh no, we thought only that there were so many people around us you had been unable to get close!" laughed Krishna.

Jesus took the boy's hands. "This is indeed wonderful. Thank you," he smiled at the old priests.

Then each of the younger children threw themselves in turn at the two men, all except for Yeshe. He kept his ground next to Norbu, holding onto his robes. Jesus walked over and squatted. Looking at the young boy, he put his right hand over his own heart. Eyes glistening, Yeshe put his little hand on his heart. He did not cry.

And so they went, remembering with gratitude the kindness of their hosts, and the love they had been shown. Though Krishna was not drawn to the vocation of teacher, he had much wisdom and generously shared of himself with all around him. And he loved to play, teaching the children new games throughout the long winter. They all adored him.

The monastery had enlisted a guide from one of the high villages to accompany them through the mountains, as none of the travelers had been that way before. He was called Zhang. Zhang shared Homer's tent, his natural shyness quickly dissipating under the young man's exuberance. They were often heard laughing late into the night.

The first several days were pleasant, a joy after the long winter. Then late the next afternoon, darkening clouds began to bunch up against one another. Zhang said they must look for a cave or overhang to protect them from snow. The temperature plunged. They went off in four directions in search of shelter, calling out periodically in case one of them became disoriented. Homer's shout could be heard over the growing wind, saying he had found something. By the time the others reached him, a heavy snow had begun to fall. It was a shallow cave, not deep enough to prevent the snow from getting in, but it would keep them from being buried by it.

They slept well in their womb, digging their way out in the morning, emerging into blinding sunlight. The two men from the west had never seen anything like it, not even during the preceding winter. It seemed they have been transported into the heavenly realms, immersed in a sea of glistening diamonds.

There had not been room in the cave for the yaks, but the creatures looked unfazed in the morning light. It is extraordinarily rare for one of their kind to perish from the cold. Their long hair and thick hides insulate them. A dense crust had formed on top of the snow in the bitter cold night, on top of which the men were able to walk. They might have made good time except the yaks with their great weight sank into the deep snow with each step. But by early afternoon the party had descended into a valley where there'd been little snow, and man and beast could walk with a lighter step.

After this the journey was blissfully uneventful. The grandeur of the mountains often held them in awe. Words were precious and measured by day, as befitted their surroundings. But Homer took advantage of his time with the two teachers, asking interminable questions in the evening hours. They did not mind, as he was an apt student, and uncomplainingly stopped when night sent them into their tents.

At last they began their final descent from the mountains into the low-lying foothills. Temperatures rose, and the humidity intensified. "Monsoons come early here," said Krishna, describing the intense rains to his companions.

It was time for Homer and Zhang to return, but no one was in a hurry to say goodbye. A flower-strewn meadow called them to relax, and they lingered a day longer before parting ways.

Chapter 24

THE GREAT TEACHINGS

They thought of the great river as their mother, the source of their own life blood. Her name was *Ganga*. The early morning mist cast a flowing veil over the scene. Krishna walked away from his friend to wade into the swirling waters, palms together, lips moving in silent prayer. The sun rose above the horizon, a blade of shining silver. Jesus watched, curious. Even the sun was different in this land.

Others stood nearby, aware only of the God to whom they opened their hearts. They prayed to be freed of karmic debt, liberating them from the wheel of rebirth. To die in this holy city was the ultimate goal. Cremation fires burned on the steep steps leading down to the river, and the ashes of the newly dead were delivered into the mother's watery embrace. But there were others too like young Krishna, standing in the waters, pledging the fruits of life yet to come. This brought great merit – and it was a good investment in the event unforeseen circumstances prevented one from returning as death drew near, or impeded one's family from delivering the body there afterward.

Jesus was moved by the devotion of the pilgrims. Even the beggars in this place seemed at peace. None grabbed at his sleeve, demanding their due, but quietly accepted that which was offered

The warming sun pierced the mist, sending platinum ripples up and down the river. Jesus descended the earthen steps and joined the others in the fast current. He was unfamiliar with the rituals for ablution, but it did not matter. The Jewish Rabbi could see the inner fire in those whose hearts had been opened, allowing the sacred waters to wash the burden of guilt and shame away.

As the mists dissipated, the devout turned their attention to cleansing their physical bodies. Many stood naked in the water, man and woman alike, as innocent as babes. Some few were clothed, self consciously washing, ingeniously wrapping and unwrapping long pieces of fabric around them in an effort to protect their modesty. Jesus had followed Krishna's lead and lifted his robes off over his head, laying them on the riverbank before entering the water. Now walking back to the water's edge both he and Krishna scrubbed the grime of the journey from their bodies.

Krishna broke the silence: "Two great traditions peacefully coexist here, a sure sign that it is sacred land. Brahmanism is the more ancient of the two, dominant along the river. And Buddhism originated very near here, in Sarnath."

Jesus had heard much of these two traditions from his teachers in Nazareth and Carmel, and during his time in Egypt. Even Jingu had said that one day his own people would embrace the teachings of Prince Siddhartha Gautama, now called the Buddha.

"And in your home, which predominates?" he asked his friend.

"It is hard to say, as both are honored. But I was raised with stories from the Ramayana and the Bhagavad-Gita, and these I love above all else." They were walking through the village now. "And besides," Krishna said, "I am named after the God Krishna from the Gita, and so I think it must be my destiny to follow him."

Jesus loved his friend, who sometimes seemed as simple as a child and other times wise as an old man. "Tell me about the Bhagavad-Gita."

"It is a part of the longer Mahabharata, a beautiful story merging poetry and drama. It tells of two ancient kingdoms from the great plains, the Kurus and their neighbors, the Panchalas. These kingdoms, two branches of the same family, are at war. The story relates a conversation between the young prince Arjuna and Krishna on the eve of a great battle. Arjuna hates war and desperately hopes to avoid taking part in the carnage. Krishna speaks to him of selfless action, of honor and righteous battles. He tells Arjuna that he cannot live for himself alone. He is subject to the collective karma of his people, and must subjugate his selfish interests in the interests of the greater good.

"It speaks to us all of those inner battles that are constantly waged between the forces of darkness and light, between evil and good. We must actively choose one or the other and then give everything, even our life if need be, to support our choice. It is an allegory for the purpose behind human evolution, told on a level that all can understand.

"The Gita is reenacted in my town each year, and people come from all over to see it. Most agree it is the best portrayal of the story they have ever seen. Any man or woman in Juggernaut would consider it an honor to take even one of the minor roles in the play. Much singing and dancing are woven into the story, and there is little we love more than music. The name Bhagavad-Gita means the Song of God. My sister Sita is one of the lead dancers," he added, flushed with pride.

Krishna hailed a cart pulled by two strong oxen whose heads and horns had been painted with turquoise and white circles. Each also wore a garland of yellow flowers, twined together with green reeds. The thin driver smiled at them.

"Why are his teeth red?" whispered Jesus. "He does not appear to be bleeding."

"He is chewing the *tambula*, a dried nut that is ground together with supari and lime. You will find it everywhere here, among all the castes. People believe it helps with digestion and purifies the blood. I do not know if that is true, but for me it has an unpleasant taste."

"Where are we going now?" asked Jesus.

"To Sarnath, where it is said Gautama gave his first sermon after becoming enlightened while meditating under the Bo tree. It is better to hear of his life where he actually lived it. And it is not so far out of our way."

The cart creaked along, both oxen and driver chewing their mash. The countryside was beautiful, a lush green punctuated with every color flower imaginable. They passed many on the side of the road, men walking with men, and women most often with other women. Children seemed to have a great deal of freedom, walking and playing in groups, shrieking with laughter. The women's eyes followed the handsome strangers, hands covering their mouths, whispering. Their brilliantly-colored saris reflected the flowers, a rainbow of color in constant motion.

Jesus found it hard to tell who was rich or who poor. Krishna said there were few wealthy people, and these never walked but were carried in palanquins or rode in carriages drawn by horses. His family was neither rich nor poor, much like our own family in Nazareth, it seemed.

"My father is a cloth merchant and though he has earned more money at his trade than many priests or noblemen, we are considered a lower caste."

"But you are training to be a priest, are you not?" asked Jesus.

Krishna laughed aloud at the question. "I do not mean to offend you your question, my friend, but such a thing would never be possible. Here we cannot cross caste lines, no matter what, at least until we are reborn. And besides, I would not choose to be a priest. Though the priestly caste is a social station with certain status, comprised of men and women, only some men from that caste actually take a vow of celibacy and become priests. But that life does not appeal to me and even if it were possible, my beautiful wife would not allow it," he laughed.

"Here we are," he said, jumping off the cart. He pressed something into the driver's hand, who nodded and drove off.

"This is Sarnath. Surrounding us is a park filled with hundreds of deer. These wild creatures have been drawn here by the magnetic quality of the place, for only those who love peace can remain here. There are no rules or laws to keep anyone out, but it is the nature of the attractive and repelling forces that keep it this way."

Deer grazed everywhere, walking among the monks and visitors alike.

"These trees are amazing! I noticed a few as we came south through the foothills, but here…." Jesus trailed off, stroking the smooth bark. The new trunks had created their own pathways down to the earth, having taken leave of the thick branches that grow outward from the main trunk. Each tree was like an entire community within itself, a family of trees.

"They are the Bo, and when we resume our journey I will take you to the very tree under which it is said Siddhartha sat meditating when he awakened. Some of the trees are ancient, expanding endlessly until even the parent trunk grows old and dies away. They remind us of enduring life and the resiliency of the form that houses this life."

They spent the following days talking with devotees of both traditions, who managed to live quietly alongside each other. A few of the priests were clearly closed-minded, fearful of stirring up clouds of personal doubt, but most were open, some even asked Jesus questions about his homeland and the beliefs of his people. They were surprised at the depth of knowledge displayed by the young traveler.

When they resumed their southerly journey to Juggernaut, they detoured to Bodh Gaya, a small steamy village that seemed to have mushroomed from the central temple.

"There it is," Krishna said, pointing to a tree that was nearly as expansive as the largest temple in Palestine. "That is the very tree where Gautama ended his search for life's meaning." A score of seekers sat amid the tangled branches and roots, each in search of his own enlightenment. Some wore the robes of monks or priests, and a few were ordinary men. "You know," Krishna explained, "Buddhism is a quest for insight or realization of our personal divinity, and not the worship of a creator God. It does not forbid the belief in such a God, but that is not its purpose."

"But what provides its unique identity then?" asked Jesus. "Are you saying its followers don't worship Gautama?"

"No, there is no worship of him or anyone else. Gautama discovered a path that anyone can walk toward realization. It is simple yet profound, guiding people along a middle path between extremes, helping them to overcome their desires or attachments to things or outcomes. It is this attachment that perpetuates suffering. He called these doctrines the Four Noble Truths and the Eightfold Path. Both Buddhism and Brahmanism remind us that life is impermanent and ever-changing. Buddha said that enlightenment follows when we surrender to the realization that life is imperfect, thus ending the cause of our suffering. We see then that we are intimately one with all of life. These are the three keys to *nirvana.* What makes it so difficult is its simplicity."

"Ah yes," laughed Jesus. "It would be so much easier if it were complicated!"

"I think that one of the things people love about Brahmanism is that it offers a range of deities from which they can pick and choose those who appeal to them. But this is a misunderstanding. At its core the Brahmanic teachings are as refined as those of Gautama. Brahma is the Supreme One from which everything emerges, the Creator giving birth to Vishnu the Preserver, who holds forth during the duration of our little lives, and Shiva the Destroyer, freeing the life essence from its imprisonment in form at death. It is the Shiva quality that makes enlightenment possible, allowing one to return to Brahma. Of course, we do not have to physically die to accomplish this, but it is the little self that we must surrender to the flames. All the other gods are but permutations of this trinity.

"Behind or before Brahma is the incomprehensible point of origin, a nothingness that cannot be described with words or conceived with the mind. Out of that were male and female breathed forth, two sides of the One. Moving in unified intent they create all that we know as life in its myriad forms. The goddesses are said to be consorts to the gods, but this has a far deeper meaning than simply serving as their mates. Those who teach that female is subjugated to male have misunderstood, or else they purposely use such false teachings to enslave women, or to avoid taking responsibility for their own awakening. Male and female are equal, complementing or completing each other. You will see in many of our temples sculpture or carvings that appear to depict the sexual joining of man and woman, but which in reality symbolize the unification of masculine and feminine principles.

"Each one of us embodies both elements, whether man or woman. And yes, sexual union offers an opportunity to approach the ecstasy of union with our supreme Source. With such intention it is a sacred act, but it still is only a dim reflection of true union. This takes place *within* oneself, when we marry our dark and light aspects. The key to this is not our spiritual studies or practices. It is forgiveness of self and others, the relinquishing of our fears and the acceptance of love."

Jesus was sure he had never heard such a pure exposition of the teachings of the ancient Brotherhood. While Krishna was not a priest, he was surely a wise teacher.

"I would like to sit awhile," he said.

"Yes, of course," said Krishna, and each found his own place under the great tree to ponder the life and teachings of

Gautama. As the sun neared setting they rose and found their way to the *dharamsala*, a modest pilgrim's inn where they stayed the night.

Approaching Juggernaut two days later, they found the road clogged with people on foot, and carts drawn by oxen or horse. Jesus imagined Rome this way, thronged with people of every description. The city was overpowering to one used to the open road and the mountain vastnesses. He gagged on the dust-thick air, and the increasing smell of human and animal waste. Stagnant water sat in pools on either side of the road. Krishna explained that the awaited monsoons had yet to arrive here, which would flush out the drainage system and clear the air.

"We live at the far side of the city, on the sea. As traders we conduct most of our business by ship." The smell of sea air filled the air, though it would be some time before the great expanse of water spread out in front of them like a deep blue fan. By then they had jumped off the cart they'd hired, when the road became hopelessly enmeshed in the traffic. Krishna stepped up the pace, eager for his homecoming. The Nazarene had never seen so many tall ships, and stopped to survey the scene. But his friend would not be slowed. "Hurry," he shouted, turning a corner.

"Swarna!" he called out to his wife, running up to a large house built of finely polished stone. "Swarna, where are you? I have come home" he called again. "Leela, Meera," he called to his daughters. "Ravi!"

He turned to his friend, a worried look on his face. He was about to call out again when a manservant ran out the door, stopping dead in his tracks. "Krishna, oh Krishna," he cried, clapping his hands together. "You are here! The gods have answered us."

"What is it, Harsha?" asked Krishna, certain something terrible had happened.

"What is it?" repeated the old servant. "What is it? Why,

Swarna is this moment giving birth to your daughter," he replied, clapping his hands again in glee.

"A daughter? How did she get a daughter?" he asked, somewhat stupidly.

"The same way as always," the man said, now puzzled.

Jesus erupted in laughter. "How indeed? To look at you now would be to think you incapable," he sputtered. "Go, you silly man."

Krishna ran into the house with his servant, just as an infant's cry burst forth into the world. After that all that could be heard were shouts, and laughter, and words tumbling out of many mouths in a language Jesus could not understand. It was some time before anyone thought to return to the courtyard for him, and to show him to a room and draw him a bath. But he did not mind. There could be no more joyful a homecoming than this.

Krishna apologized the following day, confessing he had entirely forgotten his friend. "We named her Parvati, which means *daughter of the mountain*, in honor of our journey together" he said, his voice filled with emotion. "I did not even know we had made her when I left. In fact, it must have been our last night together, since I have been gone just ten moons. I went straight from here to meet you," he said, eyes momentarily lost in the past. "How long ago that all seems."

"I am happy for you, dear friend. So you now have three daughters and a son, is that right? You seem hardly older than I am."

How old *am* I, Jesus wondered? I must be twenty now, or nearly so. His friend seemed so happy in his home, with his family. For the first time in his life he wondered if he would ever marry. The thought had never occurred to him before. He did not know if such a thing would fit into what he was beginning to see as his destiny.

"You will stay here as long as you wish – and I hope it will be a very long time," said Krishna. "We have more than enough room now that both mother and father have gone. Unless you prefer your own place," he added, hesitantly. "You are my brother, and uncle to my children."

"I will stay with you," said the Nazarene. "It would be my honor. Thank you."

From that very first night, he felt at home.

Chapter 25

SACRED FEMININE

It had been raining each afternoon for days on end, clearing only at nightfall. But on this night it did not stop. Jesus wondered how anyone could sleep with the noise, and the possibility the roof would cave in on them at any moment. He could see how simple people would believe angry gods were the cause of such rains, and seek to placate them. Around Galilee the rains came with thunder and lightning. He loved those storms. But here was only rain, incessant rain, turning everything into a breeding ground for mold...and worse. The monsoon was upon them with full force.

"Each year I forget how strong the rains are, until they come again," said Krishna. "We are glad for them, of course, for our crops depend upon them. And rice especially cannot be grown without flooded fields."

In the north chapatti made from wheat is the staple, while in the south no meal is complete without rice. In Krishna's home there was a surprising variety of foods, some brought in from as far away as Indochin. Jesus had never tasted such wonderful spices, and exotic fruits. And tea was drunk throughout the day, not just at meals. Tea, steaming hot, laced with cow's milk and a grainy, sweet substance which dissolved in the hot liquid. It was delicious and invigorating, causing him to sweat profusely in the monsoon damp. Swarna said sweating cooled their bodies so they would not overheat.

The rains went on longer than usual that year. But as it had been especially dry for several years running, it was welcomed by most people. "Our cisterns were dangerously low, and many had run dry. I do not know what we would have done with another year without rain," said Krishna.

In the early days of the monsoon children danced in the street, faces turned to the downpour, but as it wore on, the streets became deserted. No one went out if business did not require it. Jesus hated to see the coolies running their passengers through the drenching rain. They could hardly have been able to see where they were pulling their overloaded rickshaws. But as Krishna's warehouse was a goodly distance from home, he had to resort to them for transportation back and forth, else he would have spent an agonizing amount of time in the rains himself, walking. He accompanied his friend now and then, hoping to learn more about the scope of commerce in Juggernaut.

One day riding home together, he asked Krishna, "You told me I would see the Bhagavad-Gita performed here. When will that take place?"

"You will have to wait until the Phoenix moon, not far away. It is presented just once a cycle. But the principals rehearse throughout the year, occasionally putting on other minor plays and dances to keep their followers happy. Sita has been in the south studying with a famous teacher, learning a form of dance quite different from our own. She promises to be home soon."

"Have you heard from her since you've been back?" asked Jesus.

"She has sent messages. Ships ply these waters with regularity – though less often during such rain. Many of them call at a port near where she stays. We have already

received her blessings on the birth of her newest niece," he grinned.

Krishna was a loving and attentive father. It surprised Jesus that he had spoken of his family so seldom when they were traveling.

"It is more difficult when I speak their names," he said. "The sounds release a longing that is hard to bear at times. I find that if I hold the words inside, I am better able to visit them in my dreams."

"And was Swarna not with child in these dreams?" he teased. But he understood the fickle nature of such non-physical contact. He regularly sent thoughts out to his mother, to me and a few others, and while such communications are not dreams, they tend to behave like dreams, and soon lose their clarity. Sending his body of light across distances was a much higher level of projection, but that was rarely done.

While Krishna was busy with business and family, Jesus occupied himself with visits to temples and walks along the sea when the rains let up. The land ran flat into the water, resulting in extreme tides. At Carmel the land rose up sharply from the water's edge, and he assumed it dropped just as sharply down beneath the water. The tide was insignificant in comparison.

The sea had never enticed him to swim. He knew how, having learned when visiting Galilee. But that was long ago. He asked his friend about swimming here. "You should know there are sharks, and poisonous water snakes, though not in great number. If you wait, I will have some time away from business soon and we can go together."

Jesus missed the long talks they had enjoyed while traveling, and envisioned a peaceful outing where they could catch up. Instead Swarna and their four children filled two carts with food and water and Lal, their maid, and the seven of them lumbered to a beach not far from their home, already filled with others seeking to escape the city. So instead of quiet he was surrounded with the laughter and cries of children, mingled with the sounds of the surf. He was surprised to find that he enjoyed the day, perhaps more than if it had just been the two men. It reminded him of days with his family before setting out on pilgrimage, with the younger children always underfoot.

"Thank you for this day," he told Swarna that evening. "You have become like a sister to me." She smiled back at him, a gold tooth reflecting the last rays of the sun.

How different the women were, he thought, looking at his friend's wife. They surround themselves with a riotous mix of color in their clothing and their homes. They bared their midriffs, arms, and even some bosom, yet took great care not to show an ankle. And jewelry...gold shone from earrings or studs and bracelets in great profusion, if they could afford it. A woman in Nazareth or even in Jerusalem paled by comparison; no less beautiful, yet subdued in dress and demeanor. They expressed confidence differently.

Over a meal one evening they talked about these differences. Krishna told him that not all women were as free as Swarna. She explained the advantages in being born to a lower caste. "The higher the caste, the more restricted the life of women. The poorest, already considered untouchable by the rich haughty leaders of society, have nothing to lose and nothing to gain by further enslaving half their people. Women share the brutal labor of their kind, but generally their men treat them with a degree of respect. "Think about it," she said, "In our religion the goddess or consort to the god is considered to be not just his companion, but his *completion*. Together they form the whole. There can be no god without the goddess. At the most primal level we call her Shakti. She is the light of divinity that exists in everything and every being."

"In the Jewish tradition, the goddess is equally important," said Jesus. "On the more conservative line we speak of Sophia, the personification of wisdom. In the mystical realm the feminine indwelling aspect of God is *Shekkinah*. Both men and women embody Shekkinah, though women wield the scepter of her power within the world. The *soul* is feminine, without which the Divine would have no voice in us."

"You lived in Egypt, brother, as did Krishna in his youth – though he has spoken little of those years. Even here we have heard of their magnificent accomplishments. What do they say about women?" Swarna asked, as she suckled Parvati.

"Women have served as Pharaoh, though rarely. But in nearly every instance, a woman stands with her husband or brother on the throne, in some cases having more power, if only behind closed doors."

"Which, I believe is the case in all lands," laughed Krishna.

"Isis is the mother goddess in that land, the queen of heaven. In Rome they call her Venus. And Norbu, who knows more about Buddhism than he says, spoke to me once of Tara, who is the embodiment of love." Jesus laughed, remembering the conversation. "We weren't even talking about religion at all. Norbu was speaking of when he was still a novitiate at the monastery, and had gone into the village to buy provisions. He had been trying to get the price down on a piece of cloth when he turned to find the most beautiful woman he had ever seen standing there. She smiled, and he forgot everything, what he had been discussing with the shopkeeper, where he lived, *his name.*

He was paralyzed, he said, even after she turned and walked away. He dared not return to the village for months after that, afraid he would run into the White Tara in human form, the Goddess of goddesses."

"That is beautiful. It is sad they deny themselves the joys and pleasures of love," said Swarna, looking at her husband. It was obvious they did not.

"Do you know of Kwan Yin?" asked Krishna, finally looking back to his friend, his cheeks flushed.

"No, I do not."

"She is the goddess of mercy and compassion, a Bodhisattva or kind of Buddha for the Han people far to the north, much like Tara. The goddess is the intercessor with the gods in every land. Without her we would be lost. We would have no means to find our way back home."

It was growing late, and time to say goodnight. Krishna had promised to take Jesus to visit an old friend the following morning. Muktananda was a priest, his teacher and his father's teacher.

Jesus rose early and bathed, putting on clean robes. In his night travels, he had shared with his mother their discussion of the goddess. "You are growing in wisdom, my son," she had said, "even as you learn the ways of the world. This you must do, for you do not belong to us alone."

His mother's words disturbed him, though he did not know why.

"Father, what am I doing here?" he asked in his morning prayers. "I love these people, but surely there is work to be done in Nazareth, and wise people closer to home from whom I can learn." He did not know what he was asking, only that he felt a kind of restiveness, an unrealized question, and a longing....

When they arrived at the temple, they went around to the back instead of entering through the front door. He had peered in as they walked by, and saw that it was beautiful, sumptuous though not large. At one time he might have thought it gaudy, but their ways were growing on him and he could now appreciate the gilt carvings and lavishly painted walls, ceilings and doorways. There was always incense burning on the altars of their temples, and fresh flowers and offerings of food left each morning by the local women. One of these women saw them and rang a bell at their approach.

"Is someone there?" came a resonant voice from the shadows. "Come in." Upon seeing them, the old priest jumped up and embraced Krishna. "It has been too long, my son. You are always working." He knew Krishna had returned, but had not seen him before this. The priest then turned to my cousin, took both hands in his and looked into his eyes. They met each other in a deep place and the old man nodded.

"The God Krishna said that whenever there is a withering of the law he would manifest himself. 'For the salvation of the righteous and the destruction of such as do evil; for the firm establishing of the law I come to birth in age after age,'" he quoted.

Krishna stared from one to the other of them, his dark eyes round. "That is from the Bhagavad-Gita," he said to his friend. "Did I not tell you it was beautiful?" Though he said nothing more he silently wondered at the strange greeting. Muktananda never did anything without purpose, but neither would he explain himself.

"Tell me about your journey," asked the priest. "I want to hear everything, starting from the day you left here."

Krishna sighed. There was too much to tell, even if a lifetime were given him for the task. Their stories continued through the midday meal, and stopped only for the obligatory rituals of a temple at appointed hours throughout the day.

"We must leave. Swarna will be waiting for us," said Krishna as the sun neared setting.

Muktananda walked them to the road and said to Jesus, "You will come back often. We have much to learn from one another." Hands together, he bowed. "*Namaste.*"

"Namaste," the two men replied in unison.

Jesus settled into a routine, spending several days each week with the old priest, helping Krishna and Swarna with household tasks, and occasionally going with Krishna to the warehouse to assist with the inventory as new shipments came and went. He no longer thought to ask about his purpose in being there.

One day he returned from the temple to a house in tumult. Lal was shouting orders to Harsha and a delivery man standing in the doorway. "Sita is back," she called out to Jesus. "They have gone to the market and will return shortly." She turned her back on him and resumed grating the dried coconut, humming to herself.

He went to his room to wash and comb the knots out of his long hair from the rickshaw ride. By the time he came back out into the main house, the family had returned. "Come in!" Swarna called out when she caught sight of him standing in the doorway. Sita stopped in mid-sentence and turned to see who had come in. She caught her breath.

He stared at her in turn. Krishna cleared his throat. "Sita, this is my friend from Galilee."

"Nazareth," he corrected. "I am Jesus ben Joseph," he added, rather awkwardly, not sure why he used a formal title that would have no meaning there.

"Nazareth," repeated Krishna, bemused. He had never seen his friend flustered before.

"Jesus," said Sita, with a slight bow, smiling.

Everyone pretended they had not noticed, returning to their preparations for the meal with lighthearted chatter. But something *had* happened, and Jesus was not sure what it was. She was beautiful, to be sure, but Sita's beauty went deep -- and that was what had taken his breath away. A light radiated from the core of her being, shining outward into the room ... a pinwheel of colors framing her dark skin and hair, dancing across the emerald green of her sari.

He had no idea what he might have said that night, or what anyone else said for that matter. It passed in a blur. He thought he would not be able to sleep when at last they turned to their rooms, but instead fell instantly into a deep slumber, filled with a collage of dream images.

Surely we are connected from another time, he thought to

himself when he awoke the following morning. He was transfixed by her beauty, her heart and her soul. But what could he do? He could not avoid her, as she was staying in the house. He could not behave as he had the night before, but neither could he bury what he was feeling. But what *did* he feel, besides an unfamiliar attraction to a beautiful woman? He was, after all, a man of 21 years, so his response should not have surprised him.

But it did. When he returned to the Muktananda's that afternoon, the priest regarded him without words, waiting to see if the Nazarene would offer an explanation for his uncharacteristic silence. But he did not. He could not.

"If you are not going to say anything, you may as well eturn home," said the old man, at last.

Jesus' head jerked up to meet his eyes. He did not try to hide what was inside, indeed would not have known how to do so. There was no guile in him. Still no words came, and so they just sat together a while longer in silent communion. The priest had seen enough in his eyes, but wouldn't force something that was not ready to be spoken. At last the young man left, walking slowly back to the house.

This was a new kind of love to him, something known only in ancient memories, long dormant. He did not know what to do with it. Fulfilling his mission did not preclude loving another, so far as he knew. But his work lay elsewhere, far beyond the mountains and deserts and seas, in another world. And her life was there.

He saw the question in her eyes as well, when they came together for that evening's meal. The table was generally alive with conversation, but that night was too raw for superficialities, yet not ripe for heartfelt discussion. And so silence reigned. Even the children felt it, and were quiet.

Sita left the house each day to rehearse for the great event anticipated by the whole city each year, the opening of the story of Arjuna, the story of every man. My cousin was grateful for her absence, while it pained him at the same time. On the third day he sneaked into the great hall to watch from the shadows. Sita danced the backdrop to the story, drawing the rest of the world into what otherwise would have been a simple dialogue between God and one man. Though there were other dancers, he saw only her.

She was brilliant, stylized, nuanced, yet passionate, emanating the same light he beheld the first time he saw her.

He knew he had to speak with her. The next morning he waited just outside the door as she left for the theater. "Would you walk with me?" His words seemed awkward in a language still largely unfamiliar to him. She nodded. He wanted to take her hand, but was afraid of offending her. They turned toward the sea, she to his right at arm's length. They walked in silence as the city buzzed around them in their cocoon. When they reached the sea, she took his hand to let him know it was all right. They looked out over the water. After a time he turned to her.

Her calm, dark eyes smiled back at him. "There is no hurry," was all she said, and he felt his shoulders relax and all the anguish of the past days evaporate.

They parted company halfway back, as Sita was expected at the theater. Jesus returned to the house alone. When he entered the kitchen, Swarna rose from the table where she sat with Leela and gave him a quick hug, then turned her attention back to her daughter.

The play opened that night. They had left the house a little late, and found few available seats. Hundreds of people were turned away. It would run ten nights in a row, allowing everyone a chance to see it eventually.

And one man would return each night, never tiring of the story or the performers.

PART THREE

Chapter 26

DANCE OF LIFE

A solitary woman played upon her lyre, and another coaxed the heartbeat out of the earth with her small drum. We quickly transcended self-consciousness, as the music lifted us out of our smallness. The longer we danced the more powerfully the sounds moved us, the greater the sweep of our spins, the higher the jumps, and more graceful the landings.

I had once seen a great cat out in the desert jump from a ledge high above us onto the ground not far from where we stood. It made not a sound, barely disturbing the dust as it touched the earth. I wondered if had the cat entered into us, and the birds too, allowing us to soar, arms flying, backs arched ... so effortlessly.

No one observed our passion. It was for ourselves alone to discover the full range of movement of which we were capable, awakening and freeing the life force that it may flow unimpeded. Too often we see ourselves as insignificant, squeezing the vastness of spirit into ordinary physical experience. The dance, indeed all creative efforts dissolve limitations so we might expand into and be a more perfect instrument of the life force.

Hair unbound, encircled our heads like halos of bronze, brown, and black. Each woman wore a blue robe, their different hues billowing, blending like an ocean under shifting skies, seething, merging, and parting again. Arms swirled like currents of light within the seas of change, fingertips painting the air with threads of gold.

It must have been a thing of beauty, though we had no observers. Any woman who entered the building joined in, and to my knowledge, no man had ever witnessed the creation ceremony, whether the dance or that which came before or after. Though there are precise elements to the ceremony on either end, the dance itself is always unique, self-created. No one knows how long it will last; it was over when it was over. But somehow the music and the movement always seem to end at the same moment.

The dance honors *She* who stands with the Creator, giving form to thought. We who danced were her hands and arms and feet, her very self. In the dance, we also honored ourselves, acknowledging our intrinsic beauty as women and liberating our divine power. It was our meditation and our prayer, an ecstatic expression of life.

Each woman is invited into the dance after her first blood, and is forever changed by her assimilation into the Sisterhood. The sacred dance takes place at the turning of the seasons, at each equinox and solstice. I will never forget the first spring dance after I returned from Carmel. Mother had told me what to expect, but she likened it to the first time a woman enters the bed of her husband. "I can say what it was for me, my child, but even then words are inadequate to the experience. And each woman's relationship to her husband and certainly to her Creator is unique to her, and no two will share the same experience."

It was once again spring in our land, the time of rebirth. Each season's dance is different in every way, as each season expresses a different facet of the unfolding creative process. Spring carries a sense of expectancy and this one more than most. I could not say why, but felt as if I had been holding my breath for a very long while. And now the moment had arrived to surrender the old in exchange for a powerful infusion of new life. The others felt it too.

Mary approached me at the end of the ceremony. I had been standing alone at the door of the women's house, gazing at the evening sky. The stars drew a swath of pale light across the black night. The waning moon had not yet risen. "I can never decide which I prefer, the full moon or the dark of the moon," I said. I could feel her eyes join mine in the heavens.

"Each is perfect in its own time, like youth and old age, neither one better than the other," she replied. Mary slipped her arm around my shoulders, and I suddenly knew myself her peer and not just a much younger niece. Mother walked up, with Miriam and Naomi in tow.

"Come," said Mary, ushering us back into the building. She led us to a small room in the rear which contained only a low table and a pile of large pillows. We each grabbed a pillow and found a place for ourselves in the near darkness.

"Salome, would you light the candles?" Mary asked her sister.

Mother went out and returned with a burning candle from the ceremonial room, and from it lit a large candle on the table, and a score of smaller ones that encircled us. Mary filled cups from a large pitcher, handing one to each of us. I wondered why we gathered there rather than in one of our homes. The younger children would all be asleep and we could have talked there undisturbed.

"Judy will arrive here tomorrow," Mary began. Judy was old now, and rarely went out from Carmel. That she would travel such a long distance seemed propitious. "From here she will travel to Egypt."

"Such a long and difficult journey!" said Naomi. "But why...now?"

"Why now?" Mary repeated. "When Judy was about your age she spent considerable time in Egypt studying and preparing for her work. Now her part is nearly finished, and she desires to return to that ancient land to live out her life."

"But," I stopped, not knowing what I wanted to say. I could not conceive of the school without Judy at its helm. Nor could I imagine my life without Judy somewhere within it.

"Youth, old age and life beyond the veil...it is all the same," she said, looking at me.

"She does not wish to travel alone," added mother. "She has asked that you three go with her."

"Go to Egypt!" Naomi sounded incredulous, and I wondered if she had never considered the possibility. I had often dreamed of going one day, and Miriam always said she was sure we would go together.

"You will be accompanied by Simon, who has his own business there. Though I have no doubt you enjoy protection of a higher kind, the Romans would not think well of four women traveling alone. They will watch you closely as it is," she laughed, "for more than political reasons."

I was not sure I liked that, though it was true we were three women of marriageable age, and handsome enough.

"Judy will tell you all you need to know on the voyage. You leave in six day's time, at the new moon. Passage has already been arranged. In the meantime you will see little of us, as she has asked to spend the days with her old students."

There was no more discussion that evening. As we joined hands, I felt the familiar current begin to flow from one to the other, enabling us each to become more than we were on our own. We droned the sacred syllables, softly at first, growing louder as the energy increased. At a certain point I lost separate awareness, immersed in the singularity of our kinship in the light.

*

It was my job to fill the cistern in front of our house. Mother had breakfast waiting on the table for Elizabeth and me after my chores. I had been thinking about Judy. "She meant the twelve girls, didn't she?" I asked, referring to Mary's comment that Judy would be passing this time with her former students.

"Yes."

I realized I did not even know who all the twelve were, and asked mother about them. "Two have already passed on," she said. "Of the ten, just six remain here. It is interesting that we six had been the closest of friends, even then. I don't think any of us ever doubted that Mary would be the chosen one, and the five of us would remain to support her."

Elizabeth hummed a song to herself. She did not know the story yet, and seemed little interested in our conversation. It would be told her when she approached her woman's time.

"I will miss you, mother."

Her eyes glistened. "And I, you. But I envy you this opportunity. My sister spent time in Egypt after the birth, but I never had the chance. It was just not meant to be."

"There is still time," I said, without believing my own words. She smiled back, knowing as I did it was not her destiny.

"We will have many years after you return, and your time there will go by quickly – for you."

We spent most of that day together, doing little chores, speaking of everyday things. After Jesus left, and especially after the time in Carmel, mother had become my confidant and dearest friend, and we savored these moments together. Even Miriam, who by then was as close as any sister could be, never approached the same degree of intimacy. There was always a part of her she held to herself.

Just before the evening meal Martha, one of Mary's children, came to the door. "Auntie, mother said it is the gathering time. Judy has arrived." She whispered, her voice filled with awe.

"Now? Before we eat?"

"Mother said now."

"I am sorry, my dears. Veronica, would you see to Elizabeth until I return?"

"Of course," I replied, wishing I could go with her. "Will you be back tonight?"

"I do not know." Mother grabbed her shawl, kissed us, and ran out the door.

We saw little of each other before I left. Except for my trip to Britain with uncle Joseph, I had never been away from her for longer than a day at a time. Just before we left she told me that our visit to Egypt was a part of the *great plan.*

"You mean the plan that began with the twelve girls in Judy's school?"

"Oh, that was not the beginning. It was only one step on a very long journey that began at the dawn of man."

I could not imagine then what she meant – but she only smiled. "That story will be revealed to you in the red lands of Egypt. But you must listen and watch carefully, as much of the telling will be done without words."

Chapter 27

THE SISTERHOOD

With eyes closed my fingers traced the undulating furrows of the lion's mane. How real the form felt, except for the lack of a living creature's warmth. It was exactly as I had seen it in vision years before, when Jesus first arrived in Alexandria. *The stone lion.* And it was the first thing I sought out, after paying our respects to Bandar. Zar had left his body not three moons before, and Bandar had been lifted up to head the monastery by unanimous vote of the brothers.

My thoughts strayed to my cousin, wondering where he might be in that moment. He had opened his sight to me on several occasions during the preceding year. A flat sea had replaced the stunning mountains where he previously lived. The peoples of the mountains and those of the plains were vastly different as well. In the mountains it was difficult to tell man from woman. Fur hung down low over narrow eyes carved into smooth, round faces. Heavy dark clothing masked the shapes of their bodies. I surmised it was a cold and bitter landscape.

But next to the sea women bared slender arms covered in bangles, and wore brilliantly colored fabrics that floated in the wind. Men wore white, some little more than pieces of cloth wrapped around their private parts, while others wore short robes over leg coverings. People labored in the heat, but seemed not to be burdened by it, their large eyes smiling often.

As I thought about him his face came into focus before me, though his form remained clothed in mists. I felt the thrill of his presence. "Cousin," he said, looking past me to the lion. "Ah, it is good you are here." He asked who came with me, and was pleased at my reply. "How do the brothers fare without Zar?" he asked. I did not think to be surprised that he would know of Zar's passing.

"You shall have to ask me that question another time. We have only just arrived. Bandar and Judy already knew each other. It is obvious the brothers are honored by her decision to return here. That alone endeared them to me. And you, how goes your life in this distant land?" I asked him.

"I am happy to be here. There is a different language spoken at each crossroads, it seems, and I struggle to make myself understood. One minute I am an ignorant student and the next pushed in front of a crowd to answer questions. Like everywhere, people seek to understand what lies behind life's difficulties. But I fear I have little to add to their wisdom," he said.

"This I doubt. But I will be eager to hear what you have learned when you return. I see you are well ... and growing older," I teased.

"As are you -- no longer a child, but still a maiden? Has no one taken it upon themselves to find you a husband?" he joked in return.

"I am quite capable of finding a husband for myself, should I ever see need of one."

Words fell away then. There was too much to share, so many questions unasked. It would have to wait for his return ... and mine. I did not even know how long it would be until I went back to Nazareth.

"Find Hebeny and tell him he is loved. Let my brothers know they still live in my heart, and assure them we will meet once more before it is all over."

A swirling energy rose up around me, and then he was gone. We had long since left off saying goodbye to each other. *Before it is all over*? His words came back to me. What did he mean by that?

"Sister, might we disturb you? I will be preparing your bath first, and …."

The moon had risen full and I could see the acolyte's face as if it were daylight. She was young, not yet a woman, and in the silvery light her skin appeared as if carved of alabaster.

"Yes, of course. What is your name?" I asked.

"Moriah," she answered curtseying.

"You do not have to curtsey to me, Moriah. I am not much older than you, and have no need for deference. But I thank you for your kindness."

She smiled with a little bow, and turned to her chores.

I was glad to have the journey behind us, though the seas were kinder than when Miriam and I accompanied Joseph to the north countries. After that experience, I never wanted to step aboard ship again, and had been fearful for Judy's sake. At her age stresses can be intensified, but she fared as least as well as we.

They had given her a private room here, that of the former head mistress. The room had sat vacant for some time, as if awaiting her arrival. During the voyage she told us that while she would no longer teach classes she had been called there to mentor two advanced souls who would soon arrive. "Both are very young yet, a girl and a boy, unknown to each other." Her eyes told us she was looking forward to her new mission.

The great tub was filled with steaming water, and Judy took the first bath while the three of us ate a light supper in the room we shared. Hot water was added for each of us, when it was our turn. As each one left the bath, Moriah rubbed our bodies with scented oils until all the tension from the journey had gone. I slept well that first night, though my sleep was filled with strange images which spoke of things to come. By morning all the rich details of the dreams were lost in a stew of feeling and sensation, and it would take our entire stay in Egypt for them to sort themselves out again.

"What now, I wonder?" asked Naomi, who had been wandering around the room restlessly since dawn. We had hoped for more information from Judy during the voyage. But she had said only that we would study awhile in Alexandria, and then visit Memphis; nothing about how long we would be in either place or what our studies would entail. Simon had literally left us on the doorstep of the monastery, without saying if or when he would be back.

"The belief that we can plan our lives is an illusion," one of our teachers would say later. "Nothing can be as we imagine it in advance, because at each moment we are subject to an infinite number of influences, most of which are unseen and unknown to us. Imagine you throw a seed into the churning sea. Is there any way to venture where that seed may end up in the span of a heartbeat, let alone a day or year? No, there are too many forces at work, each one acting upon the other in unexpected ways. Life is like that for us as well. Anything could happen from one moment to the next, propelling us in an entirely new direction than that originally begun."

I did not understand how to reconcile that with prophecies in general, and the great plan which I knew was continuously being implemented through all of us.

That first morning we put our travel clothes away, and donned the robes that had been given us the night before. We would learn that one's robes spoke clearly of a certain status within the hierarchy of the Brotherhood. Though we had just arrived, we had already spent many years in our studies and thus were accorded a more advanced status than most new arrivals --

though not yet that of the initiate.

"Come," said a voice from the doorway. The sun shown brightly behind Moriah and all we could see was the outline of her form. She led us across the courtyard to a large wooden door, and gently knocked three times. The door opened. It was dark inside and we stood some moments in the doorway, waiting for our eyes to adjust before entering. A man's voice bade us welcome. Though early, it was already hot and I was glad for the cool air inside the room. "Sit," a hand indicated two low benches. We three sat on one, and our host took the other across from us. Before his face emerged from the darkness, I saw that his eyes sparkled, alive and curious. He was probably not much older than we, a slender man with skin like the night sky.

"I am Hebeny," he said.

"Hebeny! Oh Hebeny, I am so happy to meet you!" I could barely restrain myself from jumping up to embrace him. "My cousin told me so much about you, I feel as if you too are a cousin of mine."

"And I have heard much of you," he replied, obviously pleased. "Where is Jesus?" I relayed my short vision of the night before, and what little I knew of his life so far from us. Miriam watched me intently, as she often did when I spoke of him. Naomi seemed not to be listening, looking around the room with curiosity. This was the first time she had been away from Palestine, unless you counted the two short trips to Carmel.

He asked about our journey, inquiring after the rest of our families. I was surprised to discover he knew my uncle Joseph, and several from our village as well.

"Many Jews and Greeks, and a few Romans come here to stay, and to learn. Your village and others in Galilee, Samaria and Judea are well known to us. "No," he laughed, "I have not been there ... yet. Perhaps when your cousin returns." He sounded wistful, or sad, and I wondered why. "We are ... I am especially happy to welcome you here. I attend Bandar, and he has asked me to tell you that if you need anything, or have any questions, you are to ask me. I am at your service."

"Who will teach us?" asked Miriam.

It seemed an odd question. I would have asked instead when our classes would start, or what kind of studies we would undertake, or about the daily meditations, or how we could contribute to the community. After all, we did not know the teachers here.

Hebeny looked at her, considering her question. "Most who taught Jesus and me are still teaching."

I realized with a start that he knew exactly what Miriam was really asking. And in that same moment I understood everything about her that had long puzzled me. She was *in love* with my cousin. I felt my face flush; the cool air turned hot and sticky. It may be that until that moment I had somewhere deep inside imagined the two of us may one day marry – though the joining of cousins was uncommon among our people. But now it had come, I was happy for them. I wondered then if he knew of her feelings. Did she herself know?

"Veronica," said Hebeny, giving me a quizzical look. "Are you coming?"

The two women stood at the door, waiting.

"Yes, of course. Where are we going?"

"Hebeny just told us, he is taking us to meet our first teacher," Naomi said, impatiently.

From that day until the following autumn we rarely deviated from our routine. We rose with the sun and washed ourselves, then joined the community for meditation. Sometimes, after the morning sessions there would be a ceremony of some kind, related to the stars or a rite of passage among the acolytes or brothers. The cycle of studies shifted focus or theme at each new moon. We three were privately tutored for half the day, joining a small group of men and women our age the rest of the time. The majority of them had been there since early childhood.

To my delight, I discovered my cousin's old friend Helen had been assigned to Judy as her handmaid. We encountered Judy but rarely (which was my one regret there). But since we often met with Helen after meditations, we were kept current on the older woman's welfare. Helen did not join our classes, as she had completed most of her studies by then. Still, we got to know her well, and learned to think of her as a sister.

The students came from many places, less than half of them from Egypt itself. Sanjay came from an area near Kushan, and I peppered him with questions about his land, knowing it to be one of Jesus' destinations. Sanjay had traveled with his father throughout the area as a youth before coming to Alexandria, and loved to tell stories about the cities and villages they passed through. I could almost see through his eyes the brilliant colors, feel the dampness of the rainforest on my skin, and taste the strange spices of their food. Miriam would sit near us, saying little but listening intently.

I never mentioned my epiphany to her, or anyone else, knowing she would tell me in her own time. But the more I thought about it, the more I realized how perfect it was. Jesus and Miriam were among those closest to my heart, and nothing would bring me greater joy than to see them together.

"I am going down to the river today. Would you like to join me?" Hebeny asked us one morning.

"Yes," we sang out in unison. We had not been beyond the monastery walls since our arrival.

"Good, I will be back for you shortly."

A carriage waited at the gate, and the four of us climbed in behind the driver. The port was much larger than the one we saw when first arriving in Egypt.

"That was strictly for passengers and this for commerce,

though many of the barges also carry travelers. A messenger arrived last night, informing me that my brother's barge had arrived. We need to transfer its cargo to a larger ship, bound for Sidon. I just need to make sure everything goes alright." By the time we arrived the entire transfer was nearly finished, as the men had worked through the night. Since Hebeny had arranged to be away for the whole day, we were free to explore.

"Might we go to one of the great libraries?" I asked. Everyone spoke of the libraries with awe, in voices usually reserved for something holy. Most texts that related to the natural world, geography or history were concentrated in one of the smaller libraries, while the largest was devoted to all things sacred.

"And the temples, I would like to see the temples," said Miriam.

"And the *souks*," added Naomi.

"We shall see them all," said our friend "Or at least a sampling of each."

We arrived at a building cut from massive stones, with pillars in front so big my arms barely reached halfway around them. "Like the cedars of Phoenicia," I said, though I had only been told about them.

"Yes," replied Hebeny, "though *they* are grander still."

The building had much the same feel as the great Temple of Solomon in Jerusalem. But while the Temple was filled with noisy crowds, the library seemed to me unnaturally quiet. Everywhere were people standing or sitting, reading or engaged in whispered discussions. We were led into an enormous round room, which sat at the center of the rectangular building. Far above us was a domed ceiling, painted as the heavens themselves.

"It is covered with lapis lazuli," said Hebeny. That seemed impossible. Where could so much of that stone have come from, I wondered? "Inlaid with other stones from all over the world," he added

I do not know how long we stood there gazing into the stars above, but Hebeny had to drag us back out into the street. "Or we would never see anything else," he said. The sudden chaos of the street disoriented me.

"I am afraid the temple might disappoint you after the library." He was right about that. But then the temples of Alexandria were not the largest or most impressive in the country. Those we would see later. I had heard of Egypt's pyramids, and was curious about their form. We had been taught little of sacred geometry previous to going there, but would learn much before we ventured out into the countryside.

Hebeny had a list of things to buy for the school. We trailed along after him in the souk like ducklings, soaking up the sights and sounds and smells (though some of the latter were most disagreeable). He hired two porters who followed us about. They would deliver the purchases directly to the school, or there would have been no room for the four of us in the carriage. There were lumber and metal fittings for repairs, spices for the kitchen, a dozen lengths of cloth for the new acolytes, and a length of heavy silk for Judy. She had confided to Hebeny that while in Carmel she had never had the time to embroider, and now wished to create something to hang behind the communal altar.

We stopped at one of the many food stalls and purchased baklava, a remarkable thing dripping with honey and filled with nuts. Eating as we walked, we moved through a collage of people and animals and produce and items for the house and workshop, and repairmen of all kinds offering their services. There were dyers and spinners and tailors, shoemakers and jewelers. There were paintings and metal sculpture and carved wood of great artistry. A funny little man with a pointed hat and shoes offered to paint our portraits, but we declined. I could not imagine what I would have done with such a thing.

When we arrived back at the carriage, Hebeny retrieved a package he had left in the driver's care. With little ceremony he opened it, placing a strand of beads over each of our heads. "These are not from the souk. They were among the items being transported for trade on the barge, a symbol of Nubia, my homeland."

"They're beautiful," said Naomi.

"Of what are they made?" Miriam asked.

"They are carved from the tusks of the elephant" -- and his hands made great sweeping gestures on either side of his nose -- "an animal the size of a house," he laughed. "They are used throughout all the lands above the great river for transportation and as work animals. When they die, their tusks, which are longer than my body, are carved in many ways, including beads such as these. In my city, the carvers have high status, and the elephant is greatly valued."

"And this, what is this?" I asked of the single black bead on the strand.

"It is ebony, for which I am named, since my skin has its color."

"Is it stone?"

"No, it is a wood, nearly as hard as stone, and as difficult to shape and polish."

In Israel it is not fitting for a man to give gifts to women who are unrelated to him. But this was a different land, with its own customs, and we thanked him for his thoughtfulness.

One morning, not long after our foray into the city, Moriah stood in our doorway. "Judy has asked for you." We went to her room and kissed her affectionately, glad to see her well. She served us sweet tea and cookies, and asked many questions about our studies. Suddenly changing the subject, she asked, "Miriam, what do you know of the old prophecies?"

Miriam's head jerked, startled. I knew, as did she, that Judy said nothing without purpose.

"There are many prophecies of which we have been taught.

Where would you like me to begin?"

"Are there prophecies that pertain to our time?"

Naomi and I watched our friend, while Judy pretended to be distracted with a fresh pot of tea.

She took her time in answering. "We Jews have long awaited our Messiah, one who would lift us up out of bondage. I have heard that a similar story is told by other peoples, who say he will be born in a foreign place, pointing to our land. Some say he is now among us."

"Naomi, do you believe he is here now?" Judy asked.

"I do not know," she answered.

"How will we know him, Veronica?"

My heart beat hard against my chest, as I thought back on conversations with mother and with Mary. "It does not matter what the signs point to, because each can be interpreted in various ways, influenced by our individual hopes and fears." As I spoke, I felt calm return. "The only sure way to know is to listen to our hearts."

"Naomi, do you agree?" She nodded yes. "What does your heart tell you then?" Judy persisted.

Naomi took a deep breath before speaking. "My heart tells me he is here, but the time has not come for him to declare himself."

"He *is* here now," Judy said after a long pause, "but he will not appear as expected. The prophecies speak of him as *King of the Jews*, but this does not mean he will take an earthly crown. Indeed, the texts that claim him for Jews alone hold the least truth. Better to turn to the ancient Parsis, or to Kushan, or to the ancient tablets in Iunu. It is not so important for you to know now the details of his life.

But I am here to tell you that he will not be able to fulfill his destiny without the women around him taking up the mantle of their own power. You," she paused, looking from one to the other of us, "are numbered among these women."

A shot of energy surged up my spine. I do not know if that or Judy's words frightened me more. "What must we do?" I whispered, unable to say the words aloud.

Her eyes softened, as she touched my hand. "Do not worry about that now. Everything you have been taught, everything you are doing each day is preparing you for this. You will know what to do when the time comes. You have been trained to listen for the small voice within your heart, knowing this is the voice of soul aligned with the Holy Spirit. Nothing is more important than this ... no teachings, no prophecies, no rules or laws, nor that which other people think or might say of you. Nothing.

"Continue your studies, but pay especial attention to your meditations. Confer among yourselves as to what you perceive, but trust in that inner voice above all. Though women have long held honored positions among our people, in the outside world -- whether Jewish, Roman or Greek -- we are little valued. The authorities will hate the promised one, and look for fault with you. Do not expect special treatment. But remember that your role is critical to the ultimate success of his work. The sisterhood is sacred, and more important than you know. Watch out for each other. I will soon be gone, but you will remain, and your power will continue to grow."

Judy said many more things to us that night, introducing me to my greatest fears and finally, to that source of strength which brought me to remembrance of who I am, and my purpose in being here at this time. Without noticing, Miriam, Naomi and I took each other's hands as she spoke. I had begun to see the power of our circle while yet in Nazareth, but here it would increase. We women were called upon to create and sustain the very foundation upon which he stood.

The following day we prepared to leave Alexandria, saying goodbye to our new friends. Though he usually dined alone, Bandar joined us for the communal meal that last evening. He sat at our table across from us, chatting as if he were just another student. And then, as he stood to leave he said, "Stop back here to see me before you leave our country; I will have messages for you carry back with you. I took my first studies with some in your own village, and it is long since I have seen them."

"Of course we will come back," said Naomi.

"Judy tells me you are leaving for Heliopolis in the morning," he said.

"Heliopolis?" asked Miriam.

"Iunu is known as Heliopolis here," said Judy.

"Yes, we leave tomorrow but we know little about it, or why we are going there," said Miriam, hoping for clues. But Bandar only smiled and said goodnight, a signal for the others to return to their rooms, leaving the four women alone.

"I will not see you off in the morning," said Judy. "But Hebeny will accompany you to Iunu."

I was pleased we would see more of him, but her words struck at my heart.

"Aunt, you will be here when we return, won't you?" I asked.

"No, my dear, I will not."

Chapter 28

CEREMONY OF FIRE AND WATER

Hebeny diverted us with childhood stories on the long journey. "My brother and I had to find out everything for ourselves, which constantly got us into trouble. But our parents were loving, tolerant and patient, forever rescuing us from ourselves." In one of his stories the two of them sneaked out of their house one evening and took off alone across the desert. They were headed to a Bedouin camp to see if the women really turned into wild dogs at night, hunting in packs for the community's food. It was a story told two gullible boys by a mischievous stevedore. They were lucky not to have been stoned for the insult, nor to have been the cause of a war, given they were the sons of a chief.

"I would love to see your homeland. How far is it from where we're going?" Naomi asked him.

"From Alexandria it is five day's journey upriver in a small boat to the first cataract, and another day beyond: less coming back, as you are moving with the current. But if you were to go by land, it would take twice that, and be half as enjoyable. Maybe you *will* visit there sometime," he said, a hopeful note in his voice.

"I hope so," we answered in unison.

He drove the horses himself, and the three of us took turns sitting up front with him. The other two sat behind, burrowing into pillows and bags filled with our personal possessions. Near the end of our trip we boarded a small boat to cross the river, just upstream from where a major tributary joined in to make up the great river known here as Iteru. Heliopolis lay almost directly in front of us, connected to the river by a canal.

Heliopolis was a much smaller city than Alexandria. "It is fundamentally a temple town," explained Hebeny. "Though every rock, tree and pond in our world is sacred -- as is every person -- many believe Heliopolis is built atop a confluence of invisible rivers of energy. Since people have been practicing the spiritual arts here for an age, it possesses a high level of concentrated power. You will see for yourselves, and come to your own conclusions."

Hebeny told us the name Heliopolis had been given it by the Greeks. The word means City of the Sun. As we neared the town, the sun was setting behind us, casting the stone structures in a red-orange glow. It looked like the sun had set the whole city afire. This was the western seat for the study of heavenly bodies, the eastern center being Persepolis in Persia.

 Six barefooted men dressed in white pants that billowed out in the evening breeze lit a string of red lanterns at our approach. They bowed as we disembarked, their oiled beards touching bare chests. I cannot describe the feeling that came over me. The place bore no resemblance to anything I had known up until that moment; and I wondered if I had been transported to another world. The air crackled as the lanterns gently swayed.

I do not really remember what else happened that evening, waking the next morning as if still in a dream. Miriam and Naomi were seated next to each other at a table in front of a sunlit window, eating in silence. I wore a nightdress spun of flax, soft and lightweight. My sisters were dressed the same. I sat down across the table from them, the sun on my back.

They smiled and nodded at me. No one seemed in a hurry to speak. As I peeled a piece of fruit, I studied their faces and noticed just how beautiful they were. Maybe it was the way the sunlight fell upon them, or maybe they were especially well rested or content. I do not know, but I saw them differently. By the time we'd finished eating the spell had begun to dissipate.

"What are we to wear?" asked Naomi, of no one in particular. None of our bags were in sight, nor had any clothes been laid out for us.

"I can understand why they call this the City of the Sun," I said, ignoring the question. Sunlight drenched everything, gilding surfaces.

A woman soon appeared, holding robes and sandals decorated with feathers that would curl about our ankles. After we'd dressed Hebeny arrived. "Did you sleep well?" he asked.

Miriam replied with a yawn: "Oh yes, I feel reborn." Naomi and I agreed it was the best sleep we had had since, well, for a very long time.

"This place does that to people," he said. "It is a tonic, though none of you seemed in need of renewal last night."

"What happened?" I asked. "I remember nothing once we came on to land."

"Precisely nothing," he laughed. "It is the same every time I come here. It's as if I am being welcomed into the arms of the gods, or goddesses when I come here. They take me in and sing me to sleep, and in the morning I awaken, having had new life breathed into me. In a day or two I adjust, and am once again able to think and act in an ordinary manner. Yet in a way I cannot explain, nothing is ever the same as it was before."

We walked out of the small compound that would become our home there, and turned down a narrow, dusty street, lined with low houses on either side. Directly ahead the street ended in a plaza, which lent the impression we were emerging from a tunnel. We were surrounded suddenly with people moving this way and that, talking quietly among themselves. Vendors sold their wares at one end of the plaza; a small café was to our right, and on our left up several broad steps sat a small temple. The sides angled in as if someone had begun a pyramid, without completing it. Windows of different shapes had been cut into the facade.

I stopped to look more closely. "You will find that every detail in this town has its purpose and meaning," said Hebeny. "There is an art of form here that speaks the secret language of creation. This language has many dimensions. We could spend an entire lifetime studying just one of these buildings.

"This is where you will begin your studies," he said, when a tall, big-boned man with golden hair appeared in the doorway directly in front of us. They nodded at each other. "Thorvald will see that you get settled, and I will return for you when your lessons are finished."

Hebeny had been right. By the second day I felt like my feet had found earth again and I was able to concentrate on the lessons. Thorvald would oversee our studies, guiding us through a maze of teachers, each specializing in a single aspect of astronomy or astrology. We would spend several moons there, immersed in our heavenly studies.

Early one morning Thorvald showed up at our door. It was the first time he had come to the residence. We gathered around the table and Mirna, the tall woman who had first greeted our arrival, set out tea and fruit.

Taking a sip, he began. "We are about to mark the end of a great span of time in our planet's journey through the cosmos. Tomorrow morning the sun will be shadowed by the moon, passing from sight for a time. From this we can experience life from a new perspective. The passing moon shields us from our usual energy field, enabling us to enter a time out of time. A total solar eclipse is rare enough. But this one is a thousand fold more powerful, as it opens the doorway from one age to the next. You already know we are leaving the constellation of the ram and entering the sign of the fishes. That these two events should coincide is momentous."

Mirna returned with new robes while he spoke. They were of the finest linen, dyed purple with the signs of the zodiac appliquéd upon them, affixed with gold thread. A pair of golden slippers was laid out next to each.

He got up to leave. "When you are ready, a carriage will be waiting for you on the street. Take a warm shawl as we will travel through the night."

Mirna helped us dress, twining golden cords through our hair and smudging kohl around our eyes. I hardly recognized my friends, feeling once again drawn into that twilight between the worlds of form and spirit. It was strange, I thought, that in all this time studying the heavens, no one had prepared us for this day, or even mentioned it. Even Mirna must have known something. Our handmaid escorted us out to the street where stood a carriage with two white horses. The driver kept his gaze to the front without acknowledging us. He was dressed in a short white robe over bronzed muscles, and wore a large helmet of leather, with feathers the length of my arm trailing behind. He looked a creature of myth, and not a man at all.

We stepped into the carriage. Unseen by us, Mirna slipped a bag between our feet. Twice during the night our driver stopped at a roadside inn. He never spoke a word to us, merely indicating with a nod of his head that we were to go in. In each place we were served meals for which we were not allowed to pay. Had they too known of our coming?

We were glad for the shawls, as the wind whipped around us through the night. Sometime around dawn we boarded a barge, horses, carriage and all, to cross the river. And then we were off again, arriving at our destination not long after sunrise. The horses came to a sudden stop in front of a stepped pyramid. It was the largest such structure I had seen, ablaze in the mid-morning light. There must have been a hundred men standing around its perimeter at regular intervals. None looked at us or otherwise acknowledged our arrival. Disembarking, we took each other's hands and stood facing what looked like the entryway into the pyramid. The carriage sped off, and still we stood alone.

A voice from behind startled us, as we had neither seen nor heard anyone approach. "The hour draws near," it said. "Let us go inside."

Without turning to see who spoke we moved toward the entrance, our unknown guide following behind. We dropped hands only to draw our robes up to ascend the twelve steps. I counted them as we took each in a slow rhythm, already sensing the weight of the ceremony ahead. *Twelve.*

As Hebeny had told us, here there was no consideration of personal taste or passing fashion in the design and construction of even the most ordinary residence, let alone major government buildings or religious structures. Each angle of each cut stone had meaning. The height, width and even weight of the materials were precisely calculated. Everything was meticulously planned, the parts taken together adding up to something greater, with cosmic implications. These structures acted as energetic vehicles linking the people of the land with the higher forces, providing direct and immediate benefits. Everything that lived on the land received a constant and universal blessing.

Because of this, architects were held in highest esteem, wielding considerable political power and enjoying the respect and gratitude of the people. Pharaoh considered the success of his reign due in large part to the faithful adherence to this sacred geometry. The Egyptians, and to a lesser extent, the Greeks and others – including our own people – inherited this science from our common ancestors. We call the ancient land from whence they came, Atlantis. Most people in Egypt simply call it the Red Lands, a name they adopted for their own country. Atlantis in turn had been seeded by the stars at intervals far back in time, or perhaps, *before time.* Thorvald's version of the story differed only a little from that taught us by

Judy. It is possible his was the more accurate, given Egypt's direct line of succession from our ancient brothers.

Miriam, Naomi and I stopped at the top of the stairs. The air shimmered at the periphery of my vision, whether from heat or other cause I did not know. My attention wavered and the hand on my shoulder startled me. Thorvald's sea blue eyes met mine. He had said nothing about meeting us here, but now he gestured us to follow him inside. We walked along a low, dark passageway, one in front of the other. It seemed to me the floor banked slightly upward. It did not entail any exertion on my part but I felt the need to touch the walls now and then to steady myself. Only the sound of our breathing echoed in the stale air.

"Stop," Thorvald said under his breath. I stopped quickly to avoid bumping into him, only to have Miriam collide with me from behind. I felt suddenly dizzy and in reaching out to the walls again, discovered the passageway had narrowed considerably. "We must wait for the precise moment," he added, without elaborating.

"Proceed," he said after an interval. My mind had begun to wander again and I lost all sense of time. A few more steps brought a change to the air. I knew we had left the tunnel and entered a larger room, though it was just as dark. Miriam's hand reached for mine and I sensed Naomi had her other hand.

A burst of light cut through the darkness, momentarily blinding me. In sequence, fires ignited the other torches hung in niches around the room, raising the temperature. A figure clothed in robes stood next to each torch; I could not tell if they were male or female. In the center of the room sat a low table and on that table was a shallow bowl filled with water. *Again, the water.* Thorvald and someone who had brought up the rear of our procession moved to opposite ends of the table. They gestured for Naomi and me to stand at the other two sides, and for Miriam to move to a spot in front of a bas relief that had been hung from the ceiling about halfway between the table and what I believe to be the eastern wall. Though shadows obscured, it looked like astrological symbols had been carved into the hanging piece. At its center was an eclipse between two celestial bodies, an obvious representation of events to come.

Miriam stood with her back to that symbol, while facing Naomi's back. I stood in front of Naomi, facing the two of them. At a certain moment most of the torches were extinguished, leaving the room in deep shadow. I could no longer distinguish my friend's faces, nor see the symbols behind Miriam.

And then it began. A burst of light shot out from behind her, illuminating her form. Not simply outlined in light, her entire body was ablaze, as if lit from within. An instant later the flame surged to Naomi and from her reached across to me. I felt the explosion in my own chest and head. My body shuddered violently, as if suffering a fit. But some miracle kept me on my feet. From me, the light reached its goal, igniting the bowl of water with a single intensely-focused beam. The fire writhed with flames, building until they reached the ceiling, radiating outward from there in every direction until each person standing in the room was bathed in those flames. The wisps of mind that remained wondered if there might have been oil in the bowl, and not water after all.

Without fear I anticipated my demise. But the fire did not consume. Instead it drew back into the bowl and flickered out. I had no will to remain standing, but a hand steadied me and somehow I did not fall. The trembling subsided, and I felt suddenly strong and rooted to the stone beneath my feet, as if it were lending me its strength.

When the priests re-lit the torches I saw the dazed faces of my friends. As if on command we turned and left the room as one, passing down the long hallway by which we had entered. Outside, I noticed a notch on the sun's flank.

Horns and drums and occasional shouts sounded in the distance. The priests had long prepared the people, but still the midday disappearance of something so primal exposes the primitive fears that lie hidden in men's hearts. To me it was a thing of beauty, reaffirming the divine order behind the form side of life. Rather than a phenomenon outside myself, both during and after the ceremony I entered into the heart of the sun where I saw illuminated my little part in life's grand design.

I have no sense now of the passing of time in that day's events (not unlike our first day in Heliopolis). I do not remember being taken to the room where we spent the night, nor dealings with my friends, or any other. But, though I have no words to adequately describe the experience of entering into the sun, the person who stepped into the pyramid that day no longer lived. I still wonder how many times I will be called into the fire before the transformation is complete. It is a progressive process, peeling away the layers of illusion, discarding habits of living and being not suited to the new world taking form.

Thorvald later said that *speaking* of the ceremony could add nothing to the truth of our experience. He did say it had been water in the bowl, and not oil, and that the water had not been diminished by the fire. The age of fire, symbolized by the ram, had consumed itself. The age of water was now upon us, represented by two fish calling us to integration and balance. The entire essence and direction of human experience that had dominated since before the time of Moses was now changing. Ceremonies such as ours invoke and facilitate the shift.

Thorvald sent a messenger to us the following morning. He had set out early for Heliopolis, but said we should relax and see the sights before returning. A young woman came to the door with a plate of food, and asked if we wished a bath before going out.

"Yes, thank you," said Naomi. "But first, please tell me the name of this place."

"You are staying in the home of Menfir, second priest of the temple. He is a friend of your Thorvald."

"Which temple?"

"The temple of Saqqara, of course," she answered, turning to go.

"Wait," said Naomi. The woman stopped. "Saqqara ... in Memphis?"

She gave Naomi an odd look, perhaps thinking she was toying with her. "Yes."

"Memphis!" exclaimed Miriam. "No one said we were coming to Memphis. I had hoped to see the great step pyramid of King Zoser before leaving Egypt, and my wish was granted without me even knowing it." She flopped down on the pillows, giggling. Soon we were all rolling among the pillows, laughing.

Zoser's pyramid had been some distance out into the desert. Now, on the opposite side of the city we found the most astonishing trio of structures that could possibly exist anywhere. The largest of these dwarfed even the step pyramid. It was called by different names, but our driver said it was the Pharaoh Khufu who had commissioned it. Already ancient, much of its painted casing had sloughed off in the frequent sandstorms.

A priest met our carriage, offering to serve as guide. He asked where we were from and we told him Nazareth, in Galilee, not expecting him to know where it was. He stopped and stared. "You are from Nazareth? You then will know a man called Jesus."

"Was he here?" I asked, feeling tears well up.

"Oh yes, he was here," he answered, enigmatically. "You will need to ask *him* about his time with us though. It is not for me to speak of such things. But do tell him that Zafir asked about him. Where is he now?"

I told him he was far to the east, beyond Kushan studying with the Brahmins, and he nodded as if he knew the place.

"We will tell him of our meeting," I assured him

The pyramids were magnificent, but it was the alabaster Sphinx, stretched out like a great cat in the desert, that etched deep into my soul. It was a thing of great beauty and mystery, which would haunt my dreams in the days and years to come.

Chapter 29

TRUE POWER

"What is wrong, Naomi? Are you ill?"

"Oh Veronica, I do not know. I think not, but..."

"But what? Don't you want to go with us to the lake? The carriage will be here soon, and you haven't packed, or dressed. And you haven't eaten since yesterday!"

I had been concerned about my friend ever since the evening Thorvald congratulated us on completing our studies. We were about to leave for Lake Mareotis for the next stage of our training. Miriam and I were glad for the change. We had been given a good foundation in the study of the stars and appreciated its value, but neither of us was drawn to take it further. We were healers, and eager to learn all we could to deepen our natural talents, enabling us to fulfill what we saw as our true calling.

"Veronica...."

"Yes," I said, sitting down next to her on the cot. She had been staring vacantly, but now her eyes were moist. I pulled her to me and felt her shudder. "What is it? Tell me." I stroked her hair as the tears began to flow.

After a time she leaned back and blew her nose. There is nothing I want more than to go to the lake with you. But . . . but I am afraid I am in love with him."

"Who?" I asked. We had been nowhere, met no one while in Heliopolis.

"Thorvald. Have you not seen? I was afraid I had been acting foolishly in front of everyone, and am glad to know that at least you did not notice."

"My dear sister, hearts do not choose the objects of their affection. That comes from somewhere deeper. He is a good man, wise, and handsome too," I added, unable to resist a grin. "But would you stay here? Would you not return to our home?" I did not add 'if he would have you.' If he were a man interested in a wife, he surely was aware of Naomi's fine qualities. But he had evidenced no interest that I could see. Besides, I could not imagine what her father's response would be to such a thing. Living far away from the family in a temple town in Egypt ….

"I do not know. I sense my life purpose lies in our homeland, alongside you and Miriam. I just don't know."

"Well, the lake is not so far from here, and we could pass back this way before we leave Egypt. Nothing needs to be decided now. Wash your face and pack your bag, and travel with us this day. We have practically been with Thorvald day and night, and you need to place some distance between you if you are seeking clarity."

Thorvald saw us off. Miriam and I invited him to visit us at the lake, while Naomi barely managed a goodbye. We stopped overnight in Memphis along the way, but did not revisit the pyramids. They stood together in the distance, outlined in moonlight. We spent the next night in a nondescript village, and arrived at the lake late afternoon of the third day. It glistened on the far horizon since morning, and I expected to arrive any minute. But it just kept growing in size as the day progressed.

"It must be enormous! Are you sure it is a lake, and not a sea?" I asked our driver.

"No, my lady, it is indeed a lake," he replied, with obvious pride. "I was born on its shores. My companions and I walked around it once when I was young. It took us from the new moon almost to the full before we returned home. The waters are said to be healing. It is filled with many kinds of fish, and the daily breezes keep us cool even on the hottest of days." He would have gone on naming its virtues, but at last we had arrived at our new home.

A woman approached us with a broad smile. "You have arrived! How was your journey? I am so happy to have you with us. I am Myra," she finished, giving each of us a welcoming hug. As we introduced ourselves she pressed something into our driver's hand and thanked him for his service. He bowed to each of us and drove off, eager to join his family.

The stress and sadness had faded from Naomi's face during the journey. That evening we took our tea next to the lake, and her lighthearted laugh told me that whatever her decision might be concerning Thorvald, it would be made from a clear heart.

"I surely have lived along these shores in an earlier time," I said to Miriam as we prepared for bed that night. Heliopolis felt familiar, but this place even more so."

She hugged me. "I too feel that. It has been a healing center since ancient times, and my heart tells me the spirit of healing has called us back."

Myra made us feel at home. She bubbled with energy and goodwill, not unlike the hot springs she took us to that evening. "This is a natural healing spot," she said, indicating both the springs and the lake in the background. "It is one of many places in the area that contribute to the harmonizing of body and soul. Though we do not encourage the sick to come here, we will not turn them away either. The purpose of this center is to train teachers and healers, who then return to their native lands to do their work. In this way, we are able to help many, many more than if we just assisted the sick ourselves. It is a place of great power, but the benefits are more far reaching when people work to discover their personal source of power. That is when real healing occurs. Your goal will be to assist people find that place in themselves, rather than simply learning recipes for medicines." She laughed. "Don't worry. You will learn that as well. But it is not our primary focus."

Myra was like a special aunt whom I had not seen for awhile. I could imagine having sat on her lap as a child, or going to her to talk about my fears and hopes. One day, when the two of us were walking alone, she said to me: "We are old friends, you and I. You have noticed that the moment I begin to speak on any subject, especially related to healing, you often know ahead of time what I will say."

I nodded, hoping to hear her insights. But she left it at that...and was right to do so. Remembering is of greater use when it comes to us on its own. Coming from another, it is a story told and not yet a truth. Truth can only be revealed from within.

It didn't feel like we were studying, but more like a treasure hunt. Each gem held a clue to the next, and the next. It was an exciting time, and the three of us began to come into our own.

"Miriam, you and Veronica work similarly. Accumulating a body of knowledge is only one of your tools for healing. Information is not the first place you turn when diagnosing or determining what course of action you will take. Instead you naturally – that is, without thinking about it – align yourself with the person who has called for your help. You become one with them, and in so doing intuitively sense what needs to be done. This is something that cannot be taught. At other times, you will need to think about whether a particular tool would be most helpful -- whether a poultice, salve, oil, herb, a splint or a specific invocation or prayer is the right course of action.

"You, Naomi, have another approach. You have an ability to see the movement of life force in the body, *and* its blockages. You can see if patterns are disturbed, or if a system is discolored or distorted, all of which help you diagnose the problem and discover its solution from the same list of tools I just mentioned. These are inborn talents which simply need nurturing. That is my role."

Miriam and I worked together most of the time, while Naomi took her studies individually. But the best times were when we three came together to collaborate, which kindled and enhanced our natural abilities.

"And so it is with all things," Myra said. "This is why we do not drift through the world alone, as alone we would never discover and develop our true gifts, never awaken the sleeping giant."

"Sleeping giant?" I asked.

"It is a childish term for something that cannot be named. But it is apt. This power sleeps for our own protection. If we have not developed the capacity to wisely use our power, it would destroy us if awakened too soon. Think of it as a coiled snake, ready to spring with the right stimulus."

"Does this happen when we are healing? Is our desire to heal the right stimulus?" asked Naomi.

"Maybe. It could happen then, or it could happen when we are joined with our spiritual and temporal mate during sex, or it could happen during deep meditation, or even spontaneously without an identifiable stimulus. But let us put the questions of healing and sex aside for now. You have been taught about a force which enlivens all things. This force is the mind of our Creator in continuous motion, our life force which gives form to God's *thought*. As long as it flows unimpeded, we are healthy. When something blocks it, we suffer in one way or another – often many ways at once.

"Veronica and Miriam, when you align with the patient you automatically know where the blockage is and most often how to remove it. And Naomi, it is what you are being trained to recognize with your seeing. This life force exists in everything. The sleeping giant is a particular aspect of it, coming to us as fire. I can see that you each have already met this fire, in one way or another. If you were not prepared, you would have experienced the event as painful. Pain gives rise to fear, much as you might have at seeing a coiled snake. But in fact this snake is a powerful agent of change, just as fire is. Now you are readying yourself to bring the healing fire to others."

Myra told us about the greater and lesser centers of concentrated power housed within the human form. Taken together they provide the unique conditions for how each of us lives our life. We were to spend many, many days and nights studying these centers, learning how to move the life force through them so that the fire might be released in the right way. Eventually Myra and several other teachers with whom we occasionally met taught us to work with the force in our spiritual practice, in healing work, and to prepare for the day when we would enter into an intimate relationship with our husbands.

One day when out for a walk next to the lake, I found Naomi sitting on a large rock some distance out from shore. The gentle waves lapped around her. She must have sensed me, and turned around. "Veronica, I am glad to see you." She waded to shore and slipped on her sandals so we could walk together.

"I wish I were a painter," I told her. "You looked so beautiful

the silvery light. You seem happy. Is your heart at peace then?" I asked, not mentioning Thorvald.

"Yes. I see now my destiny does not lie here. But I am glad I opened my heart to him, and have no regrets."

I wondered, but did not ask, if they had ever met privately. Her words seemed to hint there was more to it than romantic fantasy. But it did not matter: a pure heart cannot be tainted.

"Do you hope to marry one day?" she asked me.

"I do not know about hope. But I have seen myself with another in two separate visions. We loved each other and offered great comfort in trying times. And you?"

"I have had no visions, but my heart knows there will be someone." She flushed.

We had arrived back at the place that served as both home and school. Miriam was in the kitchen, helping with the evening meal. Naomi went out for water, and I pushed my sleeves up, plunging into the floury dough.

"We have a new instructor coming tomorrow," said Miriam.

"Who?"

"I forgot to ask that. But she is coming to teach us dance!"

"Dance? I *love* to dance."

Over dinner Myra told us about her. "Leela trained as a temple dancer in Thebes.

That means different things in different places," she said. "In some temples the dancers also serve to initiate young men in the sexual arts, and while this may have been done in Thebes in the past, it is no longer so. Today dancers, and the musicians who accompany them, are trained to invoke sacred form using sound and movement. Though the results tend to be more ephemeral, they accomplish much the same thing that skilled architects do with their buildings. The results are profound, bringing about transformation in the dancers' own lives, and often in the lives of their audience."

Leela arrived the following morning. "My mother is from the east, and father was Egyptian. The dance that mother brought from her homeland was different from what she found here. What I teach is a marriage of both traditions. You could say I am the product of two such marriages," she said with a laugh, "passion being the impulse for both of them."

Leela was short -- her head just reaching my shoulders -- and powerfully built. She moved with grace, silently like a cat. But there were times in the ecstasy of dance she whirled like the storms that move across the desert, consuming everything in their path.

"I am a combination of the Dervishes and the goddess Durga, tempered by Hathor."

She grinned and dropped to the ground in a ball, turning head over heels, then sprang to her feet in a single fluid movement. Leela embodied the coiled serpent fire. Enhancing the image, she often wore the colors of fire, tinged with purple. She captivated her audiences, sometimes leaving them stunned and silent, while at other times they exploded with shouts and applause.

She worked us mercilessly during our lessons, until we tapped into a power we did not know we had. With training I began to understand how to both unleash and contain the fire at will without becoming discomfited by it. In so doing I had my first glimpse of the immense power Creator had given me, and began to appreciate what Myra had said about how our power had been hidden from us for our own protection.

"Men believe that because they are equipped with larger muscles, they are the more powerful sex. But they were given muscles to compensate for their limitations." I expected Myra's usual laughter, but she was absolutely serious. "Without the power of Shekkinah, nothing would exist," she said, using the name from our Hebrew tradition. "People in every land have their own name for the *woman of light* who contains the power of life in her womb. With proper training we learn to invoke this *power* to flow through us and into the world. She alone interprets the divine plan, and wields the life force accordingly. She shares her secrets with healers, priestesses and priests, and others of worth, at her discretion.

"But much has been lost: the forces of darkness have begun to convince women to hide their power in shame. They have even persuaded us that *we* are the source of the world's suffering, and that our sins will be assuaged if men assume worldly power through their superior might, thereby protecting us from ourselves. Compassion, our greatest strength, was turned against us as we surrendered our power to alleviate suffering in the world. Not all of us were convinced, of course. Many priestesses hid their power under the guise of temple dance or in secret ceremony, while other women concentrated it in their role as mothers or caretakers of the home. In nearly every land women have been driven from the temples, made to stand outside or behind curtains, as if their very presence tainted the sacred images or writings.

"But had we actually extinguished our power as they thought we had, life itself would have been withdrawn from the world, and it would be no more."

After Myra finished talking, Leela began to dance again. She waved us in and we danced with her until we seemed to lose our separateness, moving within a unitary vision of our power. Together we *became* Shekkinah, life itself expressing against the canvas of the world. The colors of our costumes were its pigments, blending, merging, now subtle, now bold. The dance left me breathless.

"Good!" she shouted to us. "Save nothing of yourself -- not even your breath. It is given you to release into life so that all might live. *You* are the Divine Mother, the light of the world. *You* are the sacred archetype for all women, standing alongside *he* who brings the new dispensation to mankind. He is heralded as savior, but he cannot prevail alone, indeed is powerless alone. You are more than helpmeet. You are *she* upon whose arm he leans for support. Open yourself to receive the arrow of truth and the waters of rebirth; open your womb and heart and soul so the three can become one. In this is the hope of the world"

*

One evening we took our tea down to the lake. "It seems to me," I ventured, breaking the silence, "that some of our musicians are one with us in the light as they play their accompaniment -- though they are men."

"Of course," said Leela. "I have never said women were superior to men. We enjoy superiority in the fulfillment of our unique roles, as do men in the fulfillment of theirs. I have simply pointed out the heresy in saying men are stronger or superior to women. In the dance, in your healing work and in the teaching that is to come, you will begin the process of righting this wrong, of bringing balance and healing to our world in the most elemental sense."

"But this will take a very long time," Myra added wistfully, staring out over the water.

I wished the process could be sped up, of course, that we might alleviate unnecessary pain and suffering. But my nightly visions, both waking and sleeping, confirmed what she said. These visions sometimes spoke of my personal path to awakening. But at other times they expanded to encompass vast periods, stretching far into the future. These latter visions were sometimes hard to bear, as the enormity of the challenge weighed down upon me.

We were becoming increasingly close during our time on the lake and I saw a parallel -- though our numbers were fewer -- to the six women who remain of the holy twelve that had been gathered before Mary was chosen. Those women were drawn together to love and support each other through the most difficult times, just as we will do through the dangerous times ahead. .

We continued to learn certain rituals related to the dance, specific to healing. And there were other classes that pulled together our studies of the stars with both healing and dance, such as the best cycles of the moon for applying poultices or for planting or gathering specific herbs, ritual movement to focus and enhance our power, to deflate negative activity on the part of others, and so forth. These different classes were integrating all we had learned while in Egypt, and I began to understand that our time there was drawing to a close.

Soon after, Myra came to us. "Tomorrow a boat will call here, to take us across the lake. Put a few things in a bag, as we will be gone several days."

"Is this to be our farewell?" I asked.

She turned her coal black eyes on me. "Yes, it is time. We have sent word to your families, and Simon will meet you in Alexandria at the new moon.

"So soon?" asked Naomi. "The full is almost upon us, and...."

"There will be time for every needed thing," answered Myra. "Now let us enjoy ourselves."

We spent three full days and four nights aboard the boat. The lake was indeed large, much bigger than our own Galilee.

"It is about the same as your Salt Sea," agreed Myra.

"Have you seen it? Have you been to our land?" asked Naomi.

She nodded yes.

"Why have you never spoken of this?" I asked.

"There is not enough time for everything," she replied. "It was for you to be here, not thinking about what went before or what might await you upon your return."

We docked just before sunset, and spent that last evening with our beloved teachers. We did not speak of our leaving, or whether we would ever see each other again. It wasn't that we avoided it as a painful subject, but recognized it did not matter. Of course we would miss each other's presence, but we were learning there was no going away. Not really. Whenever the heart has opened to allow another person in, that person is forever a part of us.

Instead we ate a hearty feast and drank some of their best wine. And we danced together, even Myra, who had not danced with us before. And little Greet, who quietly cleaned and cooked for us. And Brant, who did the gardening. And several of the neighbors, and a few of the younger students. It was a wonderful evening, and in the morning we were ready.

The carriage stood outside, and after the shortest of goodbyes, we were on our way to the river where a boat awaited us. We took our meals with the captain, and on the second day he announced an unscheduled stop, suggesting we join him on deck.

There, waiting on the dock was Thorvald. I looked at Naomi for her reaction, and saw the same happy surprise that registered on Miriam's face.

"How wonderful to see you again," he said, embracing each of us in turn. The captain had a table set on deck, then left us alone. "We must be off by sunset," he called over his shoulder.

We picked at the bread and honey, the fruit and nuts, but mostly we talked. Now and then I thought I saw a flicker of something else cross his face whenever our old teacher looked at Naomi, but I could not be sure. He asked many questions about our studies, saying how he wished he could see us in the dance. Myra had a reputation throughout Egypt as the finest teacher of the healing arts, and Leela, of temple dance.

"And now you will bring the best of our world back to your land."

"Including the most excellent instruction we could have received of the stars," added Naomi. A crimson blush shot up her neck to her cheeks.

And then we were off again. The journey went by quickly, and we soon arrived in Alexandria. Simon met us at the port, as if no time had elapsed from his quick departure two years earlier. "Bandar would see you before you leave," he said, as we made our way through the dusty streets to the school. I was glad to see the brothers again, though Judy had already passed on.

"She missed the morning meditation one day. And that was it," said Bandar. "I shall be forever grateful she returned to us before departing.

"And now, I have written several messages that I would ask you to deliver." As I sat closest to him, he handed them to me. I didn't really mean to read the names on the outside of the sealed and tied missives, but noticed my cousin's name on one. My heart leapt. Bandar saw my face and said, "No, he has not returned, and it will be some time before he does. But keep this safe for him, will you not?"

We passed a single night there before the ship was to leave.

Hebeny saw us off the next morning, adding a note of his own to Jesus. And then we left the Red Lands.

Chapter 30

SURRENDER

Jesus heard the shouts even before Krishna's house came into view. He felt the fear and broke into a run.

Swarna wailed, hands cutting the air frantically. Lal caught her wrists, uttering soothing sounds as one does to a baby. But she would not be comforted.

He burst through the door, out of breath. "What is it? What has happened?" But no one seemed to notice him. The man from Galilee loved these people as his own family, but he suddenly felt like an outsider.

Moans came from behind the curtain that separated them from an inner room. There in the shadows Jesus found Krishna on his knees in front of his daughter Meera's tiny mat. He cupped her hand in his. Another man, whom he had not seen before, poked and prodded her arm, his eyes full of fear. Behind them Harsha berated Ravi, the girl's brother. "How could you leave her there? What is wrong with you?" he shouted, shaking the poor child's shoulders.

Jesus went up to Harsha, turned him around and tried to meet his eyes. Ravi used the distraction to pull away and ran out the door sobbing. Harsha's eyes were wild and did not seem to recognize the man before him. Jesus led him outside. "What happened?" he asked again. His anger subsiding, the older man collapsed onto the ground in tears.

"Harsha, look at me," he said, trying to lift him up. "I must attend to Meera. Do not worry," he added, himself greatly worried.

Kneeling, he laid his hand on Krishna's shoulder. "What happened, my brother?"

Krishna turned, eyes lost in deep wells of misery, and his body began to shudder violently. "You are here!" he whispered. "Help her!"

"What happened?" he asked yet again in the softest of voices, searching those eyes for the elusive answer. Krishna took several deep breaths, then said: "Ravi and Meera were playing ball down by the water, next to the old warehouse where the grasses grow thick and tall. The ball rolled away and Ravi ran to find it." Krishna's fingers dug into his friend's arm. "He heard a scream behind him and turning around, could not see his sister." The trembling began again. "By the time he found her, she was unconscious. He saw these," and he grabbed the girl's leg, lifting it so Jesus could see the two bite marks on her ankle. In between sobs he whispered; "She is almost as big as Ravi, and he could barely carry her back here. It is not his fault."

Jesus moved his friend to the side so he could sit closer to the girl. Taking her wrist, at first he found no pulse at all, and then only the slightest indication she yet lived. Asking the man he presumed to be a doctor: "What have you done?"

"Nothing, there is nothing to do," the man said plaintively. "It was a cobra, and she is so small." Tears rolled down his cheeks.

Jesus held the tiny wrist and from that moment on, only she existed for him. Focusing his attention on the faint pulse he noticed she had begun to shudder with each new breath. Her pale skin felt clammy and two blue lines climbed her leg.

He knew that each soul chooses its own time to withdraw the life force from its form, and that it sometimes decides upon a means that appears cruel or unfair. If it is their time, the healer lovingly does what he can to help those being left behind. And if it is not, he joins forces with the soul to restore the body.

Jesus focused his thought in the light, that he might know whether she willed to return to the world of spirit, or to remain with her family. The eyes of her soul faced him and calmly replied, "The healing is for them. Take care of my family. I am finished here." In that instant she was engulfed in light and lifted away. Returning to earthly consciousness Jesus heard her last gasp.

He had not noticed Swarna come in, or the doctor leaving. Without a word he moved aside as the mother bent over Meera's small body and began to wail. Lal fell to her knees across from her, joining her mistress in the death keen.

Jesus helped Krishna to his feet, and led him out the door and into the street where he told him what Meera had said. Krishna nodded, finding comfort in her words. "She was a brave child, loving and beautiful," he said of his daughter. He straightened his shoulders. "I must be strong for Swarna." He looked around. "Where is Ravi? I must find Ravi so he may know I do not blame him."

The two went in search of the boy. They found him some time later inside the old warehouse, crouched down in the near darkness, eyes staring vacantly in a tear-stained face. Jesus left them, and returned to the house.

Neighbors had arrived, and a few family members. The women attended the girl's body, so he went in search of Leela and Parvati, Meera's little sisters. Jesus took them out for a walk, one in each hand, calming their fears at having been forgotten in the turmoil.

The body was cremated on the third day, with Muktananda officiating. Perhaps a hundred people attended, unusual for the death of a child. But Krishna and Swarna were much loved. Krishna kept Ravi close to him and was careful to let him know his love for the child had not diminished. As was the custom, after the period of ritual cleansing had been completed (required of all family members) Harsha and Krishna went out into the community to distribute food to the poor, that the gift of life might be continued.

*

The day she died, Jesus had been called to stand before an assembly. They were careful not to call it a tribunal, though that is what it was, and *being called to stand* meant he was summoned to defend himself against certain allegations. Some in the temple community had been suspicious of him from the start, simply because he was a foreigner. Their suspicions were aggravated by jealousy of his increasing popularity, especially among the younger priests and novitiates. Then jealousy had turned to fear of a loss of prestige, position and power. Something had to be done.

Three of the older priests met with a group of Brahmins who served in a judicial capacity in Juggernaut. "He is dangerous," they told them.

"How so?"

"He teaches lies to the young priests, and seeks to split them off from their temples. I have heard he has ambitions to start a new sect, placing himself at its head."

"Oh, you priests are always grumbling among yourselves. Of course he will explain things differently. It might just be a misunderstanding of language."

"And he preaches against our caste system," they added slyly.

While his interpretation of doctrine or philosophy did not concern the Brahmins, this did. The stability of their land depended upon the perpetuation of the caste system. Thus the priests got the backing of several of the most powerful Brahmins.

The questions asked in the forum were spurious. They had no real interest in what he thought or even in what he taught. Their intention was to pressure him to leave. "And what if he does not?" asked one, after Jesus left. The issue had only been insinuated, and not directly addressed.

"We will offer him a choice: to leave or to stop teaching and public speaking."

"And if he does not?" the man pressed. But no one answered his question. Their dark looks said enough.

Jesus had not returned to the temple or spoken in a public square since Meera's death. There had been no opportunity to mention the incident to Krishna before this but he spoke of it now as the two men walked to the temple.

"I know those people," his friend said. "They will not stop until you are silenced. Even Muktananda and his students labor under an uneasy truce with them. But you have no status here. I cannot help, though as a businessman I number among the caste of which they are most afraid – due to our numbers and relative affluence. But my caste would not stand by me in defiance of them, and I would be destroyed along with you."

"I cannot let that happen," Jesus responded, worried for the first time. His personal well being was one thing, but this was his family. And Sita, he thought to himself. She was away now, but soon would return. And what then?

He sought Muktananda's advice.

"I wondered when they would resort to this. They cannot abide the thought that an outsider might offer a clearer understanding of their own scriptures than they can manage. We pride ourselves in our openness and ability to accept philosophies that offer new insight into the ancient beliefs. But they hate the Pharaonic teachings which you have brought, a people whom they despise -- though most have never met one." He laughed a bitter laugh. "But the one thing they cannot forgive is the young priests love you too much, and them too little."

Jesus also had many followers among men and women of the lower castes. He was often approached with questions or appeals for healing while walking through the marketplace or out on the street. The question was as often about an everyday problem related to family or finances as it was about things spiritual. He never turned aside from their needs, as even the most ordinary question often veiled deeper concerns and issues. Instead he would stop and spend as much time with them as they needed before going on about his business. Often, others gathered to hear his words, as he had become quite well known among the people.

"Teacher," said a woman, tugging at his sleeve at the spice stand the day after the forum. He had stopped to pick up a few things for Swarna on his way home.

"Yes, sister, namaste."

"Namaste," she answered, bowing slightly, flustered that a stranger should greet her appropriately before she had done so. The greeting bestows honor, acknowledging that one stands before an embodiment of the divine.

"Teacher," she repeated, eyes welling with tears, "please help me. My husband's family wants to return me to my parents, which would end my life." She exaggerated only slightly, as such a woman could never be married again, a source of shame and a financial burden for a poor family.

He held her eyes while she continued, somewhat calmed in his presence. "I have not given him a child, not even a girl," she whispered. "And we have been married nearly three years now."

"How old are you?" he asked.

"Fifteen, I think. My blood came late, only last year." She blushed. These are not subjects talked about with a man or a stranger, but this is the way it always was for him.

He moved his hand next to hers, and waited for her approval.

She nodded. His eyes closed as he took her hand between his. Soon they were breathing as one, standing within the crowd like two lovers might, lost to all but each other.

When his breathing returned to normal he opened his eyes. "Sister, return to your husband and tell him you will conceive in three moons' time. The seed was not complete, and worry has put off the day when you would be ready. Worry no more. Your husband is a good man, and will stand between you and his parents. A girl will come first, and then two boys. Patience...."

She kissed his hand and would have knelt at his feet if he had let her. "Go now," he said, and she turned and ran off like a young girl.

He had always known he would not remain there forever. His current trouble might well be the sign it was time to begin the long return. More than once he had entertained the idea of staying there, marrying, living a *normal* life, like Krishna's. He loved children. He loved the people there. He had begun to feel at home next to the sea, even forgetting the taste of food from his native land. Days would pass without him thinking of his mother, his brothers and sisters, his friends, not thinking of....other things that awaited him.

He walked along the sea, dipping into a reservoir of emotions he had largely forgotten over the past several years. They came now with a great surge, engulfing him in shame. How could I have imagined – even for a moment – that I might turn aside from my soul purpose, he wondered? How easily I am swayed! It was so much easier to guide other people....

Back at the house he went directly to his room to pack. He planned to leave immediately, perhaps that very night. But as he gathered his things, he realized the cowardice in running away. That was not the answer either.

"You are quiet tonight," said Swarna, as she cleared the table. He rose to help her, and Krishna joined him.

"Now I am suspicious," she laughed. "Since when do the men

of the house clean up after a meal?" When they were finished he asked them to sit. Krishna would not meet his eyes, sensing what was to come.

"You are my family, as dear to me as those with whom I passed my childhood. And like them, you will forever remain in my heart."

Swarna stared at him, tears forming in her large eyes. "No," was all she could manage.

"My time here has come to an end. I must return to Nazareth." He did not mention his difficulties with the priests, or anything about destiny or purpose. Those were not things to be spoken.

"And what of Sita?" she asked, looking for something to dissuade him.

He did not answer at first. Then: "It was never meant to be," his voice trailed off.

Swarna wept. She had wondered why Sita spent so much time away, knowing her love of this man. She had prayed that in time they'd resolve the gulf of history and culture … and marry.

"I will wait for her return, so I can tell her myself," he said softly, and his friends saw the sadness in his eyes. In the meantime he continued teaching in the temple, and made himself available to everyone, as he always had. He did not tell the priests he'd decided to leave, not wanting to feed their illusory sense of power. His only concern was that his friends should not suffer on his behalf. Besides, the bitter cold of winter would have made passage through the mountains impossible if he left too early, and he was determined to keep his promise to Jingu.

Not long afterward he was summoned to a second forum. He considered ignoring it, but to do so carried a risk of rapid reprisal, and he hoped to put that off as long as possible. So he went. They berated him for continuing to speak to the lower castes, and to women of any caste. They said that he risked being branded unclean himself, unfit to enter the temples. However, they were willing to overlook past behavior if he scrupulously avoided the unworthy, and spoke only from approved texts.

He neither agreed nor disagreed. It was all he could do to refrain from spitting at their feet. My cousin was yet a young man, given to the same passions as the rest of us. It was through experiences such as this one that he would learn the difficult lessons of detachment and forgiveness, skills that he would sorely need in the future.

That evening after dinner he told his friends, "I do not know how much longer I can hold them away." Swarna had not known of the first meeting, but he decided she needed to know the risk. "It is not possible for me to agree to their demands, but I do not want to put you in any danger either."

"We are protected," said Krishna, and he hoped it was so.

Swarna nodded. "I would have you stay with us forever, no matter what their threats," Changing the subject, she said, "We received a message today. Sita will be here in two day's time."

In spite of himself, his heart jumped at the thought of seeing her again. It would have been easier to leave without saying goodbye, but he would not do that to her. Over the next two days he quietly visited those with whom he was closest. Each one promised to watch over Krishna's family, though it was unlikely harm would come to them once he had gone. The priests would consider his departure a sign of victory.

"I am sorry, but I cannot go with you when you leave," Krishna told him that evening.

"I know, but I sense we will meet again somewhere." He had planned to leave alone; his small bag was already packed. Supplies for the journey could be found along the way.

"I have arranged for someone to travel with you," his friend added with a grin.

"That is unnecessary."

Krishna hoped his message had gotten through. For his part, Jesus did not ask who would travel with him, nor did he care. He thought only of Sita's impending arrival.

The next morning he forced himself to join the family, wanting nothing more than to flee, to avoid seeing her.

Krishna's family chatted amiably, aware of his discomfort, but savoring the little time that remained with the man who had found his way into their hearts.

They had just finished eating when he heard her voice at the door. In that single instant, every trace of anxiety, fear, sadness and regret melted away, and he knew his heart was freed. "Sita." He rose to greet her.

"Jesus," she answered in a voice sweet and unburdened. They embraced like brother and sister, the heat they had borne washed away in the cool waters of acceptance.

The family moved out to a table in the jasmine-scented garden, under the towering trees. Swarna set out tea and cakes, as if they had not just eaten.

"You are leaving us," Sita said, without a hint of recrimination in her voice.

"Yes, soon." Laughing, he gently slapped his friend's shoulder. "Your brother has apparently arranged for someone to accompany me, and so you'll need to ask him when I will leave."

That afternoon he and Sita walked together along the sea, where they had felt the first stirrings of love. She took his hand for a few minutes as she had once done, gave it a squeeze it and let it go. They asked about each other's lives since the day she'd returned to the south, and what each of them hoped for the future. His heart was grateful for the loving friendship that remained between them.

The next day he wandered aimlessly through the marketplace, returning the greetings of the many people who hailed him. He decided to visit Krishna's business and as it was getting late, hailed a rickshaw. Tipping the man handsomely, he called him brother, and with that one word changed the man's life, though he would never know it.

He awoke early the following morning to shouts at the front gate. Quickly pulling his robe over his head, he went to see who was there. Krishna had gotten there first and when he sensed Jesus behind him, stepped aside to reveal their old friends Homer and Zhang. Though grimy from their trip, they seemed extremely pleased with themselves.

"How? Why?" Jesus stammered, looking at Krishna, who shared their conspiratorial grin.

"I knew after the first forum I would not be able to convince you to stay and it was only a matter of time before you would leave us. So I sent word to Norbu, to see if they might come to bring you back. I do not know how they got my message in time, but here they are!" he said, triumphantly.

At the moment, none of them could recall the words of greeting in the others' languages, but it didn't matter. They embraced, patted each other's backs and chattered away in words mostly incomprehensible to each other.

"Thank you, my brother," Jesus said, hugging the man who had so intimately shared the past four years of his life.

They left the next day. Zhang and Homer declined to linger, despite their exhaustion. They found the damp sea air oppressive, and were eager to return to their mountain home. And now the door had opened, Jesus was equally impatient for the journey to begin.

Chapter 31

THE SACRED VALLEY

The heat and humidity of the delta sapped their strength. Mosquitoes and flies plagued the three men, and everywhere people lay sick and dying of fever. But at last they broke free of the lowlands, ascending the foothills into cooler air. Jesus finally managed to get the mountain men to slow their pace, enough to stop at the occasional shrine (though not for long), and take pleasure in the many striking vistas.

The two men had left their yak at the home of a distant relative of Zhang's before descending to the lowlands. The creature would not have survived long outside its mountain environment. The men stopped back at the village to get him for the return journey. Zhang had named him Sark. The name had no special meaning; he just liked the sound of the word. One evening not long after, they stopped at the edge of a small village nestled among the high peaks. The sun had already set, but twilight lingered long that time of year. They counted six large fires burning at intervals around the periphery of the village, and an enormous one at its center.

"Zhang!" came a shout, and two men rushed out to embrace him. It seemed he had relatives there as well.

"Come dance with us," another called out. They had arrived at midsummer, and the villagers would celebrate through the night, as do people throughout the world.

Jesus had yet to adjust to the higher altitudes, and wanted only to sleep after the long day's march. But a hearty meal gave him a lift. He hadn't eaten meat in a long time and thought his body might object, but he felt fine. Neither had he drunk spirits since leaving the mountains and it went right to his head. A young woman with a crimson shawl had no trouble convincing him to join her in the dance. They whirled round the fire until he vowed not to drink any more that night -- or maybe ever.

The children banged on anything they could get their hands on, and blew into yak horns that seemed capable of only a note or two. It wasn't music as such, but no one seemed to notice. The villagers changed dance partners with great frequency. As well there seemed to be some partnering going on in the shadows beyond the glare of the fires. Numerous maidens made it clear they would not have minded going into the darkness with the exotic stranger, though their interest was not reciprocated. He was the first to find his own bed that night, and the first to rise the following morning, accustomed as he was to an early start each day. But the sun would climb high before his companions appeared.

The days varied little after midsummer. Weather was kind to them. The few trees they saw were stunted, with only a branch or two still growing among the dead wood. "Though small, those trees are as old as the mountains themselves," Zhang said reverently.

"Tomorrow we will see the monastery," he told his friend one particularly cold evening. "We will eat well then, and I will sleep next to the fire with my children." His eyes glowed in the moonlight and Jesus could see he loved them. Zhang's wife had died two winters before, and he had taken a new wife, a stranger, really, just before leaving on his journey to the south.

By late the next morning they stood on a high ridge, looking down at the green valley and walled compound off to the side. The yak, suddenly on familiar ground, bolted and began running, sensing home and rest and its own good food. The men ran after it, and were there in time to share the midday meal with Norbu.

"Jingu passed on not long after you left," he said. Jesus nodded. Jingu's spirit had come to say goodbye to him when he first arrived in Juggernaut. "Young boys keep coming in ever-greater numbers from the countryside, a sign of increasing poverty and unrest. Their parents usually just leave them at the gate, offering no opportunity to ask questions. I think they are afraid we will not accept the children, and they would have no recourse then but to abandon them somewhere else."

He noticed Jesus' startled reaction. "I know that sounds terrible, but they cannot be blamed. With one less mouth to feed, those who remain might survive. The soil is rich in our valley and food yet plentiful, but the mountains are not so generous. People live on the edge at the best of times. Though most of them would not move to the low country if given a choice, the mountains they love exact a high price."

That evening he led Jesus down by the river. "I do not wish to frighten others, but I have heard from people I trust that the Han are planning to attack us from the northeast. It is hard to imagine what they hope to gain, as we have no riches here. The hardship would not seem worth the price. There are many villages between them and us, and we will have sufficient warning here to go into hiding. This is not a problem now, but in just three moons the snows will return. It would be suicide for them to fight then, but people who send young men off to die rarely consider such things." Jesus thought back to Jingu's prediction that he would not remain long at the monastery.

He settled into their monastic life with ease. Jesus loved the prayers and chants that seemed to rise from the earth's core, vibrating through the monks and out into the world. There was nothing like it anywhere, and he thought it possible such sounds had been the instrument of original creation.

The boys he had left behind were now becoming men in the unfolding cycles of time. What changes will I find when I return to Nazareth, he wondered? It is easier to see the turning wheel of life after an absence than in the sameness of our everyday world. Surely the ancients spoke true when they advised us to look closely at the details of our lives in order to learn the secrets of the universe. Achieving intimacy with the ordinary is to discover life's real treasures. Our world helps us understand our truest selves, and in knowing ourselves we find revealed the whole of creation.

One day a shadow fell upon him while he sat next to the river. He looked up to see a figure outlined by the sun, and patted the rock in silent invitation for the boy to sit down. Only then did he see his face. "Yeshe?" The boy nodded and threw himself at his old friend, embracing him. "I hardly recognized you, you've grown so. You are almost a man," he said, hugging him back.

"I thought I would never see you again, though you said you would return ... I should have known you would not lie to me ... It is so wonderful that you have come ... Will you stay this time?" he ended, having finally run out of breath.

"Sit. Let us just sit together and listen to the water." Once Yeshe had settled down Jesus asked "Now, tell me what has happened to you since I left,"

The boy had taken a strong interest in his studies, offering to lead the prayers whenever the older monks looked for a volunteer among the novitiates. His voice had begun to change, and he was discovering the undertones that would give depth to the invocations. His eyes sparkled when he spoke and Jesus was pleased to see he had found himself. "And I am soon to take my first initiation," he added with pride.

"I am very happy for you."

Yeshe had matured. He did not hang on Jesus as he once had. Other boys would take his place, but that was to be expected among children who had been abandoned by their families. The monastery was becoming overcrowded and there were too few monks to guide too many children.

The first snow fell early that year, with hardly a pause between summer and winter. They hurried to get the grains and vegetables out of the ground and the last of the fruit before it froze on the trees. Norbu worried there would not be enough to get them through the winter. Fewer people seemed willing to leave for the low country, citing unrest in the villages. And more poured in from the smaller encampments to the north, where people would be unable to defend themselves. The population swelled.

Jesus was awakened by a knock on the door one night. He rolled over on his mat to see if Krishna had heard, forgetting for the moment that his friend had not returned with him, and he lived alone in the room. The knock came again. "Come," he said. A shadow appeared in the door. "Who is there?" he asked.

"Teacher," said a young man, "Norbu asked me to bring you to him." He grabbed a robe and the two of them ran through the moonless night to the old Abbot's room.

"It has begun," he said, a shade in the darkness.

"What? What has begun?" Jesus asked, shivering in the cold.

Norbu handed him a blanket. "A messenger from Lhasa just left. He said they are on the move."

Jesus was fully awake now and did not need to ask who *they* were. "How close?"

"Maybe seven days. It depends upon how quickly they travel and if they encounter resistance. I doubt there will be much of that," he added, quietly. They sat awhile, each man thinking his own thoughts.

"You must leave," said Norbu.

"No, I will stay." He had planned to say he would stay and fight, but he knew he would not.

"You *must* leave," the Abbot repeated, with finality. "This is not your fight, and nothing you do could change the outcome anyway. Take three of the older children, and leave this time tomorrow. You decide who will go with you. The men must stay, and the younger children would be of no use to you. It is vital you remain safe." He did not explain himself.

"There must be something I can do before leaving, to help you prepare," he insisted.

"Pray, now and later. You can also help me hide some of our most precious manuscripts."

The old man had been prepared, having already sequestered those most important to him in a corner of his room. They gathered them into bundles and wrapped them in heavy linen, then carried them to a nearby cave. It took many trips back and forth. Worn yak skins, their strong odor long dissipated, had been laid out on the cave floor.

There they wrapped the bundles in skins and tied them with tough sinew. The sinew had been freshly cut and would shrink as it dried, securing the manuscripts against the elements.

"Do not forget this cave, in case you return one day. It is likely no one will be left here who remembers." Norbu then showed him three more caves where other manuscripts had previously been secured. "They represent the totality of our learning, from countless generations before me. They are priceless, though the Han would only burn them." He sounded old, and tired. "These bodies come and go," he said, touching his own leathery hand, "but I would have these texts survive until another time."

Jesus chose Yeshe, and with his advice two other boys about the same age. Norbu nodded approval when the four of them arrived at his quarters the next night. "You have not told anyone?" he asked the boys. They assured him they had not.

Tesu was from a village to the northwest called Teksi. They decided to go there. It was the opposite direction from the line of battle, and was known to Norbu. "Tesu can guide you, as he traveled there and back himself last summer when his father lay dying. Tesu, do you know the Abbot there?"

The boy nodded yes, his face a mixture of pride and fear.

"Good. Remember, your elder brother here does not know the terrain and he will suffer more from the cold than you."

Jesus thought to disagree, but realized he was right. Already he piled the skins on at night, and winter had barely begun. Norbu insisted they take a yak with them, though the village could scarcely afford it. "And what if we are forced to abandon it?" argued Jesus. "That would be a terrible waste."

"But you cannot carry enough supplies on your own backs," he countered, indicating the boys. They assured Norbu they were stronger than they appeared, and were familiar with some of the villages through which they would pass and could re-supply themselves along the way. In the end, he relented and they left without the beast.

Walking away into the darkness, they could not see the tears in the old Abbot's eyes. Whatever happened in the village, he knew he would see none of them again.

They were blessed with good weather for the journey, and villagers openly welcomed them, considering the information they received a good trade for the supplies they provided. It was an odd group -- a grown man and three boys -- but no one asked why they traveled together, or where they headed. They were more concerned with the news of war. It had been a generation since the Han bothered with them. Why now, they wondered?

Only after the battles ended would anyone learn what had sent them on the march. The Emperor's rule was being questioned at home. Battles being fought with the Mongol armies were not going well. The Emperor sought to strengthen his authority by showing strength in another direction. The Han believed their Emperor's mandate was given and taken away by heaven, and any weakness was seen as proof it had been withdrawn. He feared the Mongols, but not the people of the mountains whom he looked down upon as ignorant barbarians. But it was a desperate act. He might prevail for a time over these people, but it would leave him vulnerable and divided. In the end he would surely fall.

Almost as soon as they arrived in Teksi, winter made a savage assault, preventing travel in or out of the area. Jesus awoke some mornings with faint images of battles seen in the night, but they were too insubstantial for him to be certain of anything. Norbu yet lived. It was the one thing of which he had any certainty. And so he did what Norbu had asked of him. He prayed. Each evening he, the three boys and a few others from their new community gathered in front of the butter lamps for prayers of protection. They asked not for themselves, but at Jesus' insistence, for all who fought and all who suffered in any way from the senselessness of war.

Their routine carried them through the winter. Jesus was keenly aware they were a burden on an already poor village. He was especially careful to respect their mores, which were if anything more conservative than in Norbu's monastery. He longed to walk through the village and talk with the men and women there, but he had been expressly asked not to do so by the Abbot. Even his discussions with their novitiates were often critiqued as straying too far from the Bon canon. Buddhism was yet considered heretical, let alone any other system of thought.

The first hint of spring brought with it memories of Jesus' final conversation with Jingu before he and Krishna left for Juggernaut, in which his old friend spoke of an ancient ceremony in a sacred valley somewhere in the great mountains. He began to ask discrete questions of people and slowly pieced together an idea of where the valley might be located. He knew the ceremony took place at the full moon of the bull or as they called it there, the buffalo moon.

One night a monk whose name he did not know knocked at his door. "You have been asking about a certain valley," he whispered.

"Yes."

"I know that valley."

"What do you know?"

"My father took me there when I was a young boy."

"Why? What did you see there?" he asked, noncommittally.

"My father had been a monk here when a young man, but left to marry. It was not the life for him, he said. But while he still lived here, the Abbot at the time, already very old, told him about a ceremony held each year in the early spring during which a spiritual renewal took place ...." The monk went on to say how, even though his father had left the priesthood, he felt drawn to the valley, and took his son with him one year. He briefly described the event that Norbu had told him about. "I was very young, and did not understand what I saw. But if you wish, I could take you there."

"You think you could find the valley again?" Jesus asked, trying to keep the excitement out of his voice.

"Yes, the first five day's journey is easy, by main road. By then we would encounter other pilgrims to whom we could attach ourselves."

"Is it so well-known then?"

"By some," he answered, enigmatically.

He did not tell the whole truth to the Abbot, but he did not have to lie either. He simply said he was going on pilgrimage in the high country, not sure of where he was headed but certain he was being guided. As he was a foreigner, they made the assumption it was customary among his people to strike out into the unknown in the spring.

It was as Bashu said it would be. On the fifth day they began to encounter others who mostly walked alone. There was little interaction among the pilgrims, each one focused inwardly as he prepared himself for what was to come. They approached from every direction, a few women but mostly men, some well dressed and others naked; dark skinned and light, all converging upon a single well-worn path.

It may have been two or three days later when the flow of their movement slowed at a narrow pass that opened onto an ample valley. It was verdant, full of bird song and the sense of rebirth that Jesus always felt at spring in his homeland. He made his way through the crowd, drawn to the far end of the valley. He did not notice he had separated from his companion. A vagrant thought said he ought to stay in the back, honoring the order in which he entered that space. But he could not resist the pull, and eventually found himself in front of a great slab of granite held aloft by two enormous stones. Altogether they comprised a table. He wondered absently how any man could have lifted that stone into place. A clear bowl cut of rock crystal had been set in the center, and filled with water.

Jesus felt the crush of humanity, but could not turn his gaze away from the bowl to look behind him. It held him with a power of its own. A rainbow of light -- barely visible -- swirled through and around the crystal. Those who stood nearby saw him lift his arms up over his head as if reaching to the heavens. Later he described it as being suspended in the rainbow light that had begun to rise from the bowl, the way one is buoyed in a salty sea.

After a time the crowd began intoning certain words of power, which, even if I attempted to repeat them here, would be lost to the ears and foreign to the mind. They can be heard and comprehended only by one who has found his way to the sacred valley, whether in or out of the body. But once heard, the words reverberate forever within the pilgrim's heart. Jesus joined in, as if he had known the words his entire life.

At the moment the invocation ended, a tiny but brilliant light appeared in the distance. It slowly approached, expanding dramatically, finally stopping above and at the edge of the valley, not far beyond the table. The image of a great Being was suspended within that light, which had begun radiating outward to fill the valley.

Jesus stood, arms still extended, and a light like that of the sun began flowing out from him in answer to that raining down from the heavenly Being. And when at last the heavenly and earthly lights merged, a mighty roar rose from the multitude behind him ... then collapsed back upon itself in silence. The Nazarene stood illuminated, an instrument of benediction for the masses of people gathered there.

And then, so fast that most assembled could not have seen the shift, the light left the Nazarene in a single, lightning-like bolt and entered the great One that overshadowed all, finally discharging into the crystal bowl. The water in the bowl absorbed the light without the slightest disturbance.

The image of the great One immediately began to fade. The trance was broken, and Jesus ben Joseph lowered his arms, dazed, staggering to keep from falling to the ground. But none dared approach to help.

Still, the ceremony was not finished. He drew himself up to approach the table and with a trembling hand picked up a ladle lying next to the bowl and dipped it into the water, then turned and waited. At first no one stirred, but finally a man approached alone, hands over his heart to receive the blessing. One by one, others came up to sup the waters of life. And so he stood until he had served each man and woman there. Afterward, the man whom he had served first stepped up to take the ladle from Jesus' hand. He smiled as he dipped it into the bowl, holding it to the Nazarene's lips so he too might drink.

And still the bowl was full.

He heard it said later that the great One was the Buddha, who returns each year in fulfillment of his promise to hold the light for humanity until all have awakened to their full measure of Divinity.

But unknown to him the word had spread throughout the crowd that in playing his part in the ritual, he had been christened the *Light of the World.*

Chapter 32

THE MAGI

"Bashu, I am so happy to see you!"

Standing alone at the edge of the crowd, Bashu turned toward the sound of his friend's voice. A wide grin spread across his face. "I feared I'd lost you for good!" Bashu exclaimed. "I waited for you here. Since this was the only way out of the valley you had to pass by sometime."

Jesus embraced his friend. He did not speak of the ceremony, but people stared as they passed, whispering and pointing at him. A few shyly approached, touching his hand or kissing his robe. A *saddhu* standing in the middle of the road burst into tears at the sight of him.

"What is happening?" Bashu asked. "Why are they acting this way?"

"They mistake the man for the light," was all he would say.

By the time they reached the monastery he knew the time had come to leave the great mountains, to begin his return journey.

"Must you go?" asked Yeshe in a soft voice, though he knew

the answer.

"Most people are content to stand in someone else's shadow, but you are primed to ignite your own light," he told his young friend.

"I will remember you always," the boy said.

"And I, you."

The Abbot had insisted Bashu accompany him to the edge of the mountains. "See him safely through," the Abbot had told him. "And when the land begins to fall away from the Kiber Pass, return to us."

Bashu was glad to be with him awhile longer. He did not understand why, but in this man's company he felt somehow a better person than when he walked alone. For his part, Jesus felt lighthearted. The weight of the world had not yet settled upon him.

Bashu asked how he could be happy when there is suffering all around. "Despite wars and hunger, the loss of loved ones, the sting of broken hearts and petty jealousies, everything is exactly as it should be, my friend. Each experience is a point from which we can awaken to our true purpose."

"And what is that purpose?" he asked.

"Neither more nor less than to forgive others and ourselves for our offenses. Only then can the Creator's love enter into our hearts so we may live as one with Him."

It would be a long journey, but neither man was in a hurry. They carried no money, so had nothing to fear from thieves. Somehow there was always enough to sustain them on the road. Water was their greatest challenge. The blue skies they now considered a blessing were in fact a serious problem, for the mountain people had seen little rainfall for three years running. After many dusty days Bashu said: "I dreamt last night I sat in the middle of a stream while the water washed over me. It was paradise."

"In my home people bathe each morning as a part of our rituals. Here it is enough that we are able to find water to drink. That alone has become my rite."

There were few travelers on the road, unusual for the time of year. That morning they met a caravan descending the mountains from Shin. They asked the lead man for news. "There are wars all around, most of them involving the Han," the man said, spitting across the wind. "They are cursed."

"How so?" asked Jesus.

"They lose each battle, yet keep choosing new ones. The devil drives them. Where are you going?" the man asked, changing the subject.

"Persia. I will look for a friend there." "And you?" he asked Bashu. "Do you travel to Persia as well?"

"No, once I am sure my friend is safely out of the mountains, I will return to my brothers in Teksi."

"Well, if you wish, you may join me. There are no extra camels, but as you are walking anyway, it doesn't really matter," he laughed.

"How far are we from Kiber?" Bashu asked.

"Two days, three at most."

"As he is now in your good hands, I will walk along with you one more day," said Bashu. "And then I will turn back, as I miss my home."

Barbar was an amiable man from Bokhara. "I travel almost constantly, driving goods back and forth between the far Fast and Phoenicia," he said, "though most often I do not venture further west than Babylon. The reach of Rome continues to grow, and I try to keep out of its way."

"That I understand," said Jesus. He had not heard the name of Rome in years.

Bashu left the following morning. After a long embrace, the

two men stood apart with arms crossed over their chests in the sign of brotherhood, then turned and walked away in opposite directions.

Barbar had given Bashu a bag filled with food and a new water skin. "A gold coin was sewn into the skin," he whispered in his ear. "But keep in mind you must cut the skin to retrieve it, and then it will no longer hold water. The coin is insurance for trouble on the road, or a bonus when you have arrived home safely!"

Jesus and Barbar kept each other entertained with stories of their travels. One night around the campfire, the man from Bokhara asked about the significance of crossed arms. Jesus answered as simply as he could. "When I put my hands upon my heart in greeting, I am saying I abide by the principle that every man and every woman is a part of my eternal family, a part of my own heart, and that I will treat each one as I would be treated myself."

Barbar nodded thoughtfully. "I have seen men do that on occasion, but never had the opportunity to ask before. So this is not tied to one country, one race or even one religion. It is the same whether a person is poor or rich?"

"Yes. It is more a way of thinking, of living and everyday behavior."

"That reminds me," said Barbar, "we will pass through Persepolis on our way to Babylon. It is a wondrous city; you will surely meet more of these brothers there."

Barbar often walked alongside him, so they could talk. Jesus learned he owned the entire caravan, the camels and all their goods, and ran it according to his own agenda.

Though he gave the appearance of an indulgent master, he was in truth a shrewd businessman, and his drivers knew to press on without his having to remind them.

They stopped a few days later at a crossroads to trade in a makeshift marketplace. That evening Barbar pointed toward a camel, saying "We have sold some goods and now this beast is free. She must work for her feed. Do you know how to lead?" he asked with a laugh, handing the rope to his friend.

"Yes, if she is willing."

They soon arrived at Persepolis. Two men approached the caravan just outside the city walls. After a quick exchange with Barbar, they turned and ran back through the gate. "You did not tell me you knew people here," he said, eyeing Jesus warily.

"I do not."

"Yet those men asked if we had one Nazarene traveling with us by the name of Jesus."

It must be Pursa, he thought, excitedly. The Persian said he would know how to find him. Jesus was awed at the sure hand of spirit that had led him to this place.

"Well?" persisted Barbar, waiting for an explanation, annoyed at himself for having trusted the stranger. As they passed through the gate Jesus explained he was not yet sure, but thought it must be his friend from whom he had parted some years before. He suggested that Krishna had somehow sent a message on to Pursa. This couldn't have been done by ordinary means but he could not say something like that. The mysteries must be revealed cautiously.

Barbar nodded, satisfied, and they left the camels in the care of his trusted overseer. "Do you know how to find your friend?" Barbar asked Jesus.

"No. I will wait here for him to find me." They went into the inn where Barbar planned to stay, and no sooner had they sat down to eat when Pursa walked in. Jesus jumped up and embraced his old friend, tears in his eyes. "Sit down and join us," he said, not wanting to abandon Barbar too abruptly.

But he waved them off. "You have much to share after so long a time," he said. "Come see me here before I leave, if you will. It will be three to four days before we have completed all our business." In fact he would miss his companion.

They walked to the house where Pursa had been staying. At his urging Jesus began to tell of his travels and the years in Juggernaut. It would take time to reveal the deeper facets of his journey, the profound teachings and mysteries seen and experienced. Though he had been reluctant at first to speak of it, their conversation eventually turned to what transpired in the sacred valley. Pursa asked many questions, and in the end understood even more than Jesus the full significance of that event. Risking his displeasure, Pursa brought the news back to his brothers that very night, as his friend lay sleeping in his home. It was one of the ancient signs passed down among them of the coming of the Son of Light. For them it provided final proof that the man now among them was the same as the infant visited by their magi twenty-five years earlier.

The following day Pursa brought Jesus to meet the assembled brothers. On the way Jesus asked his friend if they might have time later for a tour of the city. "Except for Egypt, I have not seen such magnificent stonework or beautiful carvings, and never anything of this style. It rivals Solomon's Temple." Pursa explained that most of the walls were in fact constructed of ordinary brick, overlaid with the colorfully-painted plaster, molding and friezes that adorned everything. The enormous walls were covered with relief carvings of Kings Cyrus and Darius, of battles and half-mythical lions and bulls. He talked about the might of Persia, past and present.

They approached a large complex surrounded by a high wall punctuated by small round windows at regular intervals. Jesus sensed watchful eyes behind the opaque glass. A gilded door opened onto an elegant room. There was little furniture, only a few low divans and tables. Richly dyed carpets covered the floors, and large pillows were strewn everywhere. The men sat or reclined among the pillows, talking quietly in small groups. Without a word they rose and gathered around one of the tables, leaving two stools in the circle for the two men to join them. A pipe was lit, and offered to Jesus. He looked questioningly at his friend to see if he might decline. Pursa furrowed his brow and so he touched it to his lips and then passed it on. The men studied him as they continued to smoke.

An older man seated next to him poured a small glass of pungent liquor and held it out to their guest. He accepted it gratefully. The fumes stung his eyes, but it left a pleasant aftertaste. As he sipped, he studied them in turn, wondering if differences in dress indicated status, or perhaps wealth. The older men wore a thin multicolored band around their heads, from which a single gemstone hung to a point between the eyebrows. Krishna had called this the *Ajna* center. The Essenes knew it as a center of power, separating the lower man from one spiritually awakened. Some of these men wore an emerald, a few, rubies, and only one bore a diamond.

Not knowing the protocol he was content to wait. Pursa would not have brought him into a place where he was unwelcome. Besides, he was used to silence.

"Jesus of Nazareth," said the man with the diamond. Jesus nodded. "We have waited long for your arrival. My father was one of the m*agi* who traveled to witness your birth." There was much about his birth and early years he had yet to hear, and it unnerved him that these strangers should know more about this than he himself did. Looking deep into Jesus' eyes he went on. "Pursa told us of the events in the sacred valley."

Excitement turned to shock that his friend had betrayed his confidence. The elder man continued: "We needed to know with certainty your identity before taking you into our confidence. You have trusted Pursa. He is my brother." Jesus looked at his friend, who met his gaze evenly. Why had he not told him this story of the magi, he wondered?

"The Plan must unfold at its own pace," the speaker added, sensing his thoughts. "Each one of us is simply a piece on the great game board, and must await the right time to make our move."

He smiled then and said, "We welcome you," and each man

bowed toward Jesus from where he sat. "Your time approaches. The familiar world is dying and the one being birthed remains veiled. Some will turn to you for guidance, and others will turn their backs on you as symbol of their fears. You have been called to many lands, receiving counsel from the wisest in each. You are the crucible, where the parts are transmuted into a greater whole. The few who are ready to stand with you will, through grace, see the goal for this new age and have the courage to embrace it.

"Here burns the flame of *Ahuramazda*,' he said, pointing towards the altar, "from whom we and our Kings receive our strength and wisdom. We do not worship fire or the sun – as some believe – but fire, light and the source of light are symbols of *Ormuzd*, first son of the one God, the bringer of all that is good to our world."

He stood then and embraced Jesus as a brother. The diamond worn by Zarane signified his supreme authority among the Persian Brotherhood.

Pursa circled the room with Jesus, introducing him to the brothers. As the evening wore on Jesus had a chance to look more carefully at the room, noting in particular the domed ceiling which looked like the night sky. "It was painted long ages before, though no one knows the date, or who the artists were," said a man called Ashtad. "The structure has to be renewed each time the earth shifts, and the scene touched up as needed. It has been completely renewed several times to conform to the changes in the sky due to the heavenly precession."

Blue and scarlet were the favored colors for fabrics and paints, highlighted here and there with splashes of gold, pure gold, ground to a fine powder. The wood furniture in that room and throughout their quarters and classrooms was inlaid with precious and semi-precious stones, favoring rubies and lapis lazuli.

Jesus' own room was elegant though sparse. Pursa was given the room next door, though his own home was not far away.

"You do not have to stay here, you know. I am quite grown up now," Jesus chided his friend affectionately.

"It is my sacred duty ... and I do not wish to miss out on anything. Besides," he chuckled, "my precious Anlei and I thrive on short absences."

Jesus marveled at the differences between peoples. Some are formal, inhibited and conservative, as if they hated and feared the human body and its delights, while others draw their very humanness into their sacred selves in a way that seems to enhance both. He was grateful to Krishna and Pursa for showing him the latter path. The Jewish hierarchy he had left behind exercised control through conformity, dictating what was and was not acceptable behavior and belief. The Essenes were caught between them and their Roman overlords, who exercised their own kind of control over all Jews alike. So to protect themselves they adhered to the strict codes and norms, at least in public.

Jesus eagerly assumed his hosts' lifestyle, and immediately began his studies. The Egyptians had provided him a good foundation in the study of the stars, though the Persians considered it the most sacred of the sciences. Besides astronomy and astrology, he learned of the prophet and king, Zarathustra, who ruled Persia even before the Buddha lived among men. It was he who, in a vision, first beheld the one God, and received instructions from Him to disseminate the light of understanding and compassion into all the lands.

Later, under King Darius, the Persians ruled all lands from Egypt across the great mountains to the east, even to the borders of the Brahmin heartland, spreading the doctrines of truth, purity, piety, immortality, and the ultimate perfection of humankind. Their religion does not require conversion, but only adherence to these basic principles. Each person and each nation is encouraged to worship as they wish. It had been King Cyrus before him who sent the Jews back to their homeland from Persia after they had been made to suffer in exile under Nebuchadnezzar. He commanded them only to be faithful to the worship of their God. Oh, that we should know such tolerance today, thought Jesus! This was a remarkably wise and benevolent society.

"Why are there no women among the magi?" he asked Zarane one day.

"It is not forbidden them to study the stars," the older man replied. "But in our land women traditionally assume the position of priestess. We have no priests among us, as such. Women conduct many of our ceremonies and carry out the sacred rituals at the heart of our religion. And of course it is women who run the home, and make the most important decisions related to it and our children."

"Tell me about those rituals," Jesus asked one evening not long after.

"I anticipated your request; we are on our way to one now. When it is over I want you to tell me what you saw." Many others were walking in the same direction outside the city walls, shadows within darkness. They were gathering at the top of a hill Jesus had seen from the window of his room. When they reached the low summit each one turned to face the outer perimeter of the hill, forming circles within circles.

Out of nowhere he was filled with a fear that the earth would somehow disappear beneath his feet – and he felt the ancient terrors of ignorant men long dead rise around him. For a brief moment he mistook the fear as his own. This is ridiculous, he told himself, and with a force of will he turned his attention to the inner light, which snuffed out the darkness in a single breath.

A memory rose up in his mind. His old teacher Judy was explaining the importance of differentiating his thoughts from those of others. "Fears congeal, taking on forms that correspond to the nature of the fear," she had said. "If one is afraid of death, then death appears as a rotting corpse. If a whole city becomes afraid of disease, they may draw to themselves an army of death, whether an actual army whose greed and power lust feed on their fear, or the disease itself. Know your fears for the ghosts they are, and take care not to provide haven for those of others."

Each one gathered there had been trained in soul contact. Once they had stilled their minds a great light began to blaze forth from them, illumining the hillside. The tension slowly evaporated from the crowd, and a sense of expectation took its place. Jesus looked at Zarane and was surprised that despite the darkness he could see his face as clear as day. In fact, everything, near and far alike was illuminated -- though the clouds still clustered in dense patches around the hill.

A sudden explosion ripped through the crowd, and many dropped to their knees. Though he could not have explained it, he knew that the darkness had somehow *turned itself inside out*, releasing a brilliant light that illuminated everything. He looked for the source of the light, but could not see through it to its center. It had grown so bright that Jesus could no longer distinguish the features of Zarane's face, or anything else.

"The eye has been opened," said his teacher next to him.

"But how?"

"By your refusal, and mine, to give refuge to the darkness. Together, we recommit to all that is real within this unreal world. Some will say the darkness was vanquished by the priestess who stood within the circle of protection, out of range of our fears. In either case it was the work of many. Tomorrow the days will begin to grow longer."

They moved through a throng of people gathered at the bottom of the hill as they made their way back to the city. The magi and priestesses of Ahura Mazda use ceremony, and sometimes theater, to enact the mysteries for people who have not yet sought or found the deeper teachings. The fire which burns unseen within their hearts is reflected back to them through the play of light and fire on hillsides and along streams and rivers. These people have no need to build temples of stone when the entire landscape is, for them, sacred ground.

Chapter 33

CALLED

"There are too many Marys and Miriams! I never know which one you are talking about. And Elizabeths...ours and Mary's," I said, gesturing toward my aunt. She had recently returned from Bethany, after an extended visit with Zebedee and his wife.

The two women did not try to hide their amusement, which only fueled my frustration. It was late and mother had asked me to go find Mary and bring her back to the house. I had been out all day working in the fields, and was dirty and exhausted. And now I had brought back the wrong Mary.

"Don't forget, Mary is my second name as well," mother said, unable to resist. "It's alright, my daughter," she added when she saw my reaction.

But I did not want to be mollified and walked out into the chill night, soon wishing I had grabbed a shawl before rushing out. I don't know why I was so upset. I knew the naming customs under Jewish tradition and Hebrew law. And both Elizabeths had been named in honor of my aunt, John's mother. I was just tired....

My memories of the elder Elizabeth were sketchy, but she was beloved by everyone who knew her. She had already been old when her first child, John, was born, and did not live to see him become a man ... nor had Zacharias, his father. I hadn't seen my cousin for many years. Rumors came and went of a man of his description on the edge of some small village or other, soon disappearing back into the desert. He might have been a character in a play, and not flesh and blood, for all I knew of him.

"Cousin," I called out from the doorway, having arrived at Mary's house. A light came from an inner room, so I knew she was awake. "Mary," I called again, and she appeared from behind the curtain.

"Veronica. Is something wrong?" she asked, her brow furrowed.

"No, but mother asked if you would return with me to our house. She did not say why, but as she was laughing when I left so I know there's nothing wrong."

I was shivering and she wrapped her cloak around both of us. On the way back she asked if I had heard from Jesus recently. She was one of few who knew of my occasional contact with him. "I had a strong dream several nights ago." It was easier to call them dreams than try to explain. "He did not speak to me, but I know he sensed my presence because just before the dream ended, I felt his hand on my shoulder...as I often do. He and another man were riding camels across the desert, talking about their destination. The last time I had seen him he was amidst great mountains, within a walled compound that looked something like the school in Egypt. But the people around him now looked much like the traders who came through here last year. Do you remember? The ones with almond eyes and skin the color of burnished copper."

Mary nodded.

"Both of them wore turbans." The memory of Jesus in a turban made me laugh. "I did not recognize him, until I saw the eyes. His eyes are unmistakable."

"Where were they going?" prodded Mary.

"*Persep*, or something like that. *Persib*. I don't know. But Jesus was excited. Neither mother nor Mary knew of the place, so I' sure it's nowhere nearby." I heard myself sigh. Though he had been gone a long time now, life still seemed somehow incomplete without him.

"Mary!" mother called out when we came through the door. "Thank you for coming. Sit, both of you." She took a pot of water off the fire while we made ourselves comfortable at the table. Cousin Mary was several years my junior and while I had always liked her, until recently we'd had little in common. Mother sat down across from us. "Starting tomorrow we will begin a new study group. Do you remember Elois?" she asked Mary.

"She took over in Carmel when Judy left, did she not?"

"Yes. Your aunt Mary spent some time with her recently and they agreed the time has come to accelerate the women's studies. You both know there is increasing unrest in the countryside, and tension in the cities between zealots and the Romans. It doesn't matter whether we wish to be involved or not, as the Romans do not distinguish among us. And ... there are other changes coming soon, very soon." I sensed the urgency behind Mother's calm.

My sister Elizabeth came into the room as she spoke, rubbing her eyes. She sat down on the bench next to mother, and I wondered if she would be allowed to stay. We had begun preparations for her first woman's ceremony, and she would soon be included in everything. Mother put her arm around her, and continued.

"It is to us the burden falls when chaos comes. The only thing we know for sure is that conflict is growing and is likely to engulf us all in some way or other. We women must hold our people together. This is the way it has always been. And if the worst should happen, we will be the foundation upon which a new world is built. What happens here will reverberate far beyond our nation, and long into the future."

"You will be entering into your own training very soon," mother said, giving Elizabeth a reassuring hug. "As soon as you have had your ceremony, you may join the classes with Elois. And you will have the benefit of many older sisters to guide you."

Elizabeth stared at mother, her eyes large. From the moment we come of age all women are guided in the unfolding of our power, though the training for some is more comprehensive than it is for others. We learn scores of rituals, invocations and exercises to help us understand the impersonal nature of this power, which protects us from its misuse -- whether intentional or otherwise.

"*You are healers.* There will be much need for healing, on every level and at every juncture. Prepare yourselves well. Veronica, you and Miriam will assist Elois, since you have certain experiences even she has not had." This was true. Our studies in Egypt had been extensive, and then there was the journey with uncle to Britain. "That training has changed you in more ways than you know, and will provide critical support to your cousin when he returns from his own travels."

Not long ago her words would have struck fear in my heart, but now I knew only a deep calm. For the first time in my life I felt an absolute certainty that I was in harmony with the Father's purpose for me, and in the process of becoming a useful instrument for the divine Mother. Looking up I met mother's eyes. She gave me an almost imperceptible nod, and I knew she saw me as an equal. So much had changed while we were in Egypt. We might have left as girls, but we returned as women.

Our loss of innocence was reflected in the growing political tumult around us. Many of the boys we had grown up with were calling for insurrection against our occupiers. The rest were being pressured to take sides, either with or against their childhood friends. No matter the outcome, there would be much need of healing.

The following morning twelve women gathered in the community room, which would serve as our classroom. "Worldly power is a tenuous thing," Elois began. "The only certainty is that it will ultimately be surrendered, whether through old age or death, or having it taken away by other more talented or unscrupulous men. It is temporary, as are all things of the world. Men in power tend to be fearful, and like animals will strike out at any perceived threat. Be assured they will strike not just at the zealots, but at anyone associated with them by birth, religion, proximity or allegiance.

"Thus we dare not meet in the synagogue or school, lest we draw their wrath upon others who are still more innocent than we. In truth, the Romans and even the Jews who actively support them do have cause to fear us."

"Surely that is not true," interrupted Martha. "We are trained to heal, and mean harm to no one."

"That is exactly why they will come to fear us. They believe any person not with them must be against them. As healers, we must help any who suffer. Because of this, some of our own people will turn against us. We serve the light, while many – on both sides of the divide – serve the darkness, though they do not know it."

Elizabeth, Martha's sister and Mary's youngest daughter, wept quietly at the back of the room. Sophia put her arm around the younger woman to comfort her. Elois went on. "It is a hard thing, I know. But it is better you are prepared so you can make your choices with full understanding of what is to come."

"But what *is* to come?" whispered Elizabeth, afraid of her own question.

Elois paused, looking at each woman, as if assessing her capacity to hear the truth. "An end … and a beginning. We are witnessing the change from one age to another, though this interval encompasses the full duration of our lives. In trying times it will seem like an eternity. But remember, it is also a precious time, a hallowed time. Our Father-Mother God has chosen each one of you for your special gifts, even if you do not yet see them yourself."

And then she named us, one by one, pausing between each name so we may hear the sound in our ears and hearts. There were no strangers among us, but I later understood that she had spoken for the angels. She named first the sisters of Jesus, from youngest to oldest.

Elizabeth, Ruth, Martha, Miriam, and Rhea

...and continued with the rest of us.

Edithia, Margil, Sophia, Cleopia, Veronica, Miriam, Naomi, Beatrice

Edithia asked, "Why are Mary and Salome not among us?"

"There are others who will join us in time, but not Mary and Salome. Their training is complete. But we will stand together as one when need arises."

No one who wished to join us was turned away, and soon others who lived at a distance began to arrive with one excuse or another to visit old friends or family, staying on to study. There soon were so many of us that Elois broke us into three groups, according to level of training and experience. Miriam took one of the new groups, and I the other one, while we both continued to study with Elois. It wasn't long before we were approached by some of the men who wished to take the training. While it had been designed specifically for women, some components were adapted and a separate class was created for them.

In the meantime Mother and Mary were planning the first blood ceremony for my sister Elizabeth, and Mary's two youngest, Ruth and Elizabeth. We stopped the classes for an entire moon so we could travel to Carmel together for the rites. The women who remained behind in Carmel during Elois' absence had done all the shopping, and decorated the place in preparation for the happy event. When those of us from

Nazareth arrived, we had only to prepare the feast.

"Now you will be able to join us in our studies," I said, happy for my sister.

"Yes, I am looking forward to that," she replied, but did not appear happy all the same.

"What is wrong, little sister?" I asked, drawing her outside so we could speak openly. "Many women have gathered here to accompany you onto the woman's path. How can you be sad?"

"What is to become of us?" she asked in a shaky voice.

"What do you mean? Who?"

"You and Miriam and Naomi and some of the others are all unmarried. And you are getting *old*. Are you not interested in marriage? Do you not want children of your own? You are concentrating so hard on being healers that sacred duty and earthly happiness seems to have been forgotten!"

"Yes, I see." I did not really know what to say to her, having pushed aside such thoughts myself. "These are not ordinary times," I began, feeling my way. "Yes, we are old by tradition, but we are not really *old.*" I hoped I was right about that. Would a man still want us at our age?

"Why hasn't mother looked for a husband for you?" she asked plaintively. "I will not be able to marry until you are married."

"Mother knows that a husband has never been my first priority, but she also knows I haven't decided *not* to marry." That sounded ambivalent, even to me. "Besides, we have stepped outside tradition so often in recent times that I would not refuse my sister happiness, should she find her love before me."

We went back inside, so Elizabeth and the others could be bathed and prepared. The ceremonies were as beautiful as any I had ever seen. I stood for Elizabeth alongside Sophia, and the two sisters were flanked by their older sisters, Miriam and Martha. Mary and mother stood at the center of our powerful sisterhood.

I wondered about Elizabeth's words though. On our way back I spoke of it with Miriam, Naomi and Rebecca (who had since joined the classes). Though we all agreed that such things can only happen in the right time, I saw a small knot of concern in the face of each woman, and recognized it in myself as well.

One evening when mother and I were home alone I brought the subject up.

"I have been meaning to talk with you about something," she said softly. I was stunned at what came next.

"What would you think about your mother remarrying?"

"My mother? You?" I asked, rather stupidly.

"Well," she laughed. "Elizabeth was concerned about the elder marrying first. Am I not the oldest of us all?"

"But who?" I was unaware of anyone courting mother. While widows did remarry, they were usually much younger than mother, who must have been forty.

"Matthias," she answered shyly. "He stops by here nearly every day on his way to temple."

"Every day?" I was incredulous. I knew Matthias, and liked him. His wife died before I went to Egypt, and he had been left with two children, both younger than Elizabeth. I had been spending a good deal of my time with the classes, but still did not know how I had missed it. "Oh mother, that *is* wonderful!" I exclaimed, hugging her to me. "Matthias! He is a good man. Though is he not younger than you?" I joked.

"I am just setting a good example for you," she teased back. We were dancing around the kitchen like two girls when Elizabeth returned from a friend's house. Without even knowing the reason she danced with us, intoxicated by our joy.

Having gotten his children's blessing and ours, and that of Simeon, the elder Rabbi and Matthias' superior, the wedding took place the following new moon. The entire village came out to celebrate the joining of two families. Uncle Joseph had returned from another trip to his mines in time to announce his gift.

"Construction will begin tomorrow," he said, describing the new home he was having built on the edge of town. It was at the very place where mother often went to watch the sunsets and -- we discovered -- the spot where Matthias had asked her to become his wife.

I loved having another brother and sister. It took awhile for young John to overcome his shyness around all the women, but Judy acted as if we had all lived together from the start. We invited the spirit of Sara, their mother, to join us at the hearth, so they might never forget her or be shy of speaking of her with us. Matthias' maid (another Mary) came with them, so now we were seven.

Seeing Matthias and mother together brought Elizabeth's words back to me, and I realized I too hoped for such a union one day. But all the same I believed what I told her then, that such a thing cannot be rushed.

Elois asked if Miriam and I would mind taking on a small group of the male students in addition to the younger women. While each of us was responsible for our own group of women, we banded together for the men ... for moral support, I guess. It was customary among our people for men to teach men and women to teach women after the child's initiation into adulthood. There was little precedent for what we were doing.

"Use your intuition," Elois advised. "And ask for guidance in prayer and meditation. If you have questions or problems, bring them to me. You should know it was my own such guidance that prompted me to ask you to lead these classes. So I trust it is the right thing. Men and women will be called upon to work closely together in times to come, and it is better you get to know and trust each other now, at leisure."

Jesus' brothers numbered among our students. I had not known any of them well before this. Andrew, the youngest, was shy with his older brothers around. He alone remained uninitiated among all the men, though his time was close enough for him to join the class. It was the first time he found himself on a par with them, and the elevation in self-esteem changed him overnight. He loved the classes, at first as a means to prove himself, soon developing into genuine interest. I saw the makings of a strong healer.

James was the eldest of Mary's children (after Jesus), a handsome, thoughtful man. He was followed by Simon and Amos. Only Jude (or Judas as he was sometimes called) did not join us, as he had recently apprenticed to uncle Joseph. He seemed to have a natural trader's sensibility. We seldom saw their eldest brother (not Mary's son), who was also called James -- though he would rejoin us in days to come. They were wonderful children, all. Mary had done an extraordinary job with her large family after her husband died.

There were other young men, though none so dedicated to their studies as these brothers. I do not recall all their names now, but Thomas and Bartholomew and another James were among them.

We had been meeting for half a year already when late one morning a burly man appeared at the door. Neither Miriam nor I recognized him and when we asked his name, he said he was John, the son of Elizabeth and Zacharias. And thus he was my cousin, and cousin to half the class. "You are most welcome!" I told him. I would ordinarily have hugged a cousin, especially one not seen for so long, but there was something about him that did not permit intimacy. I never knew of anyone except Jesus who could penetrate his stiff reserve, no one else who could make him laugh (though his followers might disagree with me).

John did not take part in discussions unless prodded. He was never rude or unkind, and I concluded he was shy and driven. He remained detached from most all subjects, save one. At the mere mention of Romans his face reddened, and a vein on his right temple would start to throb. He was loathe to have the subject changed, yet would not relax until it was. These outbursts created a highly charged and uncomfortable atmosphere at times. While there were others who agreed with him, none matched his passion. John would not rest nor would he find peace until the Romans were driven from the land. He would do it himself, if necessary.

I feared for him and increasingly for my people, as the numbers of his kind grew daily. He did not consider himself a zealot, dismissing them with a wave of his hand. "They do not know what they are doing," he said without explaining. The younger men looked up to him, all except Andrew. He kept his distance, almost as if he were afraid of the big man with the unkempt beard. John would disappear for a moon or two at a time. No one knew where he went or inquired after him. He was a force unto himself.

Miriam's and my training as healers had taken place in Egypt, where we were referred to as *Therapeutae*. "Osiris said we must become *Tem-akh*, which means we become one with our spirit or spiritual self," I told the class. "Sickness occurs when the self has been split."

"We are physicians of the soul," Miriam added. "Healing must involve every part of us, or it cannot last." My friend and I worked together with ease, as if we both operated from the same thought.

People from the community had begun showing up before class, and on several occasions of late, at our homes, in search of healing. At first we turned them away, telling them they should look for help elsewhere, among professionals.

"Why do you refuse to help?" Elois asked us one day.

"We are still learning," Miriam replied, and I nodded agreement.

Our teacher turned her back on us and I sensed she was angry. After a time she turned back and placing a hand on our shoulders, led us outside. She walked fast and despite her age, we had a hard time keeping up with her. At the top of a hill she stopped and pointed back to the valley over our shoulders. "Today it is calm. One of these first tomorrows, the valley will fill with blood."

I shuddered and turned to look, but all I saw was the peaceful valley I had always known. "Close your eyes," she commanded. What I saw sickened me. Not rivers of blood as I had expected, but the prelude to it. From across the width and breadth of the valley rose shouts of anguish and pain, brother fighting brother. There were crosses on a hillside, and fear rising up like black clouds to block out the sun.

"Enough," she said, shaking me gently. Miriam knelt on the ground, her face twisted in pain. "Enough," she repeated, helping Miriam to her feet. "I am sorry to have shocked you this way. But you needed to see that you cannot wait until you know everything about healing before offering it to the world. You were born healers, and are only now bridging your inner and outer knowing. By ministering to those who suffer you hasten the memory, coming into your power now rather than later.

Remember, healing does not come *from* you, but flows *through* you, at your invitation. The Goddess of Mercy cannot do it without you. The God of Love needs your helping hand. It is not for you to choose when you are ready. You are needed now."

And so began our ministry.

Chapter 34

TURNING POINT

"We should not go to his funeral," said Amos. "The Romans or their spies will be there and take note of his sympathizers. It is dangerous."

"While I do not entirely agree with his opinion of the Romans, or approve of the things he and his companions had been doing, he was my *friend*," countered James.

Mary stood in the doorway, listening to their argument.

"We will go to the funeral," she interrupted.

"But...."

"I just came from his mother. Though they are not related to us by blood, she is my sister ... and he is your brother. We will go," she repeated with finality.

Luke, their neighbor and boyhood friend, had been killed in a skirmish near Bethany three days before. There had been rumors of Roman soldiers encamped just outside town. By all accounts – and even those sympathetic to the men believed – the zealots were planning a nighttime attack on a nearby Roman garrison. When the soldiers confronted them on the road, they raised spears and a fight ensued. Luke was killed and the others scattered into the wilderness. The soldiers dragged his body into town and left it next to the well. A cousin recognized him, put the body into a cart and rode through the night to bring him to Nazareth.

The four brothers, four sisters and their mother gathered in the courtyard just before sundown and walked together to the synagogue. (Rhea, Joseph's daughter, was not often with us in those days.) Similar arguments were going on outside the main door. Even in death he was bringing danger to their doorsteps, some said, and he should not be allowed to have his last rites read on temple ground. There was fear -- not unfounded -- they would draw the wrath of the local authorities.

Theirs was a close-knit community, one that survived precisely because they had always supported one another, despite their differences. Now, however, two distinct factions were forming, threatening to erode that solidarity. One headed toward confrontation with Rome, and the other adamantly opposed it. All feared the Roman giant might crush the Jewish nation, and especially their sect within it. The Sadducees and Pharisees themselves were divided in their attitude toward the Essenes, who traditionally espoused peaceful resistance, yet they were united against the zealots and their calls for violent resistance. While everyone argued their position with confidence, in their hearts most were uncertain of God's will in the matter.

Roman guards stood in the shadows outside the synagogue, hardly bothering to conceal themselves. It was the custom for everyone in town to attend funerals, no matter the deceased's relationship to them. It provided an opportunity to say goodbye and share memories of a friend or family member. But this day seemed filled with a dread of something more far-reaching than a single death, and only a few volunteered to speak.

"I am glad you insisted, mother," said James afterward. "It was hard to see the room so empty."

"And I am glad you spoke so well of your friend," she replied.

Simon was silent, walking behind them with clenched jaw. Luke was his friend too, a man who believed as he did, that the only way to rid themselves of the hated Romans was to meet them on their own terms. He was unaware his mother knew of their nighttime meetings, and occasional skirmishes. He sometimes forgot her ability to see beyond form, forgotten much, indeed, of his own training that would argue against the value of blood loss for worldly gain or a superficial peace.

"They are watching you as well," Mary told Miriam and me one day.

"We know. But we have nothing to hide in our teachings. We take care not to meet with the young men in any but public places where our conversations can be heard by all," answered Miriam.

"Except for the classes," Mary said.

"Yes, except for the classes."

"I sense a growing distrust among the students themselves. The suspicion of outsiders is corrupting our faith in each other," I said to Miriam and Mary. The loss of innocence among even the children saddened me.

But violence was yet a rarity, and as days passed the clouds began to lift. Laughter was heard once again on the streets, and people met each other's eyes when they spoke.

Chapter 35

A NEW KIND OF LOVE

"I ran into James," mother said, coming in the door. I nodded, my mind on other things. Later, over dinner, she said, "He asked about you."

"Who?"

"James asked about you." Her eyes were on Elizabeth as she passed the bread, though her words were meant for me.

Several days later after we finished our mending, mother put her hands on my shoulders and steered me toward the door, leading me out into the warm sun. We walked to a hill, then scrambled up a mound of boulders and sat down. I kicked off my sandals and gathered my knees under my chin, feeling the hot rock beneath bare feet.

"Change is on our doorstep," she said without preamble. "Much of it steeped in happiness." Mother sometimes made enigmatic statements, an incentive to use my intuition to discover what she really wanted to talk about.

"Yes, I sense that, despite some of the dark things that are taking place." I had learned that the edges of our thoughts are where the truly important insights are found, things that are ready for discovery and exploration. And then I saw it. "Jesus will be home soon, won't he?" I asked in a sudden flush of excitement

"Yes, though not right away. He is not yet finished, and then there is the journey, but he will be here before the winter planting." She waited patiently for me to continue.

My heart still beat hard in my chest. "Does Miriam know?" I asked, the question a distraction to give my mind a chance to settle.

"I have not said anything to her."

Then suddenly James' face was before me ... and I understood what she wanted me to see. I remembered her remark over dinner, and certain things he had said to me after classes lately. How could I not have seen?

Mother laughed. "Daughter, open your heart. It should not all be about the work.

Suddenly I could not wait to see him again. In the days ahead I tried to camouflage my feelings. But it seemed I could do nothing right, stumbling over my own feet, forgetting what I was saying while teaching, and blushing for no reason at all. I was much too old for such girlish behavior, and yet I could not help myself. I had never been in love before and did not know how to handle it.

"Do not worry," said mother one evening. "It will sort itself out, now that you are both aware of the other.

I asked about her experiences and at first she insisted they were not really relevant, the first being when she was barely more than a child and the second when she was already middle aged. She sighed. "But love is love, and when it first comes to you, everything in the world seems new. It takes awhile to bring the old world and the new together in a way that honors both. Be patient."

One day after class James caught up with me as I walked home. "There is a change in you," he said. "It has brought a new light into your eyes, making you more beautiful than ever."

I wanted to argue that I was not beautiful, but could not find any words. He took my hand, walking me home every night after that. He wanted to marry right away, but I insisted we wait until Jesus returned.

One evening Mary summoned me after everyone was asleep. The night sky glistened overhead as I walked through the silent streets. My aunt met me at the door and we walked together in silence to the women's house. Miriam sat waiting for us just outside the door. We joined her on the bench.

Mary spoke quietly, as if she did not wish to disturb the night. "I want to thank you for all you have done with the classes. The girls, especially Ruth and Elizabeth, talk about little else." We listened to the night insects, and I wondered why she had asked us there. "We are going to stop all classes for a time, except those within the school. You two need a rest, and Elois is going to return to Carmel and resume her duties there."

"Is there a problem? Have we done something wrong?" asked Miriam.

"No to both questions. It is just time. The classes have served their purpose. The students have gained much and you have become accomplished teachers." Again my aunt went silent, as though listening for something. I looked around but did not sense any other presence. "Might one of you have something you wish to tell me about Jesus?" she asked. The sudden change of direction startled me.

This time the silence felt strained. I spoke to break the tension, though I was sure I had nothing to offer that was not already known to both of them. "The last time he and I met I thought at first he took me on a journey through the heavens until I saw it was the painted ceiling of the room in which we stood. But I do not believe this is the kind of thing you are looking for, Aunt, as interesting as it was to me."

She did not reply.

Finally Miriam spoke up, knowing Mary was going to sit there until she did. "He came to me last night in a dream. Well, it was not a dream or even a vision. He appeared in his form of light, standing in the doorway to my room. He had never done such a thing before, and for a moment I was frightened, thinking it the form of one who has left his body in death. But he assured me he was still very much alive in Persepolis."

"And...? prompted Mary.

Mary sat between us and I could not see my friend's face. "He said there was a power struggle within the halls of learning there and he feared his friend's life is at risk."

"Is *he* in any danger?" I wondered aloud.

"I asked the same question, and he replied 'not yet.' He would know when it was time for him to leave, he assured me. Until then he would stay, hoping to help Pursa and a few of the others."

"Why do you think he came to you, Miriam?" asked my aunt.

"I do not know," she whispered.

"Yes, you do."

Again, silence. And then, "He said he had been shown in a vision that he would work alongside others when he returned here."

"Others?"

"He said his effectiveness would be increased if he did not work alone."

"And...?"

"... that it would be a help, a support to him to have the feminine energy alongside him in his work."

It seemed to take enormous effort to say those last words, and she ended with a great sigh. We walked Mary home after that and left her on the doorstep. Miriam and I continued on in the dark without talking, parting company with a quick embrace midway between her home and mine.

The following day we announced to our students their studies were finished, charging them to put what they had learned to work in their daily lives. "To heal is to point people in the direction of their natural wholeness," we reminded them. "To heal is to love wholly."

The classes had begun to define me and for a time after they ended I felt lost. Then one evening James came to the door, dispelling the illusion of our separateness forever. It wasn't that he filled a space left by the classes, or even that he was the answer to my questions or needs. It was almost the opposite of that. Without words, he reminded me I was complete in myself and had no need of anything outside of my connection to *That* which my people call God.

This was the beauty of our love. We each reflected divinity to the other. I recalled seeing the goddess looking back at me from the mirror before my first woman's ceremony so many years before. What I had seen now was the goddess within myself. This is what my love showed me.

Chapter 36

TERROR IN THE NIGHT

The next cycle passed, bringing a lunar eclipse. A headache followed me throughout the day, and I could not focus my eyes. That evening mother prepared a special tea, and I went to bed early. The next thing I knew I heard a voice screaming for everyone to run outside, or we would all die. I had been running and fell over something in the darkness, landing hard on the floor. What happened, I wondered ... feeling the cold through my nightclothes.

"Are you alright, Veronica?" Mother asked, her hand on my arm in the dark.

"I don't know. What happened?"

My voice sounded shaky, and I could scarcely stand when Matthias pulled me to my feet. He led me over to a chair while mother lit a lamp, his eyes reflecting concern in the flickering light. She disappeared into the shadows and returned with a blanket. I wasn't cold, but trembled violently.

And then the dream or vision returned. Though mother and Matthias stood over me my hands began to tear at the air, and I could not stop them. "Stop it! Stop!" I shouted, the words catching in my throat.

"Stop what? What is it?" asked Matthias, pulling up a stool across from me.

I took a deep breath and tried to make sense of the scene being replayed behind my eyes. "Everything was shaking. Everything was shaking, and roaring, and nothing left standing! The walls crumbled, and people fell, and were crushed!" My cries turned to sobs, and I began to shake again. "It won't stop!" I shouted. "Make it stop!"

Matthias took my hands in his. "Veronica, look at me. Nothing is shaking here. Nobody is falling down. There is no noise but our own voices. We're all right." And he continued in this way, slowly, quietly, in an even voice, until I began to breathe with him, and my shoulders relaxed, and the tears stopped.

I looked around the room, and saw that what he said was true. The earth had not gone mad here as it had in my vision. Elizabeth and Judy and John stood with mother looking terrified, and I realized it was I who scared them. My nightshirt was wet with tears, and my body ached with the terror that had washed over me, wave upon endless wave.

"It was not a dream," I whispered, somewhat self-consciously.

"No, I do not think it was. You saw something real. But it was not real for you or for us here. We are all safe. It may be better you do not try to relive it just now, as there would be nothing you could do for anyone there, wherever they are.

"Come, daughter, go back to bed and call for sleep," said mother gently. "In the morning we will seek guidance."

Sleep came slowly. When I awoke the next morning I found Mary, Miriam and mother at the table, talking quietly. Mother kissed me on the forehead and sat me down among them. "After you have eaten, we will talk."

I did not feel like eating, but knew I needed something to settle my stomach. The new goat cheese and bread helped. Miriam's special tea helped even more. But most of all, it was the everydayness of the voices of those I loved that soothed my heart.

It was a beautiful fall day, warm and dry, with a sweet smell in the air. The four of us walked together, talking of little things and I think I loved those women more that day than ever before. Mary set a blanket down under a tree for me. The grass underneath was crackly and dry, thirsty for the winter rains to come. Through lowered lids I watched the last of the butterflies coasting on the gentle breeze.

When I awoke they gathered around me in a semi-circle. "Tell us," coaxed mother. "What did you see?" The three women watched me carefully.

"You remember the day when the earth shook, bringing the roof down on that family in the next village as they slept? I think I might have been around six at the time, but I shall never forget my own fear at the shaking. Father was still alive, and he grabbed me while you picked up Elizabeth from her cradle and ran outside with us."

"I am surprised you remember those details," said mother.

"I vaguely remember something about that, but the shaking must have been stronger here than where I lived," said Miriam.

"The shaking in my vision last night was much, much stronger." I did not really want to go back into it, but knew I had to. "Much stronger," I repeated. My eyes were closed and I felt the trembling return. Mother's hand closed over mine.

"Even before I understood what was happening in the vision, I heard a deep growl coming from all around me. It was like the crazed dog last year, but scores of dogs

making so much noise it pained my ears, my whole body. Then buildings began to tumble, adding to the roar, and people started screaming and running in every direction, as if they did not see each other. Though I feared for my own life, I could not make myself move.

"People were trapped under falling rock, and no one stopped

to help them. Children stood in the middle of the road, frozen, or screaming for their mothers. No one paid any attention.

"And then I found myself on the floor, with you and Matthias shaking me."

Hearing my own words helped me surrender the fear ... my fear and that of the others in the unknown city that had somehow laid claim to me.

PART FOUR

Chapter 37

NO SAFE GROUND

Some sat on the ground staring vacantly, others wandered like the living dead. A small cadre of men and women pulled together to comb through the wreckage, hoping to rescue those who still lived. The groans all too often stopped before the heavy stones could be lifted away. Many died who might have been saved. Only a few escaped without injuries of some kind, and all suffered from the horrors of the devastation.

The great dome was cracked, but did not fall. The men had been dining in the next room when the shaking began. Most of them ran into the street, tucking their long robes into their belts, or stripping them off altogether to work in loincloths alongside the people of the city. A few ran and hid.

The Nazarene looked into the eerie sky, darkened with dust and debris from a sudden wind. It stung his eyes and made him cough. He tore a strip from his robe and wrapped it around his face to help him breathe.

A woman shrieked while clawing at the dirt around a huge slab of stone that had pinned the leg of a child. Jesus took her hand and gently pulled her back. At his touch she fell silent, eyes wide with shock. Squatting, he slid both hands under the marble slab. With closed eyes engaged the stone to serve his purpose. He did not need to lift it very high, for the mother rallied, grabbing her son and pulling him out before it fell again with a thud. In her joy she forgot the man, who left them to see where else he was needed. The boy's leg was broken, but he would live to be among the wisest of the magi. Jesus had seen the hidden signs.

He labored all that day, and the next, pulling people from the wreckage, later helping to bring the bodies of those who perished to a place where their families could find them. In the end many went unclaimed, cremated together in a fire that reached to the heavens so their spirits might rejoin the one God.

Their land was prone to such upheavals, but this was the worst any had seen in their lifetimes. Much of the city lay in ruins, and people sought solace and understanding from the wise men. "Why did you not warn us?" some asked.

"Not everything is written in the stars. We are meant to learn through hardship," they told the people, "and now we must come together to help those who suffer."

"But we all suffer."

"Yes, there is not one among us who hasn't lost our home, our loved ones. Seek light within the darkness. Turn your back on no one."

"But why did *your* buildings not fall?" a few asked suspiciously, making the sign of protection over themselves.

"They were well designed and strongly constructed. And perhaps the earth did not shake so violently here as in other places." Outside the cracked doom (later mended), only a few tiles had fallen, and just one of the outer walls of the magi's compound had collapsed.

Even before the current disaster, the magi had been going through their own internal crisis. Two factions had formed over the previous year, those who sought to open their doors to outside influences and teachings, and those who wished to remain cloistered, protecting the old ways and their personal power and prestige. The first group spoke of the Brotherhood in inclusive terms, embracing all those who uphold the sacred traditions no matter where they were born or the language they spoke, while the latter group sought to exclude any not born among them, or of their own rank.

A secret alliance had been struck between certain townspeople and priests to sift out those who threatened their ancient way of life. Jesus' name was often mentioned, as were other foreigners from east and west. And now, with destruction all around them, fear and anger conjoined in a fevered pitch.

"Surely Ahuramazda has punished us for allowing such men to sit in the sacred halls," said some. "...and to spread their teachings among our women and our young!" added others.

It went on this way for days, their numbers swelling until they spilled into the streets one night, surrounding the great domed complex. Some of their sympathizers among the priests slipped out to join them, while others sat innocently among the rest, clucking their tongues and wagging their heads at the mob outside. Later it would be seen that those who spoke most aggressively against the 'ignorant rabble' were those in league with them. Those who held true to the spirit of the Brotherhood spoke sympathetically, understanding the fear that comes of such trauma and loss.

Their shouts escalated, threatening to erupt in violence. Some threw stones and overturned statues. The outer wall had already been repaired and it was unlikely they could breach the immense doors -- but neither did the men inside wish to become prisoners in their stronghold. While the priests argued, Jesus slipped out a side door into the courtyard. Only one man had seen him go.

"What are you doing?" asked Pursa, who had followed him out

"I will talk with them," he answered softly.

"They will stone you, as symbol of their fear. Come back inside. We must talk." He would not release his friend's arm, finally pulling him back inside.

He was right, of course. They would have taken their frustration out on the stranger, and nothing would have been gained. The two men sat down across from each other in Pursa's room. Jesus slumped in his chair. "I must leave here."

"It may be that you must, but now is not the moment."

Pursa buried his face in his arms. "I fear my country is slipping into the shadows. Oh, where are our great kings now?" he asked, with a moan.

"It is only the turning of the tides," Jesus answered, in turn comforting his friend. "Until the last day, when each man and woman has reclaimed his *Sonship* with the Father, there will be an ebb and flow, turns through darkness and light until the circle has completed itself. And then the Brotherhood will be known to include all people without exception, even those who had not known of its existence before."

The two men stayed there most of the night, a small lamp casting shadows across their faces. They spoke of the times they lived in, bringing waves of change across many lands, and talked about what might be done to alleviate the suffering of the people of Persepolis as they rebuilt their city. And last they talked about Jesus' next step. The noise of the crowd had long since dissipated, and the first hint of dawn could be seen in the distance when they rose to their feet.

"Stay here in my room today," said Pursa.

"You will arrange everything then?" asked Jesus, his voice sad.

"Yes, for tonight. Others are also in danger and I will try to convince them to leave with you. You will want to pass through the Lion's Gate just before it is closed, after the city is asleep." He looked away from his friend and added, "I am sorry."

"I too, though it is no one's fault. We are all pieces on a board, moved according to men's caprice. They are yet children, requiring our love and patience."

Pursa took a chance in inviting every man within the great halls to dinner that night, including those whose jealousy threatened the foreigners. There was a risk they'd cause problems at the gate that night, but he hoped they would see that the men's departure served their ambitions, and let them go. Those who hated Jesus most made the greatest show of distress at his leaving. 'Oh, you are our brothers and our family will not be the same without you. You enriched our knowledge with the wisdom you brought. You will be sorely missed...' and the like.

Only Pursa accompanied the four men to the gate, embracing his friend under a darkened sky. They could not read each other's faces, though the light from their eyes shown out into the night.

"Travel well, my brother. I will see you again one day, before it is over," he said.

The gate closed behind them with a loud thud as they began their westward journey into the night.

Chapter 38

THE RETURN

On their third day out the four men encountered a small caravan bound for Damascus, its camels laden with spices and other goods for the royal court. They had sufficient gold pieces among them to convince Arahn, the headman, to provide them safe passage. Devastation from the earthquake was widespread, and many were abroad begging and stealing to survive. This created competition for the professional thieves who increasingly turned to violence. Arahn extracted a heavy price from them.

The night temperatures dipped close to freezing, the days brought fierce winds. It was an exhausting journey, and they were glad to finally see buildings take form in the afternoon haze. They had come to the great city of Babylon, situated at the crossroads of several major trade routes. "We will spend the night here," Arahn announced.

"But why not press on, as we are so close?" asked Mikel, one of the men who traveled with Jesus.

"Do not be deceived by appearances," he replied, as he shouted orders to his men. "The sun will set before long and the city is yet half a day's journey from here. It is foolhardy to travel by night." He narrowed his eyes: "You would not survive long."

Mikel and Jesus left the caravan the next day after learning that Arahn ran roving bands of thieves, taking a percentage of their spoils. What the thieves did to their victims was of no concern to him. Jesus would always be grateful to Pursa for the gold he pressed into his hand when they left Persepolis. It had obviously been sufficient to buy Arahn's protection, but he harbored no illusions of the man's friendship.

The other two men who traveled with them from Persepolis decided to stay on with Arahn, and said their goodbyes. Mikel and Jesus set up at a local inn. After supping on a rich stew and beer, they went out for a walk. There was little wind within the city walls, a welcome reprieve. Still, the tension in the city was palpable. Mikel kept watch over his shoulder to make sure they weren't being followed. "I do not wish to stay here any longer than necessary," he whispered in the darkness. Jesus agreed.

The innkeeper gave them the name of a man who had frequent business dealings with Jerusalem. "Barak is a savvy man, and honest," he said. "He has never cheated me, which is not something I could say about most."

It was impossible to guess Barak's age. His right eye was completely closed by scars, a fearsome sight. But his hands bespoke openness, and his voice was gentle, without the cloying overtones of one who has something to hide. They instinctively trusted him and decided to forgo a caravan leaving the following day in order to travel with him three day's hence.

In the meantime, inside a small Zoroastrian temple at the edge of the city they met a priest who was tending the sacred fire. "There are temples of every kind here," he said," but you will find few people inside any of them. We conduct our ceremonies on a hilltop outside the city walls, without spectacle of any kind, and it is rare they are witnessed by any but us priests. We would be honored to have you with us this night."

Jesus and Mikel returned at sunset. His arms filled with wood for the fire, Jesus' thoughts drifted to events yet to come in his own land. Another hill stood against a setting sun, when the earth began to shake as he had seen it do in Persepolis. A deep pain shot through him and he stumbled, dropping his load. When Pursa came to help him pick the wood up, he waved him away and bent to the task himself. It was a simple ceremony with only a handful of men, but a salve to the soul of these weary travelers.

Two days later a man came to their hotel to say the camels were being readied and they would leave at sunrise. They awoke early and went to the appointed spot. Two of the beasts had been reserved for them, with thick blankets to ease the ride. Heavily armed guards rode at the front and rear of the caravan, guaranteeing their safety. Of all the men, only the two brothers carried no weapons.

The days flowed together with the waxing of the moon, finally delivering them to Jerusalem. The last rays of the sun cast the gate in gold. Jesus dismounted the camel and dropped to his knees, his eyes filled with tears. His friend stood beside him, and the restless caravan waited. Barak had gathered a small group to accompany the two men to Joseph's estate, but Jesus declined. Barak knew of Joseph and might have savored the idea of an introduction for future business dealings, but Jesus sought a quiet homecoming. He would speak highly of the caravan owner to his uncle, in any case, knowing that Joseph always remembered honesty and rewarded it when he could.

Jesus encouraged Mikel to go with him to Joseph's, but his friend claimed he had something to attend to in the city, and would meet him back there later that evening.

He found his uncle Joseph standing at the gate, as if waiting for him. The two men embraced, weeping. Jesus pushed back a moment to look at his uncle. Both men had aged since the last time they'd seen each other when Jesus returned for the death of his father (though Joseph was twice his nephew's age).

Joseph wanted to hear of the journey, but Jesus won out, insisting first on news of his family. "So they are all well?" Jesus pressed, though he knew they were.

"Yes, yes, they are all well. You will see many changes. Those who were children are now full grown, and there are other young ones to take their place. Salome has married again, and only a few days ago gave birth to a son." This in itself was astonishing, as she was not young, with many years between the infant and Elizabeth.

"And you say Veronica is soon to marry. That is wonderful news!"

"She waited for your return," said Joseph.

"They all know then? They know that I have returned?"

"They knew you were on your way and would soon be here. Each one's heart thrills to know you will be with them once again...and none more than Miriam," added Joseph as he walked out the door to relieve himself. He purposely left his nephew to absorb his comment in private.

For the moment his thoughts turned to Sita. He understood for the first time she had been right to refuse him. Though he had loved her, his destiny was here. Somehow she had understood this better than he. He felt great affection for her and admired her courage, as he knew she loved him too. He hoped she had found someone else who would be worthy of her.

"You will not recognize your brothers and sisters," continued Joseph, coming back into the room. "Even Elizabeth and Andrew have taken their adult rituals." They were infants when Jesus left, and complete strangers to him. "I am surprised at you," his uncle teased. "You have not asked whom Veronica is to marry."

"Do I know him?"

"*Do you know him*?" he countered.

"Well, who is it then?" Most women in Nazareth, especially among the inner families, married someone from outside, and Jesus assumed he would not know the man.

"It is your brother, James." This time Joseph did watch for his nephew's reaction.

"James! James is a good boy. I am glad! It is hard to imagine the two of them old enough to marry," he added, wistfully.

"Old enough! They are more than old enough! Our young people are not marrying, causing some of the elders to think the Romans have cast a spell upon us so we would die out." Neither man laughed.

While he longed to hear of his family, friends and events in Nazareth, he could not keep his thoughts from straying back to Miriam. He too was more than old enough for marriage, though except for Sita, he had never considered it. How old am I now, he wondered? More than twenty five and less than thirty; he would have to ask his mother.

*

Word reached Nazareth of his arrival in Jerusalem. Some wanted to plan a big celebration for his homecoming, but his mother had the final say. "Let him come to each one as he is ready. We want to welcome him, not scare him away."

She knew his aversion to crowds. The world would press in on him soon enough.

So when he and Mikel arrived late one afternoon, the townspeople watched through open windows or doors as the two men passed, a few calling out to him in welcome. Jesus acknowledged them with a smile. Mary stood alone at the gate when they arrived at the home of his youth, much as Joseph had waited for him in Jerusalem. Mother and son embraced, and Mary reached her hand out to Mikel. "Welcome. You have my gratitude for coming this long way with my son. Come in," she said, leading them both inside.

It seemed a mob awaited him, though they were all his

brothers and sisters. He grabbed James and drew him close. "Congratulations, brother. You have chosen wisely," he whispered, referring to our upcoming wedding. Thus he made his way around the circle, posing questions of each as if meeting them for the first time – asking their ages and occupations or favorite subjects in school. He coaxed names out of Jude and Andrew so he would not have to admit he had no idea which one was which. Mary stood back and watched, beaming, wishing their father could be there. She knew Joseph watched over her and the children, and would do so until each had fulfilled their purpose and returned to the other side of the veil. She felt his presence now, and knew he shared her joy.

Mary and her eldest daughters, Miriam and Martha, left Jesus and the others to help the servants prepare for the evening meal. Mary had told them to expect forty, though there could be more. It was an unusually warm evening for the time of year. She was glad as the house would not have held everyone who wished to be there. I arrived while they were in the kitchen. James saw me first, and took my hand.

How can I describe that wondrous moment, standing between the two men I loved most in the world? I sometimes marveled that I hadn't noticed James earlier in my life. But I guess his brother overshadowed him, overshadowed everyone in fact. He could not help it; his inner light was like the brightest star in the heavens. And yet, from this moment on, I saw them both as equals.

I do not recall much of that first evening. I only knew I was happier than I had ever been in my life. A number of our cousins were there, and mother and Matthias, of course. I saw that he and Jesus took an immediate liking to each other, and was glad. Jesus spoke with my sister Elizabeth and Matthias' two children, then took Judah from mother's arms. My baby brother stopped his fidgeting and looked into his cousin's eyes as if surprised to see him again. This made me laugh, as he had barely begun to recognize the rest of us. Jesus touched his forehead to the infant's and whispered something to him. After he handed him back to Salome, Naomi, Ruth, and Sophia went up to him, followed by Matthew and Leroi, all old friends of his.

Our cousin John came – a surprise to all. He did not mingle much, barely speaking even to Jesus. He mostly sat off by himself, a great brooding presence not unlike a wild animal, preferring a solitary existence to the company of people. It was not a judgment against us, as much as a shy unfamiliarity.

And then there was Miriam. The way I remember it is everyone fell silent when Jesus walked across the room to her, though mother insisted they had kept right on talking. He took both her hands and smiled at her. She smiled back, and that was it. They exchanged few words throughout the evening, but it seemed to me their eyes found many opportunities to meet.

Jesus looked older than I expected, but many years had passed and I knew he had endured hardships. In some ways he had always been much older than his years, so perhaps his face had just caught up with him. He was still handsome, with striking eyes that captured anyone upon whom he cast his gaze.

Chapter 39

TRUE HEALING

I was thirteen when I first had the dream, though it has returned to me many times since then. I am sitting in a place much like the great Temple in Jerusalem. But it is not that or any synagogue I know, because men and women are treated as equals there, sitting next to each other instead of separated as we now are. James is usually at my side, though when I was younger I didn't know who the man was. I know some of the others too, even if most of them do not look quite as they do in waking life.

This dream or vision unfolds in an ongoing discussion that seems to go on and on throughout time. We are always debating the important issues of the day, whether they pertain to the people of Nazareth, to Palestine, Rome, or the rest of the world. We seem to have a say in all of it. Whenever we stop talking, we go to Jesus' well to replenish our reserves. While he distributes the sweet water, he offers to show us how to create and enrich our own wells, so we in turn may give what we have to others.

During our waking reality, now he is back among us, he will tell us many times and in many ways there is nothing he does that we cannot do as well. "I walk only a few steps ahead of you, to shine the light upon your path until you remember who you are. There is no difference between us. None." But no sooner would he finish these words than another comes and kneels at his feet.

It was hard for all of us at times to accept this admonition, because his light appeared to shine so much brighter than anyone else's. "I only polish it more frequently through use of the gifts the Father has given each of us," he insisted.

There *were* days when I truly saw my own light and that of his other disciples, but there were also days when frustration and despair seemed to blot it out altogether.

"I too become tired, and tempted to give up," he confessed once when we were alone. His words shocked me. Then he put his hand on mine, smiling that tender smile only he wore. "Do not worry, my sister, I will not give up or turn aside from my path."

In my recurring dreams we talk about the path that lay ahead. Our dream discussions seem to evolve and change, according to our experiences in the world. I can only recall the smallest portion of our debates in the great hall when I awake. When my cousin began his travels the group in the dreams debated where he should go, and for what purpose he should travel. He was asked to learn certain things, and to bring those teachings back to us. As the dream evolved, our future history was transformed. As we changed, our world changed.

The dream held possible outcomes, some we hoped for and some not. There were few ready to follow the light, which tested our courage and resolve. At the same time polarization was intensifying among both zealots and Romans in our waking world. And it seemed the Sadducees and Pharisees, our own countrymen, were increasingly siding with the Romans against us. The simmering stew was becoming explosive.

I spoke of these dreams only with mother, Mary and occasionally with Miriam. I did not want to frighten the others.

These three women, closest to my heart, were familiar with the *council* where we met and planned our destinies, though they saw it somewhat differently than I. The only thing we knew for sure was that a great deal of work lay ahead of us.

The school continued to function for the children, but we no longer used any formal venue for our own training. Only at the end of each meeting would we decide where and when to meet the next time. We kept our gatherings small, so as not to draw attention to ourselves.

Innocence was one of our greatest strengths and potential weaknesses. Matthias' son, John, told us about a new friend at dinner one night. Bruno was a few years older than John, who was then fourteen. Mother invited Bruno to join us for dinner the following night. He accepted, but then did not show up. Worried, Matthias asked around about him and discovered Bruno was a Roman soldier. The Romans had exploited his youthful appearance to have him befriend the young men, to learn what he could of the zealots and even to report back on our own small groups. John was devastated that he had compromised our security. It unsettled all of us to see the extent they would go to, to undermine our community. Bruno was never heard from again, though there were surely others to replace him.

Jesus was at the center of many of the small gatherings in our homes, though by no means all. We never tired hearing of his travels. The telling brought events back to life for him as well.

"What happened in Juggernaut?" I asked one of those rare times when just the two of us sat talking. There was a hole in his story of that place, something he spoke *around*. "What saddened you there?"

He hesitated. He had been back with us half a year by then, and some of our old intimacy had returned – though it would never be the same as when we were children.

"I loved a woman," he said, not looking at me. He told me about Krishna's sister and how they had loved each other. "At the time I knew little of my purpose, only that my coming back here was inevitable. It seemed natural we would marry and return here together. But Sita asked why I could not stay among them, where I was also loved. I did not have an answer for her question. I only knew I couldn't stay, which was not sufficient answer for her. She seemed to avoid me after that. Unknown to me she called on my teacher, Muktananda. He had long been Krishna's teacher too, and priest to the family. It was only upon the eve of my departure that Krishna told me of that meeting.

"'My daughter,' Muktananda had said, 'The Nazarene carries the mantle of Lord Krishna, and does not belong to himself as you and I do. You must not ask him to do this thing.'"

Jesus stared off across the room, and I could see the vestiges of pain. "At first I felt betrayed, and was angry at my old friend and teacher. You see, Sita just disappeared after her conversation with him. She was a dancer and often traveled with her teacher, to study or perform, but I was hurt she had not said goodbye. And then, when she returned several moons later she told me we could not be together, but would not give the reason.

"I hoped to dissuade her at first. But by the time I left Juggernaut I knew she had done the right thing, and did it the only way that would have succeeded. If she had told me what happened at the time, told me the real reason, I would have resisted, even subverted those things which had long been put into motion here – things to which I myself had acquiesced in an earlier time." He heaved a great sigh.

"I cannot imagine what life would be like if you had never returned. Maybe I would have gone to visit you. Maybe...." I didn't know what else to say. What would it take to abandon one's deepest soul purpose, I wondered? My head shook from side to side, to drive away the unthinkable.

"Sita must have been an amazing person, to have captured your heart, and then to have acted so unselfishly. Surely she has been blessed in other ways." Though I was sincere, my words sounded hollow in my own ears.

"Yes, I have to trust that," he replied.

The man was on the verge of his healing. Miriam served as a true blessing in his life. Of course, she would never *replace* Sita, as one love is not interchangeable with another. But she would come to play a most unique role, supporting him as no other. That too had surely been a part of the grand design from the beginning.

Miriam was a profound healer, which eventually brought her as many enemies as friends. She refused to conform to social norms, especially as they pertained to the distinctive, often inferior status of women meted out by the ruling elite -- both Roman and Jewish. (The one thing they agreed upon.) She bristled at standing in the shadows when there was something she could do to alleviate pain of any description.

It was obvious to all that she held a special place in Jesus' heart. He did not love her more. Later he would tell us so. Increasingly all were equal to him, whether Roman soldier or zealot or cousin or mother. But he loved her differently, and by the time he was cast into the public eye, she was rarely away from his side. This, of course, increased the jealousy, suspicion and hatred of some. But none of that mattered to her, or to him, except as he was concerned for her well-being.

"You three have been given the highest level of training in the healing arts," Elois had told Miriam, Naomi and me just before returning to Carmel. "Your only payment for the selflessness of your teachers is to pass those skills on to as many people as you can. Turn no one away who wishes to learn, whether you deem them capable or not. Everyone has some capacity if their heart is open, and their hands willing. Even if you suspect someone's motives, do not withhold your knowledge. The Holy Spirit will see to it that nothing learned in your classes will serve evil."

Even Jesus came to learn, which confused Naomi and me, and flustered Miriam. How could we presume to teach him, he whom I had shortly before seen drive out leprosy at the touch of his hand? He saw our hesitation, and said: "Each of us is a teacher and each one a student. It is arrogance to believe you are less than or more than another, just as it would be arrogant for me to think I had nothing left to learn."

How many times had I compared myself negatively to others, never realizing that too was a sign of arrogance?

"We are all one and equal in the Father's eyes. To diminish your self is to diminish our common Source, which cannot be less than perfect."

What we had been taught in Egypt and with Elois and others came intuitively to Jesus. But he wished to learn our techniques, the healing oils, herbs and poultices we used, and especially the words of power that we had been taught. He also went now and then to spend time with our brothers in Qumran, where he studied the ways of the ascetic, discovering the special powers that come from living a life of solitude and renunciation..

In turn he shared with us certain attitudes of mind and avenues into spirit to help us as we progressed in our work. "A day approaches when I will pass from sight, and you must step up to light the way for others."

Alarmed, we questioned what he meant. But he would not explain himself, saying only "through you I go ahead of myself, leaving signposts along the path of return."

He said many such things. "If I tell you too much," he said gently, "I would deprive you of the joy found in discovering the power that comes in awakening on your own. You are your own teachers."

One day his mother, Mary, appeared at the door of Jacob's house. We were showing some people how to set a broken limb. Jacob had fallen off a roof he was working on that morning and broken his leg. Naomi laid a poultice under the splint, which would speed healing, then stood back. Mary walked up and placed her left hand over the break and her right hand just below his navel, closing her eyes.

Mary's position in the community was unique, both because of her son's stature, but also because of her unassailable character and quiet power. She had tended to stay in the background, until recently. There was a palpable increase in energy in the room as she stood there. The sound of people's breathing seemed to grow louder until it echoed unnaturally in my ears. Everyone's eyes were closed, even Jacob's, and so I closed mine as well. As soon as I did that, the noise and pressure I had been feeling immediately decreased. At the same time, I saw a flowing palate of colors behind my eyes. Jacob moaned and the colors disappeared.

When I opened my eyes I saw Mary had stood back from him, her arms crossed in front of her chest, surveying her patient. "*Stand*," she quietly commanded. He sat up on the table, and swung his legs over unto the floor, then stood without hesitation. I half expected him to collapse when he put weight on the broken leg, as he had been in a good deal of pain earlier. But he stood unfaltering.

"*Walk*," said Mary. He gingerly pressed forward onto the leg with the splint. It held while he moved the other leg in front of him. Slowly, one step after the other he made it to the other side of the room, and lowered himself onto a bench with a grin.

"You want to know what I did?" asked Mary before any of us could say a word. "I did nothing but speak to Jacob's body spirit, which knows only wholeness. With my hand on the break, I *saw* the healthy bone as it exists within that spirit. I used my will to create a temporary bridge for transferring the perfect image onto the physical bone. Spirit and man were one. Such healing is instantaneous, and natural."

She turned to Naomi and said, "It is no different than the flower you see in your mind before you put needle and thread to the garment. It is already finished before you begin." Naomi nodded. To the rest of us she said, "You do this when using the healing skills learned from your teachers. They are only the needle and thread for the flower of health lying perfect within the body, awaiting your command to appear for your eyes to see. And in this case," she went on, turning back to Jacob, "for your leg to heal."

"But are the poultice and splint even necessary then?" asked Naomi.

"No. And yes," replied Mary. "One day, when we are strong enough to overcome doubts caused by appearances, such things will no longer be necessary."

Looking at Jacob she said, "Because you trust me, and believe in me, you were made strong enough to accept the truth of your wholeness." She laughed. "But why you should trust me more than yourself, or each other, I do not know.

A broken bone," she went on, "is one of the most difficult things to heal, especially the larger bones. Maybe that is because they are so heavy that our right thinking is unable to penetrate." We all laughed, even though I thought it made sense.

"You have been taught as healers to help your patient see themselves as they really are -- whole and perfect. Healing then comes either when you are powerful enough to impose your true vision on their false vision of themselves as sick or injured or weak, or – and this is the better way – when they decide to agree with your vision, and accept they are perfect, even as God made them.

"There is nothing that can withstand the power of true healing, not even death." She pointedly looked at the three of us.

"Now, you must become your own healer," she told Jacob.

"How do I do that?"

She led him outside, and the rest of us followed. Picking up a stick she drew an image in the sand. "This is what your healthy bone looks like within the flesh. I want you to draw the healthy bone yourself. And each time you feel pain in your leg draw the picture again until you can see nothing but wholeness, and *feel* nothing but wholeness.

You all can do this, with your body, your thoughts, and in your relationships. Most importantly, you must learn to feel such wholeness when those you consider your enemies come to mind." Mary looked at each of us. Her eyes blazed with an inner fire. She turned to leave, pausing only a moment to put her hand on Jacob's arm as he stood next to his astonished wife.

The rest of us stayed late into the night, talking about what we had seen and especially, about Mary's words. She had seeded a vision of a new kind of healing within our minds.

Though there would be great need of healing bodies in time to come, this was a higher calling, a healing of the soul.

Chapter 40

THE WEDDING

It made no sense. James and I had known each other for a long time. We had been promised for nearly two years now. And yet my stomach ached, and my mind wandered. It was a good thing the many details of the wedding were in the hands of others.

James had agreed to wait for Jesus to return. And then Samuel, the chief *Kabbalist* had come to ask us to wait a while longer, until a certain day just before Passover. "James has been patient, and it seems unfair to ask this of him." I argued.

Samuel took my hand and led me to a stream, flush with winter rain. He picked up a small stone and tossed it into an eddy where the water had seemed motionless. A succession of circles rippled out from the point of impact, one after the other.

"You see, your wedding is that small stone. It strikes the world like the stone strikes the water, impacting upon ever-greater numbers of people and events as time passes. Most of what is changed by your personal decision will forever be unknown to you. But all acts are universal acts...especially now."

"What do you mean – especially now?" He brushed aside my

question.

"You are already old," he said, and I felt my jaw clench. Old, how dare he! But I knew what he meant. I was indeed old to marry in a land where most women married a full ten years younger than I was. "It will not matter if you wait a little longer." Samuel sat me down next to the stream, and like a patient father explained to me that it would soon be Jesus' time, and our wedding was in some way a part of that. It had been written, he said, in the great cycles of stars and numbers, that this step is taken at the appropriate moment, and not before. "Will you do this?" he asked. "It is not just for your cousin, but the fulfillment of ancient prophecy."

In the end I agreed, though it seemed preposterous to me that our little wedding should have an impact upon things of real importance. James listened attentively as I relayed the old Kabbalist's message, and hoped he would not think me silly to have gone along with him.

"You were right to do so. After all, we have not suffered in our wait," he said with a grin. That was true enough. Though I looked forward to having our own place, James and I already spent most of our time together under Matthias' roof. Such a thing was unusual among our people, but tolerated. After all, as Samuel said, we were both *old* already, and capable of making our own decisions. Our Rabbi had given his blessing, as had our families.

Mother had asked me my wishes about each element of the ceremony and the feast to follow, and I tried to provide sensible answers. But on the wedding day I could remember none of it. James and I had not seen each other for seven days. The Rabbi insisted upon it, and our families encouraged us to agree – especially as he had been so tolerant in these other matters.

"Hold still, Veronica," said Mary. "You are fidgeting like a child," she teased. While mother was putting the last stitches to my new robe, Mary braided the first spring flowers into my hair.

Elizabeth sat on a chair next to me, a dreamy look on her face. She had recently been promised to Simon, the master carpenter with whom Jesus first apprenticed so many years before. He was at least ten years her elder, but they seemed suited to one another. They planned an autumn wedding, but I had a feeling they would not wait so long. "You see, little sister, all works for the best when we trust."

She laughed. "Yes, I am happy for you and James ... *and* for myself!"

Mother slipped the robe over my head. It wasn't anything like the one she'd made for my first woman's ceremony. Instead of all the bright colors, this had cream colored threads stitched onto newly spun creamy linen. Ribbons twined my ankles and sandals, and a single bracelet of gold encircled each wrist. Mother held a mirror up so I could see myself. My cheeks were red, and my eyes flashed like sun reflecting off water. I could not remember when I last looked upon my face, and was fascinated to see small lines at my eyes and mouth.

She set the mirror down, and Elizabeth went out to join the others. The three of us linked hands and closed our eyes. Mother spoke. "I call upon the great Mother to join with Her daughter, Veronica." In the silence that followed a profound sense of calm settled over me, and I knew myself to be *She who nurtures and sustains all life.*

She continued. "I call upon the eternal Father to merge with His consort, Veronica." A lightning bolt of power shot through me, the heat radiating outward in great pulsating waves that would last throughout the ceremony.

James later told me that uncle Joseph had similarly called upon the Father to enter into him, followed by the Mother Goddess. Only when They have merged within each individual are we capable of entering into a true marriage.

Mary went out and mother walked me to the door of the hall where Matthias waited. The sound of a flute came from the front of the room, and I saw it was Jesus. It was the first time

I had ever heard him play. Matthias and mother walked me to the front, and right behind us walked James with Mary, his mother, and uncle Joseph, who would stand as his father.

Not a virgin, I chose against wearing a veil. And instead of circling my husband, as was the custom, James came up on my left and stopped, facing me. His right hand took mine and he guided me under the white cloth that stretched above us. Together we slowly began to move under the cloud-like cover, tracing three circles. When we stopped, the Rabbi began to speak and I felt lifted out of the room and into the heavenly realms.

When the Rabbi had finished his blessing Jesus came up and placed his right hand upon our joined hands. The Rabbi's blessing always signals the end of any ceremony and the guests pressed forward, encircling us to see what would happen next. I suddenly remembered my dreams where everyone stood together as one – men and women, children and old people. I felt their closeness and knew that Jesus' silent blessing settled upon each of us. We walked in silence out of the sanctuary and into the pavilion next door, savoring the moment.

The music broke the spell. Men lined up on one side of the room, and women on the other, the groups facing each other. Women put their arms around those on either side of them, and the men did the same. The musicians struck a slow beat, deliberately building its pace until feet were flying and dancers struggled just to stay afoot. Had they not been holding on to each other, I'm sure some of them would have landed on the floor. And just when the laughter and music reached a crescendo, the musicians paused, and reverted to their original slow tempo.

James and I had been standing hand in hand at one end of the room, facing the space between the dancers, enjoying the spectacle. The shift in tempo was a signal for us to join in. Everyone gently swayed to the rhythm, standing in place. My left hand moved to James' outstretched forearm and we began to move down the middle, our feet following the age-old steps that signified two people coming together to dance through life as one.

There were tears in more than one eye as we made our way from one end of the room to the other, and I felt – as I never had before – a sense of loving support from the entire community. When we had reached the other end of the room we turned around to face the two lines again, a sign for them to break rank and dance with whomever they wished, or leave the floor to find something to drink or eat. It was a wonderful party, many staying to dance through the night, even after the musicians tired and left.

James and I slept that night in our own home for the first time. Jesus and the other brothers had worked hard to have it ready for us. It was customary for a young couple to live with parents until the birth of their first child, but we were nearing the age of thirty -- and I was not altogether sure there would be children.

Chapter 41

TELLING OUR STORIES

Our new home became the central gathering place for our friends, where we could talk through the night if we wished, knowing we would disturb no one. And as time went by more and more of our study groups met there. We knew we were being watched, and tried to make those gatherings appear as spontaneous social events.

One night Jesus and Miriam stayed on after everyone else had left. We had come to the full moon of the Ram. "I am reminded of the same moon two years ago, celebrated in a valley high in the mountains." Jesus looked into the steaming cup of tea as he spoke, almost as if he were talking to himself.

"I do not know how many people were there, but some had come from great distances, representing every people and land. Such is the nature of the ceremony that it brings together all humanity, no matter their traditions or beliefs, just as it unifies the old and new, spirit and matter." His voice sounded as if it were coming to us from a great distance, and I knew that in some way he walked with the throngs in that valley.

In the silence my own thoughts drifted into a scene filled with people milling about a large open area surrounded by mountain peaks. The air was highly charged as if a storm had just passed by.

"You see," said Jesus, looking at me, "you are indeed beginning to walk the two worlds."

"What does that mean?" I asked.

"It is only another step beyond what you were doing just now, allowing your imagination to take you away. Eventually you will learn to separate your consciousness to be in more than one place at once."

"Is this what you did when you visited me in your shining body?" I did not know what else to call it.

"That is more complicated yet," he replied. "Each of you has already taken the first steps toward this yourself, though the techniques were buried within the guise of another kind of lesson."

"Which lesson? Where?" Miriam and I spoke at once.

"How can we uncover the technique, separate it from all that we have learned?" I added.

"You will arrive at understanding on your own, learning more along the way than if I or another were to give you a simple answer."

I thought that would be the end of it and got up to refresh the teapot, when he began again.

"You have been told there are men and women who live always in the light. Some of these were once like us, having awakened and gone beyond. But there are others who come from afar, never having walked the path of men. Together they guide us along our path. They do not care if we are aware of them; they do not need our allegiance or gratitude. They are concerned only that in some fashion we serve the same goal as they. They know us by the way we conduct our lives, especially the little things, the little kindnesses when we think no one is watching us.

"The many people in that valley are guided there by these unseen helpers, until one day they can find the way on their own. And when that happens they join the ranks of the guides. Though they will appear as ordinary people, they are not. They are called gods or saints, or other names peculiar to each race. But their path is our path, the same for every man and woman, now and in the distant future. This same path is being offered to us -- our time is now, should we choose it."

It was difficult to place myself in such company, despite the many things I had learned in Egypt and with Judy and Elois and others. Yes, in some other lifetime, I could believe that: but as Veronica, here and now?

"Each of you doubts this, as we sit here tonight," he said, reading our thoughts. "And it is only your doubt that prevents it from taking place. In the meantime, this Brotherhood of Light is the next step from our own Brotherhood, which already serves to guide and protect and teach us. The one is prelude to the other. You have already been initiated into the Brotherhood, and when you have had enough of fear and doubt, you will cross the threshold into the higher realms."

"But what of the valley?" Miriam persisted, speaking the question for each of us.

"*The valley.* There is an ancient ceremony, during which the eldest of these Brothers of Light returns to bestow a peculiar blessing upon humanity that can only be safely given during this moon."

"Safely?' repeated James.

"It is a blessing of such potency that if circumstances were not as they are during this moon – that is, when certain planetary and solar forces are in place to extend and in some ways diminish the power of the blessing – humankind could not survive it. The ceremony assures this will not happen. People have long gathered in that valley, but with the passing of an age the blessing has been multiplied. And thus the risk and the benefits have also increased."

He went on to tell us something of the ceremony itself, explaining its method and purpose to us. But it would be a very long time to come before any of us would see the fruits of what was birthed there – in the next age of water and rebirth.

Shortly before dawn we laid out mats for Jesus and Miriam. It was better they stayed than to be seen leaving together at that hour, for it is the way of close communities that people occupy themselves with idle gossip.

When we broke bread the next morning Jesus announced: "A small group will be leaving at the new moon for a retreat to the desert … after which John and I will travel to Egypt together."

Miriam looked stunned. "Will you be gone long?" she asked.

"To Egypt? No, but our work necessitates our going."

There could be few people as different as Jesus and our cousin John, and it was hard to imagine them collaborating on anything

"You have not spoken of your own journeys," said Jesus, changing the subject.

"I have asked Veronica," agreed James, "and she keeps putting me off, saying another time, another time. Now must be the time, then, with the four of us together."

"If you wish to hear about both Brittany and Egypt, we will need a day and more. And there are some things I need to do first. There is no group here tonight, so come for dinner, and stay late," I said, pointing to the stack of mats.

*

Jesus arrived before Miriam. "Here, a gift from mother," he said, handing me a crock filled with honey.

I stuck my finger in, and put it in my mouth. "Mmmm. Thank her for us."

"She misses you, and asked that you come by tomorrow. You can When Miriam arrived the four of us moved out into the courtyard under the shade of an ancient olive tree. James had built a table and benches for the spot, large enough to accommodate ten people. He was not as good a carpenter as Jesus, but they were sturdy and would last a

"Well?" prodded James.

"Well?" added Jesus, grinning. They were ready to be entertained.

I began with the day Joseph told us of his impending journey, not inviting, but *telling* us we would accompany him. Miriam joined in whenever I stopped for breath, adding to the tale. The two men asked many questions about the ceremonies in Brittany and on the Holy Isle. In turn we asked Jesus if he knew could tell us the meaning of 'the seeding,' and he said not really. I could see that Miriam would like to have pressed him on that as much as I, but Jesus will only say what he is ready to say.

It was the far edge of twilight when we stopped for supper. James and I set out fresh bread and Mary's honey, and salted fish. It was too early for fresh fruit, but we still had a good stock of dried from the previous year.

"Pistachios!" exclaimed Miriam, lifting the lid off another crock.

"I bought them on my last trip to Jerusalem," said James.

"They are my favorites."

"And mine as well," said Jesus.

The pile of shells grew as we resumed our narrative, this time of Egypt.

"Where is Naomi these days?" interrupted Jesus. "I did not see her at the wedding feast."

"No, she has been away for some time now," I told the men. "She took her mother's sister to a spa near Jericho, in hopes her wasting disease could be arrested. It is especially hard for a healer not to be able to help those you love the most. I haven't heard from her for some time, and recently sent word to discover how she and her aunt are doing."

"I miss her," said Miriam. "She should be here tonight to add her own perspective of events. She nearly stayed behind when we returned here."

Our story resumed with Thorvald and Naomi, and Lake Mareotis, Myra and the dance with Leela.

"It was all I could do to keep from lapsing into the sacred dance at your wedding!" Miriam told us. "Some of the music moved me so. Those last days on the lake were transcendent."

The glow in my friend's eyes brought it back to me in a rush. I could almost hear the music again, and feel the ecstatic movement that lifted me out of myself and into another world.

"I wish I could have been there," James said in a wistful voice, touching my hand.

Jesus was looking at Miriam and his face held a look I had never seen before. It surprised me to see so much vulnerability written on one whom I had always considered invincible.

"I want to hear about Alexandria," he said, breaking the trance. And so we backtracked to our time at the school, telling him about Zar's passing. He had expected that, of course, as Zar had already been old when he was there. We talked of the temple, the city's markets, and our visit to the great library. "The dome was extraordinary, and the huge collection of books and manuscripts from all over the world took my breath away. It made me feel somehow connected with all those people, knowing we are on the same path of discovery."

"Yes, this is true," said Jesus. "We are on the same path, assisting each other along the way. It's easy to forget that since we use different names for the one God, and set forth countless, sometimes contradictory guidelines for walking the path. But one by one we will awaken to discover that not only is there only one journey to one destination, but that there is but one person taking that journey."

Before we could comment, he asked after Judy.

Miriam said it simply. "Judy and Zar are together. When we left to travel south, she hinted she would not be there when we returned, but we hoped we'd misunderstood. I am glad she spent her last days there; she loved that place more than any."

"Zar told me he and Judy had once spoken of marriage. But she could not stay in Egypt, as her work was here. And his was there." Jesus sighed.

"I remember the dome in Alexandria," he said, changing the subject again. "I think the great dome in Persepolis is older than that one, though no one can be sure of the age of anything in those ancient cities."

"You haven't finished your story," James coaxed.

"Travel is difficult. I thought we would die shipboard between Brittany and Penzance, or at least never be able to eat again. But each voyage after that was easier than the last.

"I cannot imagine what it was like for you when you left, barely a man, on your own crossing the desert on foot."

Jesus' eyes seemed to travel across time. "I valued every single day of my journey, and each person met – every one bringing a lesson, all teachers. We are who we are because of the experiences we have been given. Without each one of those events we would be unprepared for what is to come.

"It is all perfect."

Chapter 42

AN INVITATION TO REMEMBER

We came in ones and twos over a span of two days, arriving from different directions. And we would leave the same way, setting a pattern for the year ahead. Our growing numbers had made it increasingly dangerous to meet at our home.

I'd stopped off to see Mary on the way out of town. "The honey is delicious. Thank you."

"Marcus has been experimenting, blending honey from different hives. It seems to have become his passion. He did not say which flowers contributed to this batch."

Marcus was a distant cousin to Mary and mother. I had only met him once in Jerusalem when visiting uncle Joseph. He had a huge red beard, was awfully shy at first, but smiled a lot when he got to know you. It was easy to imagine him among the hives.

"How long will you be gone?" she asked, changing the subject.

"Four, maybe five days. Won't you join us?"

"No, I think it better I remain here."

"Mother said the same thing."

"Few are called to brave the desert in this heat, and fewer to risk the wrath of the Romans, should your meetings be discovered."

"Yes, it is hot for this time of year; the blossoms weren't on the trees long enough for proper pollination. As for the Romans, we are doing nothing wrong."

Mary did not reply, but gave me a look that said 'you know better.'

"We will get together when you return, at Salome's"

I kissed her and left, meeting James on the edge of town He hoisted the pack of provisions onto his back and took my hand. We struck out across the desert. I pulled the scarf down over my forehead, hoping to keep the glare out of my eyes and lifted my robe away from the endless thorny bushes.

Jesus had asked us to meet him at a small river the other side of Nain. No one would expect us to travel in that direction. The summer heat had come upon us so suddenly that we found a sluggish stream along the way with enough water to refill a depleted pouch and refresh ourselves. In a few days even that would be gone.

Several others had arrived ahead of us. "He left early this morning." Matthew referred to Jesus. "He'll be back by nightfall."

The setting sun turned the landscape to orange and gold, highlighting the contours of each rock, each thorn and drying blade of grass. We sat alongside the small river sharing our food and talking of everyday things when a long shadow came over a distant hill. No one mentioned his approach, though each one glanced up now and then to note his progress as we continued talking. By the time he arrived, the sky had turned to rose and darkness had overtaken the light upon the purple hills.

He sat among us, silently accepting the water and food offered him. There were enough dead branches lying around to build a fire, but we were not far from one of the roads into Nain and did not want to draw attention to ourselves. A new moon hung low in the sky, preparing to set, leaving us in near darkness. Though I could not see the faces of my friends I was keenly aware of each one and could pick them out among the shadows. No one seemed in a hurry to speak.

"Later on, these days will seem a dream," Jesus said, breaking the silence, "a peaceful dream. Drink it in, savor it. It will sustain you in time to come. Each of us makes choices and acts according to the guiding spirit that lives within our hearts.

"Each morning when you rise I want you to think about this, to pray and meditate and then decide anew whether you will continue on this course of action. It is foolish to take a pledge today for all time. You will not be the same person tomorrow as you are tonight, much less a year from now. And you cannot know now to what you are pledging yourself. Therefore, be cautious in your words and actions, yet strive to be steadfast to your principles."

I imagined then I knew something of what was to come. A confrontation between our people and the Romans seemed inevitable, brought on by the actions of the zealots whom Rome thought represented all of us. Like many, I harbored the hope that Jesus would then step in and somehow save us from a violent end, taking upon himself some of Herod's power to beneficently guide our people. Or if not that, then at least ally himself with the more progressive Sadducees in seeking a new relationship with the Romans. Surely they and the Pharisees would come to see the wisdom of allowing this man, so beloved by our people, so wise and tempered in speech and action, to guide us all.

After all, the plan upon which our personal destinies are written is like a river, whose course and direction can be altered by weather and the nature of the surrounding landscape. Every event depends upon the people who participate in it. Our choices either enslave or liberate us, and when there are many people engaged in the act of choice then the outcome is always in the process of being written.

But underneath this wishful thinking I believe I knew more of what was to come than I wanted to acknowledge.

Silence reigned over the rocky outcropping as people settled in for the night. I saw Jesus rise and disappear into the darkness, seeking his own place. Miriam remained with us, though on other occasions she would go with him. I discovered a subtle sign between them that signaled his willingness to share the night with her, a certain nod of his head. I once asked if he sought solitude because we asked too many questions. 'You are an insistent lot," he grinned. "But mostly I go because it is easier to hear my Father's voice in the night stillness."

That next day he spoke to us of good and evil.

"Take care you do not judge one person as being good, while calling another evil. Evil and its offspring, sin requires of the virtuous judgment and punishment. 'An eye for an eye, and a tooth for a tooth' says the Torah.

"Some priests tell us we are inherently evil, subject to temptation by Satan. Who is this Satan? It is not a man or fallen God that seeks your downfall. It is the *fallen God in you* that has convinced you of your unworthiness to enter into the kingdom of heaven. This Satan convinces you that you are evil because of past unclean thoughts and deeds, or perhaps that you are inherently evil simply being born to woman. You therefore are judged, even onto death.

"This is not death of the body but eternal self-condemnation that casts you into the fires of hell – the torment of the mind and heart that comes from believing you have been cut off from God. You have created your own hell and cast yourself into it.

"How can we break this cycle of ignorance?" he asked, eyes like fire. "We do not need to forgive anyone else, no matter what we think they have done. We forgive ourselves the trespass of judging others. We have become enslaved by an unending cycle of judgment and punishment, forgetting that while every person makes mistakes *we are perfect, even as our Father in heaven is perfect*. You and you and you are Son of the living God," he said, pointing to man and woman alike. "The light of God shines without fail in every one of us, from first breath to last...in every Jew and Gentile, rich man and poor, master and slave.

"God wants only to have you awaken and remember you were created in His image. Without this awareness and acceptance of your divinity, you will forever suffer the punishment of the damned, sick in body, mind and spirit, separated from each other and feeling like we are separated from God. In desperation we blame and condemn each other, bringing about the ills of our world – hatred, poverty and war. *This* is an 'eye for an eye,' not God's vengeance, but our own, turned against ourselves."

He spoke further of forgiveness.

"Forgiving another person is a distraction from where the true forgiveness must take place. That is within your own heart. Seek only the light of love and when you succeed in finding it there, you will begin to see it in the hearts of all others, including those whom you thought were your enemies. And when you find that light, you will no longer remember what you thought needed forgiving. You will know that everyone is perfect in the eyes of the Father, Who never condemned them in the first place."

He stopped then, and left us. That night I looked deeply into my heart and saw how I had judged myself of each little failing, building them one upon the other until I too had distanced myself from all I loved, and all who loved me. I saw how everything I feared, whether Roman soldier or zealot or wild dog was really fear of my own weakness or unworthiness.

He returned the following morning to a torrent of questions, answering each one patiently. But there were times when Jesus seemed to ignore certain questions. Later that morning Jonah stopped Jesus in his discourse, insisting he answer a particular question. My cousin gently explained that in this case Jonah already knew the answer, and the greater gain came from his bringing it to light on his own. He turned red, got up and walked away, returning two days later to sit at the edge of the group. In time he would find his way back to the center of the circle, becoming one of Jesus' most enthusiastic followers.

"You know what is right and what is wrong," he began another day. "And if it is not apparent to you, go within to the fount of divine wisdom and ask. Whatever you ask of God in the name of truth and light shall be given to you, even the answers to the greatest mysteries of life, or the healing of that which appears beyond healing. If you ask in fear and doubt, it cannot be given. If you ask from love, it cannot be withheld.

"Live from love, and that is all you will see. Remember, I said to find the light within your own heart, and you will then see the light in all others. What you see outside yourself is only a reflection. So if you first look for the Kingdom of God within, then all good will be given you.

"I can see the questions in your eyes – and yes, the time when all men and women have given up their fears and learned to live in love is still a long ways off. And until that time, the ills of the world will remain with us. For even when you discover the lies called sickness and death, you cannot force that truth upon others. They must learn it for themselves. This will be your greatest challenge, as the world weighs heavily upon us. That which seems real is difficult to deny. When it is night, the darkness is pervasive," he said, his arm sweeping across the night sky.

"But I tell you, the light of God's love within you shines so brightly it will cast out the darkness if you would open your eyes to it. And when another seems held tightly in the arms of death, you either give way to the fears of death and decay yourself, or stand within your own light, knowing with certainty that it is only a passing from light into light."

The next night someone asked the question that would be

asked of him so many times before the end.

"Who are you? When you speak such things you seem a different person than the Jesus with whom I played as a child. From where do these thoughts arise?"

"There is no difference between the child and the man, or between you and me. The source from which I draw these words is available to each one of you. You do not need me to have the truth, for it already is known within the heart of every person.

"But the world tells us one thing, and our hearts another. Why do we listen to a world that has given birth to so much suffering, and close ourselves off to our own hearts, which promise us release from suffering? Why choose the long road, when a short one stands before you?"

No one rose to the challenge, waiting instead for him to answer the questions for them.

He sighed, and went on. "I stand before you, a beloved Son of the Father-Mother God, Son of the Sun. My name is holy. But there is nothing I say about myself that is not true of you as well."

His eyes moved from one to the other of us, and in the instant his met mine, I knew the truth of what he said. It is easy to believe this in his presence -- but oh, how hard it is to remember when I am back in a world that speaks to us only of our smallness!

"I have told you before, as have the patriarchs, that you are made in the image of God. All power, love, and mercy are yours. But you have not believed it, preferring to put these gifts into the hands of others to wield in your name. And then, having surrendered your *Sonship*, you blame those others when they disappoint or fail you. But it was not their responsibility to begin with!

"I am here to remind you of who you are, rather than speak of who I am. I am here to help you assume your power and authority, to encourage you to accept responsibility for your own life.

"Look into my eyes and you look into the eyes of God. I look into *your* eyes and look into the eyes of God. There is no difference among us, no separation from our Source."

He waited a while before speaking again so his words might find understanding and acceptance – though he saw little of either.

"There is no separation," he repeated. "I am no different than any of you, except I have seen who I am, who you are, and know us to be one in *That* which birthed us into the world of form. You have a choice. You can choose to believe in a parentage of darkness, or of light. You can sow suffering and disease or bring healing. You can serve fear or serve love. Which do you choose? *Who do you say you*

are? That is the only important question, and you must find your own answer."

The following day another asked him: "Rabbi, why did you call us here?"

"I did not call you," he answered.

"But...."

"The Holy Spirit called you to gather here so you may help each other in your awakening.

"But who is this Holy Spirit?" the woman persisted. "I do not recall any summons but yours."

"The Holy Spirit resides within you. It is your personal emissary from God, and the only true teacher. I too was summoned."

"But you speak as one who knows that teacher, while I do not," said another.

"You do, but you do not trust yourself. This is the only

difference between you and me. We are here to remember who we are," he repeated. "We gather to help each other in our remembering. And when we forget now and then, when we seem to fail in the tasks given us, we will stand in for the other until their strength returns. Where two or three of us come together, the light of eternity shines through us to dispel even the most powerful illusion of darkness. Together we cannot fail. Only in the eyes of another can we recognize our true selves, knowing we are not separate from each other and can never be separated from our common Source.

"Do not make the mistake of putting me above you, nor another below you, nor put your God apart from you, in some far away heaven. God does not need to be supplicated, but asks only your love ... love not demonstrated by offerings or sacrifices, rote prayers or false modesty, or charitable acts done out of a sense of duty. Love speaks its own language through selfless and spontaneous thoughts, words and deeds that harmonize and heal. They are not premeditated nor done for gain of reputation, position or wealth. You do not need to ponder how to love, but only how to open your heart so love can find its way through you. In love you will remember who you are, and unerringly find your way home."

The next day we all lingered, reluctant to turn our faces back toward our everyday lives. But we could not stay away longer without drawing attention to our absence.

"You found your way here," said Jesus. "Do not fear you will miss the summons to our next gathering. You must learn to trust your inner voice, and not depend upon mine."

He then rose and walked away from us, with Miriam at his side.

Chapter 43

THE WAY TO LIBERATION

We met whenever we could. It was a fluid group; new people were brought in along the way and old ones left. Sometimes certain members of the core group were not called to join us. I never heard anyone question this, or take offense. There were times when even James or I went without the other. The only constant was Jesus.

Some were formal discourses and others casual discussions with no obvious unifying theme. The teachings themselves were similar to what Miriam, Naomi and I had received in Egypt and which I assume Jesus had learned in his travels. The group was being shown a map to our celestial home. Jesus told us we were all healers, some through herbs or the touch of their hands, some with words.

Now and then someone would show up, unknown to any of the original group. The first time this happened, I wondered who the man was, where he came from. Was he a spy? But my cousin embraced him as a brother and I felt ashamed, and tried to open my heart as he had.

"Some of us have known each other from our first childhood memories," he said. "Our families have been entwined since the return from Babylon. We were brought up with the same traditions, taught in the same schools, attending the same synagogue. We hardly consider whether the other is trustworthy, assuming him to be so simply because he has always been there. Still others enter our lives unexpectedly, in uncertain times, representing ways and histories unfamiliar to us. This often provokes fear and mistrust.

"For much of my life I have been a stranger, wandering through foreign lands. Many people opened their hearts and their homes to me, without questioning who I was, where I came from or even why I was among them. These people understood we are all brothers, living from the wisdom of their hearts. Others, and often the most educated and highly placed, saw in me a threat. These men lived in fear because, no matter what they had been taught, or taught others, they did not believe we are all one. They are the ones who castigated me, some even seeking my death. But death comes in its own time and despite appearances, I was never in real danger. So put aside your suspicions and surrender your fears to the One who watches over us all."

I noticed he never told us we would be free from danger, but the ancient teachings say that nothing comes to us of good or ill, unless it is our time for such experiences. There is a vast plan for humanity that is beyond the understanding of all but the greatest seers. If we ally with the plan it will lift us onto the higher road to our true home. And what is this home? Some think it is a place like any other, except that it holds no suffering. Many believe we arrive there as a reward for right behavior or speech, or lavish gifts to the temples. Jesus had this to say about it.

"Even well-intentioned men can go astray when they presume to know who may enter the Presence. There is a scale, they say, that weighs the good against the bad. Of course, they expect these scales to be in the possession of one of their own, whether Pharisee, or Parsi or Pharaoh or Priest by another name. This leads them to the conclusion that anyone who believes or practices or speaks other than they do will not measure up, and be excluded from the heavenly city. The glory of that city is constantly enhanced in the telling, and the evil that awaits those poor souls denied entrance likewise increases, until we come to an enormous, irrevocable divide between those who are accepted and those rejected. Out of imagined division and separation come suspicion, fear and hatred. Out of division and separation arise slavery and murder and wars. In the end those who claim to hold the keys to heaven are often those standing furthest from it.

"Open your heart and the truth will find *you*. We can never be lost to each other, or to our Father. The city of light is a place of the spirit, accessed by a bridge of many colors, arising from a pure heart. Having crossed the bridge it dissolves back into the primordial light ... and we are home."

Such imagery was familiar to me from my own training, but I wondered why he spoke this way to those who'd had no such preparation. "Think back to the early years," he told me when I asked him about this. "You and I began our training as children. Judy often used such language so we could begin to think in a new way, to see the world we live in differently than the solid one perceived by our eyes and ears and touch. The student is offered a new world to inhabit, if they are willing to risk it.

"Children are naturally braver than most adults, though some mistakenly think them more foolish. But only one whose mind has become unalterably fixed on their illusions would say such a thing. Because of our early training, we have less *unlearning* to do now that we are older. These are brave souls indeed, who come to hear me speak to them as children. Those with the soul of a child will have no trouble creating their bridge, or finding the courage to cross it or the wisdom to discover the key to the gate within their own heart. Only the innocent and pure will be found on the other side. Wisdom they have as well, but not the sort espoused by arrogance of learning."

I noticed when he spoke in parables or using the imagery of dreams, his listeners often nodded their heads in comprehension whereas when he spoke the language of the educated elite, they struggled to understand, asking unanswerable questions in turn.

"Some do learn better through the thinking mind. And so I use both methods, as the spirit moves me. For most people weaving the two together anchors the higher truths in a practical, meaningful way."

One day he led a small number of us over a rise away from the rest of the group. There were others -- even some who would later be known as his disciples – who had yet to join us, but this particular group would be with him from beginning to end.

Someone asked how best to teach others. "Teaching and healing are not distinct arts, though they are often treated as separate paths. To be a true teacher, one must also heal that which stands in the way of understanding. To be a true healer, one also teaches a higher path, else healing cannot take place. We have talked about healing, and you have learned many excellent techniques. And it is important that you (he said, pointing to Miriam and myself) continue to share the knowledge that was given you in Egypt. But I ask all of you to expand your idea of who you are, and what you have been called to do."

Jesus paused and looked out over the hills and valleys. His eyes moved back and forth as if seeing a world beyond the barren desert that stretched out below us. "You must teach the language of the soul," he went on. "Even the word 'teach' is inadequate, as teaching and healing are one. We are able to transmit through our words and images only tiny portions of the wholeness of being, of the truth of who we are. Remember: we are one with the Father-Mother God that breathed into us Its life. That tells you we have within us *all* the wisdom, power and glory of that One Life?"

We were ten women and ten men. I looked around and saw in some eyes the dawning recognition of the inner God. But on other faces were furrowed brows over worried eyes, as they pondered whether his statement carried in it some sacrilege.

"Of what are we made? For what purpose are we here? The answer is the same for each question. Love. There is nothing else you need to know, nothing else to be taught. We are made of love, even as is God. We are here to teach love … *here to love*."

"But what is love, master?" asked one of the men. Others nodded.

"This is the only question, isn't it?" he replied, but said nothing more for a time.

I lay down on my back, looking up into the late afternoon sky. I know what love *feels* like, the wonderful, joyous buoyancy. And I had experienced the ache when I felt it lacking. But … since we are one with God, and God is love, we can never be left without love. It would be impossible, nothing more than our inability to perceive it at times.

After giving us time to ponder the question, he resumed.

"*You are love*. And not just when you are thinking loving thoughts either." He grinned. "If that were the case, you and I would have died long before this. You are never separated from your Source, which is love. You might think you have severed the connection to love, but that is an illusion. Some would say it is the devil that has cut you off, but that would be giving this devil more power than God has. Would this not be the supreme blasphemy?

"No, there is nothing with more power than the All. It is only your small, fearful mind that imagines it has lost its way, never to return home again. This fear *is* the Satan to which *you* attribute such power. In truth, you have offered up your own power to a lie, and the lie dictates your life." He paused. "But you have never separated from God, never separated from love. You never really gave away or lost your power. It only seems that way. Love is the way home. Remembrance of love is the substance of which you are building your bridge. Love is the key that will open the gate. Love is all you are. Love is all there is to teach those who will come to you for guidance. If another harms you, love them back. If they harm your brother, take your brother out of harm's way if possible, returning love for pain. If they speak hateful words, speak to them only of love."

"But how do we speak of love?" asked another.

"We speak with and without words. Most of the time when we speak of *love* we do so without ever uttering the word. We speak through acts of kindness. Whenever we help or heal another, we have spoken love. Most of all, we love by not judging. And if we have judged, we love through forgiveness.

"You must begin with yourself. Do not think it arrogance to love yourself, for to do so is to love your Creator. To love yourself is to love your sister, your brother – and to love your neighbor is to love yourself. To hate one is to hate all, though as I said, even that is an illusion, because in the end there is nothing but love. Hate is simply a refusal to see that. But in time all will see it, and know the one truth of their being. I am not saying that what I ask of you will always be easy. But if you awaken each morning with a desire to learn more of love that day, and lay yourself down at night with the word of love on your lips, then with each day it will become easier, more natural, and eventually there will be nothing else for you but love."

He stood and walked away from us then. Even *his* words could only carry us so far in the direction of understanding. It would have to be birthed within the heart cave of each one, for them to know.

*

One day after we'd returned to Nazareth Miriam and I were in the marketplace to do some shopping. I had always been greeted warmly by the shopkeepers, if only to draw my attention to their wares. But this day they seemed unusually reserved. Just as we were about to leave, one of the men grabbed Miriam's arm and said something to her beyond my hearing. His eyes were cold, and my friend's face flushed.

I took her other arm and pulled her away. We walked quickly back to mother's house where I set the herbs I'd bought on the table, and turned to my friend.

"What happened back there?" She looked away. "Miriam, what did he say to you?" I demanded

"What did who say?" asked mother. I had not seen her standing in the doorway. She sat down across from Miriam. I pulled up a chair and took my friend's hand.

"Tell me sister, what did that man say?" I repeated, more gently. While waiting for her answer, I told mother what just happened.

Mother drew Miriam's eyes to her own calm gaze, and I sensed my friend's shoulders relax. Her eyes filled with tears as she whispered, "He called me a whore."

I gasped, though mother did not flinch as she continued to hold Miriam's eyes. James and I had all but lived together without marriage, but to my knowledge no one had said that of me. Or had they?

"And so they called my sister," said mother, "before she and Joseph married."

For the moment I was so shocked I forgot about Miriam.

"Jesus' mother? Mary? Why....?"

"Each had their own reason, I suppose. People speak from ignorance, from self-righteousness arising from an empty heart. They are to be pitied more than anything else, attacking those who seem to have what they do not feel in their own lives."

"Love," said Miriam.

"Yes.

"Daughters," said mother, taking our hands in hers, "remember that there really is no such thing as hatred. It is simply love unawakened. Our job is to find whatever means we have to kindle it. But do not be discouraged when your efforts only harden the hearts of such as that man. One day he too will dare to open to love. But there are many who are ready now, who *will* open to you, to your teaching, your healing, and yes, your demonstrations of love with another. Turn your attention to them, but never turn your back on those who turn their backs on you. There will be more such taunts and worse for him. Do not forget your purpose."

"And what is that purpose, mother?" asked Miriam.

"To serve love."

I do not know if Miriam told Jesus about the incident. I would guess not. It was likely he already endured much abuse himself.

Our group was growing, despite efforts to limit its numbers. It wasn't that Jesus wanted to surround himself with an elite assemblage, but – as he explained it – it was becoming difficult to speak on the level he felt necessary to prepare us for the task ahead. There were many newcomers who did not understand the esoteric nature of the teachings, so my cousin turned more and more to the use of parable. And once again our inner group began to meet in one or another of our homes.

"Can you tell me the difference between women and men?" asked Jesus on another of our outings into the desert. I heard giggles higher up on the rocks where people sat in the shadows of a dense cloud cover. "What does the *Zohar* say?" he prodded, when no one answered.

"The *Kabbalah* teaches us that man and woman together is God immanent," said someone. I could not see who spoke but it must be one who had studied under Elois, for those were her words.

"Yes, that is right. But why then are we separate? What is served by our separation?"

"Through our desires to know each other, we are moved along our path of self-discovery. We learn of ourselves through each other," said a woman's voice.

"Yes, as we come together in an act of physical love, we rediscover in that single instant our true nature, and thrill at the sense of the Divine that has been revealed through our beloved. Woman is as the night, and man the day; woman the moon and man the sun. Together we form a whole cycle, representing God in the world."

"But must we marry and come together through this act?" asked a timid voice, too young for me to know if it was a boy or girl in the gathering shadows.

"No, it is but one means to help us remember the ecstasy of union, or reunion with our Creator. Man and woman represent different aspects of Divinity. This is why you will sometimes hear me or another speak of Father-Mother God, referring to the dual aspects as Source reveals itself to us. Father is that which remains at Source, seeding itself in the world of form through the body of the Mother. You might think of the Father as remaining in what we call heaven, and the Mother as taking form through the earth beneath our feet. She is the divine presence of God in all things we can touch, that which sustains our bodies in the form of food and water. She moves through us in our feelings. In her highest form *She is Love,* the fulfillment of God in our world. This is why the female head of each household assumes the role and form of the divine feminine, Shekkinah, at each sacred meal, each *Shabbat* ritual. God is unrealized in the world until He unites with Shekkinah, his partner in an unending revelation of the sacred in life.

"There is no man who does not carry the essence of Shekkinah within him, and no woman who does not carry the seed of the Holy One in her. And so no, my dear, you do not need to enter into marriage to experience divine union. One day each of us will know that union independently of such artifice. Then, as the Zohar tells us, we shall shine like the radiance of all the stars in heaven, forever. When we are seen through the eyes of truth, all that will be seen of us is light."

Not long after, a few of us came together in James' and my home. That night Jesus spoke of Shakti, the divine feminine essence as it is called in the Brahmanic lands. "Shakti is thought of as a coiled serpent sleeping at the base of the spine. This serpent is aroused through meditation, certain movements, special sounds and through the power of the fire of mind. Aroused, it rises like an uncoiling snake, opening the gateway to the sacred city at the top of the head. The awakened snake is our rainbow bridge not made with hands, which I have spoken of many times before. The serpent awakens our sleeping powers one by one, until we pass through the gate, reunited with divine mind, which is called Shiva in their tradition. In the process our hearts have been set afire, and love is unleashed through us. There is nothing for this awakened one then but a life of living love. This is God manifest on earth."

Miriam, Naomi and I had also learned in Egypt of the awakened serpent, represented in many of their paintings and carvings as a cobra stretching up the initiate's back and over the top of his head, spread out over the forehead where sits the single eye of light. It is said the eye of God is then one with ours, enabling us to see as God sees.

"At some point," Jesus continued, "often without our awareness, we stop running away from home, and begin the return journey. The awakened serpent is the end result of that return. Some people are well along the return journey, while many still refuse to acknowledge even the existence of this home. The only certainty is that all of us will eventually awaken. Whether we travel slowly or quickly, each one will find a Father's welcome waiting for them."

"What then?" Mark asked. "What does that mean?"

"We remember who we are, sons of the living God. In remembering, we have the choice to remain with the Father, or go out again into the world. But such words will only find meaning when we have made the return. In the meantime be comforted in knowing there are some who have already arrived at this point of choice – and returned to light the way of return for the rest of us. The Brahmins call it the Great Renunciation,"

Chapter 44

CIRCLE OF PROPHECY

Jesus admonished us to continue meeting without him. We should have been used to his comings and goings, but it felt like we were a boat being cast out to sea without a sail. The night before he left he said, "You have been in training, not to follow me, but to assume your own power and authority so you can serve as guides to others on their path."

"But we do not know the way ourselves," insisted Rebecca, who had rejoined the group not long before.

"You *do* know. But you are afraid of your own power," he countered, looking at each of us so we would understand his words were meant for each one. "Do not be so quick to relinquish it, as others will eagerly seize yours to enhance their own. Of course, real power cannot be stolen. Only those who have trained, studied, fasted and meditated with sincerity will be found worthy of wielding true power."

"Fasted? Is that necessary?" asked Luke, whose girth showed a fondness of food.

Jesus rolled his eyes, no doubt wondering how his talk on power had so suddenly changed course. "In fasting," he said, "we voluntarily abandon for a time that which anchors us to the everyday world, whether food or sex or gambling or gossiping or judging others. Some will tell you this body is a curse, and its appetites must be denied to enter the kingdom of heaven. But the body, in its true form, is a creation of love cast into light. It is the mansion for the soul, not made with human hands – despite its genesis through sexual union between man and woman." His smile dazzled us. He had often talked about the sacredness of such joining, cautioning us to ignore those who injected their personal shame into what is a sacred and joyful act.

"In fasting, we step outside our habits and observe our relationship with this holy vessel. Does our body serve the plan that spirit has for us? Do we honor it in our daily habits, or ignore or denigrate it? The occasional fast reminds us to dedicate all earthly acts to a higher purpose. So, for you it might be a day without food, while for another it might be abstinence from sex for awhile, or being more careful of one's speech. You will learn much about yourself in the process."

"Where will you go?" I asked, changing the subject back to his departure. "And who will go with you?"

"I go alone. This is my fast from your wonderful company. Each day among you and the others changes me more than you can imagine. It is through our talks that I come to understand all the teachings I have been given, as well as my own path."

I wondered what my addiction might be, from which I would benefit most by fasting. I rarely spent time alone anymore, though until James and I came together I often went out into the hills alone. In the stillness of the night I was able to commune with my cousin as he traveled, and it was there I felt closest to my Source. Thinking about this I realized that no one, not even my beloved, could substitute for this sense of connection.

Jesus went on: "Tomorrow is the new moon and I will travel to Mt. Hermon, returning at the full."

It would not be so long then. I saw my own relief mirrored in the faces of the others. After everyone left that night, James and I lay talking together.

"I was reminded tonight of my need for time to myself out under the stars. It has been so long, I'd almost forgotten how it nourishes me. I am afraid we have become too dependent upon each other."

"Of course. I always recognized that in you even before I found the courage to speak of my feelings. You are such a free spirit ... and I would not take that from you." He drew me close to him in the darkness, and I felt his acceptance in the way he held me.

I began to return to the hill where I used to go to meditate. James always seemed to know, even before I did, that I needed to get away. He'd look at me with a knowing smile as I gathered my things, sometimes reminding me to take a shawl or pressing a bag filled with dates or a water skin into my hands.

One night out on the hill, Jesus came to me in a vision as he used to do on his long journey. He asked me to gather a small number of the group to meet him in Caeserea at the full moon. No one questioned me whether my vision was true or not when I told them about it the following day, but just set about preparing for the journey. We arranged for horse-driven carts, which shortened the journey to two days. He had not said where in town we should meet him. There were two inns, so half of us went to one and the rest to the other.

The actual full moon would be the following night, though it already appeared in all its glory. I felt the familiar pull to go out into the hills on my own. "Not here, Veronica," said James. "I cannot let you go out alone in this borderland. It is too remote." The innkeeper told us there was a zealot training camp not far away, and there were rumors of a Roman encampment in the opposite direction from the city. So Miriam and Thaddeus went out with James and me. We all gravitated in the same direction, veering off the road onto a singular hill outlined in moonlight. Each plant and tree threw impossibly long shadows across the earth. The moon cast a silvery sheen on our skin, causing Thaddeus to suggest that we looked like the walking dead.

"Not so, you are the ever-living," said a familiar voice. A shadow appeared at the crest of the hill, where it stopped to wait. Miriam ran to him, and the rest of us followed, almost knocking him off his feet. The night made us giddy and we danced around the top of the hill like children, until we collapsed in a laughing heap on the soft grass. By then it was so bright we were able to see each other's eyes in the otherworldly glow.

Returning to town we met up with the rest of our group for dinner. We passed the evening talking and laughing about little things. But underneath the levity I discerned a change in him. Now and then his eyes drifted away from the conversation at the table. That night in Caeserea I noticed the youthful fullness of my cousin's face had gone. His firm jaw reflected an inner resolve; the muscles around his mouth seemed ready to deflect any challenge. And his eyes ... his eyes had always conveyed depth, but now the waters had become the sea, and none could follow when he dove deep. Miriam saw as well. By night's end her joy had mixed with melancholy, a fusion that would be her signature to the last of her days.

As we prepared for sleep he told us, "Tomorrow night we will return to the hill where you found me, to celebrate the arrival of the Bull."

Was it that time again, already, I thought to myself? A year and a half had passed since his return, and a full year since he spoke to us of his experience in the far-off valley of Tibet.

As we walked in silence toward the hill the next night, I noticed we were equal numbers men and women. This often happened, though if by design it was on another level of awareness. The sun was near to setting when we arrived at the top. The previous night I had noticed a huge flat-topped stone right at the peak. Upon that stone now sat a polished bowl, as if put there by the spirit of the mountain. None of us had carried it, though we had brought water which we now poured into the bowl.

Jesus had not told us what to do or what to expect, but we naturally moved quickly, seamlessly, according to some plan unknown to us. We set small lamps in an oval pattern with points on each end facing east and west. Just moments before the sun set, we lit the lamps and gathered at the western side of the stone … all except my cousin who stood on the other side, facing back toward us.

The timing was exquisite. The sun set below the flat horizon to the west just as the moon rose over a low hill to the east. During that brief interlude, a burst of light shot out from both heavenly bodies, settling upon Jesus' face at the exact same moment. He stood with arms outstretched, eyes closed. His inner light seemed to eclipse the other, bathing the hilltop and us.

"Veronica, drink," came a gentle voice.

For a moment I did not know where I was. My thoughts tried to focus upon the ladle held before my lips. Sweet, sparkling water filled my mouth, refreshing my whole body as I drank it down. A breeze against my face told me I had been weeping, and I knew I had been taken away from myself – though had no memory of it.

And then I saw my cousin's smiling eyes. It was he who held the ladle for me. James took my hand and we stood back, so the others could have their turn. Jesus repeatedly dipped the ladle into the shimmering water and held it forth, until each had received the blessing of light. Then he nodded to Miriam, who stepped up and took the ladle from him, dipped it into the water and held it to his lips. He too drank, as one of us.

*

We left Caeserea together the next day.

Not long afterward some friends were gathered in our home.

We had just finished eating when a stranger appeared in the doorway. All turned to the man with eyes like fire. Jesus went up and embraced him, drawing him into the room. I realized it was our cousin John. Again, I was struck with the image of a wild animal caged in human flesh. His eyes had the look of trapped prey, but Jesus kept his arm on his shoulder until John's face softened to a gentleness that belied the wild appearance. I had never beheld a face like that, both child-like and old at the same time.

The last time I had seen him he wore nothing but a skin of some animal around his waist, himself a creature of the wilds. This time he had on ordinary robes, a sign that he planned to remain among people. Still, his whole demeanor was otherworldly. He would never be like other men.

It was impossible to know if he remembered me, or anyone else save Jesus. My cheeks burned after our eyes met, as if he had ignited something inside of me that would smolder as long as he remained in the room. No wonder he had been unable to live among people. In the end they would either come to worship him or destroy him.

"When I arrived on Mt. Hermon," said Jesus, "I discovered John waiting there for me." He turned an affectionate look on the burly man. "Remember how you found me waiting for you on the hilltop?" he asked us.

"Yes," replied Thaddeus. "It could not have been by chance."

"No, it wasn't, nor was my meeting John on the mountain. Nor, as you are discovering, is anything now taking place a matter of chance."

I had been hearing things about John, things that disturbed me. He was said to be one of the zealots, and maybe even one of their leaders. It seemed dangerous for him to be among us now. Even if the rumors were false, others would have heard and believed them, associating us with their increasing pattern of violence.

Jesus interrupted my thoughts. "From birth the two of us have been joined, as were our mothers before us, working toward a single end. Despite that, our paths have rarely crossed, except in the world of dream and vision. Even now, the flame will be bright but brief."

Jesus looked at John as he spoke, and sighed. None of us knew what he meant in those words, but each felt their weight. "Pay no heed to what you hear of him in the marketplace or the streets. There are many who wish all our people ill, and some of our own view him as their enemy. He stands neither with us nor with the zealots. John is his own man. He is God's man."

I had never heard such a thing said about any man before that.

"Trust the path he walks." I note Jesus did not tell us to trust John, but only his path. In my later years I understood that John had so completely given himself over as God's hand in fulfilling his role, that "We must journey to Egypt together, in fulfillment of prophecy."

Again, that icy feeling ran up my back.

"As some of you know, my mother's father was the high priest at the Temple of Helios in Jerusalem, a position greatly feared *and* respected among both Sadducees and Pharisees, though they would never admit it. Indeed even to acknowledge the Temple's existence would be to recognize its power. And so it is generally ignored by Herod and Romans alike, which has been the temple's saving grace. Despite this, many of the most highly regarded Hebrew prophecies since ancient times have come from the priests in this temple." He hesitated.

"Nothing in these times takes place by accident. Even dear Apsafar, a confidant of the Brotherhood, directed my mother to the cave behind his inn when it was her time to give birth, so the prophecies might be fulfilled. He would have given her his own rooms and everything he owned if it were not so. They forecast that my family would flee to Egypt to avoid the carnage Herod would soon visit upon the Jewish infants of our land. And now it comes that the circle must be completed. The brothers await us in Egypt."

"When?" we asked.

"We leave tomorrow."

I think the groan came from all of us. This seemed to be John's cue. He rose and bowed slightly, then departed without having said a single word.

Chapter 45

THE TEMPLE OF DEATH AND REBIRTH

The two men laid their bedrolls on top of wooden planks suspended above deck. The crew hung curtains which they could draw around themselves for privacy or protection against the elements. Only the very wealthy enjoyed greater luxury. Jesus was grateful for the space to do his inner work without interruption or questions from others. There was no getting away from the noise or the smells, but he could deal with them. He didn't know if John was even aware of his surroundings. He was the most single-minded person he had ever known, rarely speaking, and totally devoid of social graces.

A runner met the ship when it docked at Alexandria, and escorted them to a waiting carriage. He threw their bags inside and the two men were about to climb in, when something about the driver caught Jesus' attention. "Hebeny! I hardly knew you from behind, with all the white in your hair."

The black man turned to his old friend with a wide grin. They embraced, slapping each other on the back. "We are getting older, my brother," replied the handsome Nubian. "It will harder to find the white in your pale hair," he teased. Ah, there they are," he yelped, running his fingers through Jesus' hair. "Moonbeams across the setting sun! See, you are not immune from time, after all," he laughed.

"Indeed?" Jesus lifted his own hair, and pulled it in front of his eyes to see for himself. He had never thought about aging, never looked at himself in the mirror that he could recall. But his hair was not quite long enough. "I will just have to take your word for it. But, why are you here? Why are you not with your brother, in your village? Weren't you supposed to return there? And why did you not announce yourself, instead pretending to be an ordinary driver?"

"I wondered how long it would take you to recognize me. And as for serving with my brother -- I tried, but it was not for me. The same night I was going to tell Arony of my decision to leave, Ambos asked if we could talk. He is the brother next in age to me. He told me of his unhappiness in business, and asked my advice. He'd always had a great talent for mediating among men, and it occurred to me he could serve in my place. So we held a family council and it was decided Ambos would stand alongside my elder brother, now well established as Chief. And I was allowed to return here, to the life I love!" He grinned.

"And you'll like this. Our eldest sister took over the family business from Ambos. It was a scandal among our people, as women had never before worked in commerce. But she is talented, and has already increased the family holdings."

"That is excellent," said Jesus, suddenly remembering John. He turned to introduce the two men, but John had already wandered off toward the docks. A moment later and he would have been lost to view. "John!" he called out. "John, come back here. I want you to meet my brother."

At hearing his name he turned and ambled back up the dusty slope. He took one look at Hebeny and broke into a grin, pulling him into a hearty embrace. Jesus was startled at the unexpected display of warmth. Something about his friend must have struck a chord with him. Hebeny was tall and thin, and looked as if a modest wind could lift him up, while John was built like the yaks of the eastern mountains. Jesus could not imagine a single force of nature strong enough to move him when he had planted himself. Stubborn as a yak, as Zhang would say.

"Where are we going?" asked Jesus, when he saw they were not heading in the direction of the monastery. Hebeny had turned the horses south, to the open highway.

"Heliopolis," he replied.

"We are going directly to the pyramid then?" he asked, referring to the place of his initiation.

"Yes and no. We will pass by it, but not stop. There is little time," he added, looking at his friend out of the corner of his eye. He had been conferring with Bandar about the prophecies related to the man from Nazareth. There was much he had not known about him before, and he wondered if even Jesus knew all of it.

My cousin noticed the comment about time, but asked no questions. He himself had felt the urgency, though did not wish to think about it. It was all moving too fast. While at sea Jesus had told John stories of the monastery, the school housed within, and the people with whom he had shared his life there. Though he was sure John would not care, he felt a pang of regret at not seeing it again.

The two old friends sat alongside each other in front, while John snored behind them, nestled into a pile of blankets under the midday sun. "I have never seen such hair," said the dark man. "Especially not on the face," he laughed. "He is indeed a lion among men. Is all that hair not hot? And itchy?"

Jesus laughed. He had tied his own hair back, to keep it out of his face, and his beard was fine and well trimmed.

Hebeny kept his hair short, and that on his chin was naturally spare. Like the men of the great mountains, thought Jesus.

He gave himself over to the moment, enjoying the passing

sights. They traveled the major highway between Lower and Upper Egypt, passing through a stream of villages. The Romans, to their credit, had remarkably improved upon the road originally built by the Egyptians. They had little interest in pyramids and traditional temple architecture, but they had a passion and peculiar talent for roads and aqueducts.

Children ran out to wave at them. Old men planted themselves next to the road, so the world might come to them. The women ignored passersby as they labored in the fields or at other chores within their compounds. Only a few of the younger women looked up -- carrying enormous water jugs balanced on their heads -- giggling behind veils drawn across their faces to keep the dust out.

The three men came to Heliopolis late the second day, but did not stop. The sun set red across the desert and still they traveled on. Jesus moved to the back with John, and Hebeny drove the tired horses. A shout out of the darkness startled them.

"Here they are! They have come!"

"We have arrived?" asked John in his deep voice.

"Yes, we have arrived."

Their knees shook when they stood, as they had when first stepping off the ship. Someone led them through a gate, barely seen in the darkness. From there they passed through a second, smaller gate leading to a large courtyard. Trees swayed in the breeze, like ghosts in the night, and the men heard a fountain burbling somewhere ahead.

Lamps were lit, revealing a score of faces. An elderly man approached, right hand across his heart in the greeting of the Brotherhood. He bowed, first to John, and then to Jesus. "I am called Thothmus. All men in the succession are given this name. My birth name has long been forgotten ... even by me." The man seemed uncertain, as if unused to speaking.

Hebeny had been standing in the background and stepped

forward to introduce himself and his visitors. The three men bowed in turn, hands across their hearts.

"We are honored to have you here," said Thothmus, gesturing to indicate both the assemblage and the place.

"And we are honored to be here," Jesus said. John and Hebeny nodded their assent. "Where are we, exactly?"

Thothmus laughed and looked at Hebeny. "Did you not tell them?"

"I know *where* we are, though I have never been here before myself. And I thought it better they learn from you the *why* and the *what* of where we are, than to have me speculate about it."

"Good. Good. Well, let us eat first. Explanations will come in their own time."

While Thothmus was a man spare of words, he became eloquent when talking about food. He told his visitors that fish was brought in daily from the great river, and their cook understood the nuances of herbs to season the bounty from river and garden.

"I have rarely eaten so well," said Jesus when they had finished. John belched in agreement, which made them all laugh.

"That was the highest compliment in my father's household," said Thothmus. "Come, you will wish to bathe and find your beds. I will come for you at sunrise tomorrow." And he left them in the care of a novitiate.

The old man appeared on their doorstep just as the sun breached the horizon. He had been in good humor the night before, laughter at the ready. But this morning he was all business. Jesus turned to say goodbye to Hebeny, but he had already disappeared. And by the time he looked back, Thothmus was walking at a brisk pace away from them, and the two men had to run to catch up. They left through the outer gate. The old priest walked in front and the two men from Palestine followed, shoulder to shoulder – a triangle of energy moving with intent across the desert.

There had no time for food or drink before starting their quest. As the sun continued to rise, so did their thirst. They saw nothing on the horizon and could not imagine what their destination may be or how long it would take to arrive there. John was more accustomed to going without sustenance than was Jesus. There had been times of deprivation on his journeys, but that seemed long behind him.

The old man suddenly stopped, and they nearly collided with him. He told them to wait, and walked on another forty paces or so before disappearing. The cousins looked at each other, but did not speculate about where he'd gone.

Then suddenly he was back. "Come, we are ready," he told them. On their approach they saw a narrow stone staircase that descended into shadows. A low wall lined the stairs, upon which was inscribed an array of ancient symbols. Nothing would have indicated to a passerby from even a short distance away that there was something worthy of exploration there. It was simply invisible until standing directly in front of it.

Thothmus descended the stairs, with his two charges following close behind. A passageway stretched out before them at the bottom, dimly lit by small lamps set into niches. Jesus noticed little discoloration of the stone above or behind the lamps, an indication the passageway was seldom used.

At the end of the corridor the old priest said, "This place was prepared for one purpose only, long before any of us was born. We priests here have been taught about the *son born out of the star from the East*, and have prepared ourselves for our own small part in the momentous event soon to be visited upon us. Now I will leave you," he said, abruptly disappearing back down the dim hall.

John looked at Jesus, who shrugged his shoulders. They stood in front of a recess in the wall at the end of the passageway, upon which was painted a man, slightly taller than either of them. Not knowing what else to do, they waited. It began to look like the lamps would go out before anyone would come for them, if indeed anyone was to come. And just as the first of the lamps began to sputter, a form seemed to move out of the wall, as if the painting were coming to life. They instinctively stepped back, not from fear, but to give the man room to move.

"*Elohim.*"

The voice came not from the man, but arose from a gust of wind. The word startled them, speaking as it did the name of God.

"*Elohim,*" this time the sound came from somewhere inside of them, echoing in their heads and through their bodies. A flash of light exploded, and they fell to their knees, blinded. The boundaries of their individuation dissolved into *It* and they were lost to themselves.

Later, Thothmus had them brought to his rooms.

"Before you tell me of your experience of the *chamber of death and rebirth*, I want to tell you something of the chamber itself. The design and dimensions of the structure had been given in a vision to the Pharaoh Sankara at the very beginning of the Age of the Bull, a vision that would be fulfilled only now, at the advent of the Fish. It was not constructed until long after his death, at a precise moment in the movement of the stars, and since that time has been patiently and lovingly tended by a succession of priests who were given cosmological training specifically related to its ultimate purpose. I am the last of these priests," he said, in a voice both sad and proud. "At my initiation I was told there was no need to train a successor."

He looked at Jesus. "Giza, you already know. And many others who come after you will be initiated into its secrets in their own time. But this ... this ... had only one purpose, to bridge the crossroads of the ages. And now it will be filled in and never used again. So let me hear of your time in the chamber."

"We waited," said Jesus, "for a long while as the lamps burned down, when the man stepped out of the wall toward us."

"What man?" asked Thothmus. "No one was anywhere near there but the two of you."

"The man, the painting, it came alive and took on form in front of us. I do not truly understand what happened, but the painting, this form somehow provided the entry point for God or His emissary to appear to us. But when the light came …."

"The light?"

"John and I … and the Being or God were all lost in it together." He looked to John for help, who only nodded in agreement. "In this light there were no more walls, no ground above or below, no separation of anything or anyone. I felt I floated in it, died and was born back into it …." He stopped, struggling for words, then said, "I do not know how to speak of something unknowable to me."

The old priest stood, watching Jesus' face, trying to fathom beyond his words, piecing together his description with what he had been told at his own initiation into the Brotherhood about the significance of the event.

Jesus made another attempt. "I saw every moment of my life replayed before my eyes, and every moment of every lifetime before this one. Like knots in a child's game, I saw how certain events throughout time were strung together to build the pattern of what happened in the chamber and what it will mean for the days to come. Everything up until now has been preparation for … this.

"I think we were taken on a journey into the stars then, and shown a similar series of future events throughout the heavens that were set into motion this very day. I cannot explain it more than this -- as it took place in a world all but unimaginable to me as I stand here with you."

Jesus looked to John again, hoping he might have something to add. But his cousin stared off into space … and he wondered if he had even been listening. John was one of those men who one day people call a genius or a saint, and the next an idiot or even criminal. He was wholly unpredictable, and for the most part unknowable.

But he surprised them, speaking thus: "Yes, all that has ever happened and all that ever will take place among mankind was shown me in that light. But the moment I tried to understand what I saw, it moved away from me. Struggling against it, I felt I would drown in the cosmic vision. But when I surrendered, the vision washed over me, and I was filled it. I do not wish to struggle now, or even to speak of it for you, or I fear I may lose it altogether."

"Brother," said Thothmus, addressing John, "we are finished here. And your work is soon done in your own land. You have served well, and the time quickly comes when the light will come for you. You are right: it is better for men not to seek understanding of something that comes as spirit."

And then John did something unexpected, I think, even to him. He raised his right hand to Thothmus' brow, and the old man fell into a swoon. Jesus caught him just before he hit the floor. John seemed unaware of what he had just done, and looked surprised to see the priest in his cousin's arms.

They called his aides, who persuaded them to leave him in their care. "No harm could possibly come to him from this," one of the priests assured them.

The following morning he arrived on their doorstep to escort them to the waiting carriage. The old man brushed away their questions about his well being, and refused to consider John's efforts to apologize. "I assure you the experience was a great blessing, and no hardship at all. Because of you my heart is free."

He kissed their hands, and with tears in his eyes thanked them. "We stand here together in the eternal now, at the point of endings and beginnings. My whole life has brought me to this, and it is enough. We are each ready now for what is to come."

"I am grateful it was you who brought us here," Jesus said to Hebeny as they rode across the desert. "Where did you go these two days? We are far from any city."

"I was taken to a Bedouin camp not far away, and had a pleasant enough time. And now we return to Alexandria. Hopefully we have a few days yet together. You will leave with the same ship on which you arrived."

Chapter 46

THE GREAT AWAKENING

The sun had not yet risen over the eastern hills. Men and women slept here and there, wherever they could find a patch of earth on that rocky hillside. Some had been there for a moon, though new people arrived daily. The fishmongers would soon appear with the morning's catch. They had quickly caught on to an opportunity to expand their market, frying the fish before bringing them up from Galilee, not far below. Women would later arrive with jugs of water in the early summer sun. They timed their arrival for midday, when the pilgrims' own water bags had run dry. Other peddlers brought bread or dried fruit, which could be had for a pittance.

The crowd had been in this particular spot for some days, using a nearby cluster of trees to relieve themselves. Soon they would be forced to move on, as the place became unfit for further use.

But it was easy to forget such unpleasantness in the magnificent sunrise. Its red and gold fingers reached across the boulders and bushes, washing over the people as it rose above the lake. A breeze swept across the water and up the hill, lifting wisps of hair, fluttering robes. A sense of expectancy filled the air, and the sea of faces turned to gaze upon an imposing figure at the top of the hill. From below he seemed a giant, though the man was not overly tall.

No one knew this man. Oh yes, they knew his name was John. There were rumors whispered about him, where he came from, the strange story of his parentage, and so on. They guessed at his motives, assuming him to be a zealot since he often spoke like one. Many believed he was the Messiah, the one long promised as savior and liberator of the Jews, to free them from the Roman yoke.

John strode down the hill as if he owned it, not looking where he stepped yet never disturbing the loose stones that caused others such trouble. He was as sure footed as he was sure of himself. And this man had no thought of himself separate from his mission. Finding an appropriate ledge, he stopped. Today he wore sandals under his tattered robe. They were new, strapped over his calloused feet. One of his followers had made a gift of them the day before, and he wore them out of deference to the man's kindness. He preferred the feel of the earth beneath his feet and in truth, the feel of the sun against his skin. But he knew his nakedness, and even the worn skins of the mountain cats only distracted from his mission. He had enemies enough without that.

His mere presence commanded respect, devotion, fanaticism, fear, even hatred. And his words breathed fire into each of these emotions, intensifying them. It was impossible to be neutral in the presence of such a man.

James and I sat among the crowd, having come with a few other friends to experience his power for ourselves. Jesus had said little or nothing of consequence about him since their return from Egypt, deflecting our questions.

"Awaken!" his voice boomed across the landscape. "Awaken from your sleep, the sleep of ages. Tear away the veil that covers your eyes. Cast off the darkness that clouds your vision!" he shouted, ending with a crescendo. Each phrase was thrust into the now still air as if it were a knife to serve the masses in cutting away their offenses. His passion stirred them. But to what end? People would interpret his words according to their own preconceived agenda.

His unruly hair sprang out from his head, encircling it like the sun's corona, mesmerizing the crowd. He paced back and forth on the rock -- his throne -- beard jutting out before him, punctuating each word. "You walk as if asleep, dragged about by demons, demons you created and to whom you have given your power. You have spurned the angels, refused the willing hand of God, turned your face from the sun and invited instead the night so that now you can do nothing but stumble blindly through life. And you blame all but yourself for this madness."

John continued in this vein throughout the day, hardly pausing for breath, never stopping for food or even drink, unless one of his followers dared to force it upon him. He was a man quick to anger, and quick to forgive, or at least to forget. He was so one-pointed that he gave no further thought to the moment just passed or that yet to come, living wholly in the word or movement in which he was engaged. Nothing of himself was frittered away in a divided life. This is what fueled his fanaticism. It was also his greatest weakness, taking no thought for the consequences s of his words. He was fearless, and thus formidable.

We did not try to approach him ourselves, not sure he would even know us, if we tried. Besides, we had come to learn, to see for ourselves what it seemed the whole world was talking about. We walked around the hillside that evening and through the village below over the next several days, to hear what people were saying.

A group of men gathered below the overhang where we sat in the dark, unaware of our presence. "I do not care if he calls himself a zealot, or ever refers to our cause," said one emphatic voice. "He serves our purpose. Many have begun to rally around Jared since hearing this man, thinking he has told them to do so." The men laughed.

Another said, more thoughtfully, "Yes, if you listen carefully, it is hard to know *what* he is urging people to do. I am only certain he is telling us to turn aside from our old ways in preparation for what is to come. And for me that means to withdraw support from the Romans, so someone else can take their place."

"Ha! Withdraw our support," someone snarled. "I will withdraw nothing but a sword from the heart of my enemy, so I may use it on another!"

The men roared with laughter, sounding increasingly drunk as they goaded each other to take violent oaths. We left when they started discussing plans to attack a Roman garrison at the changing of the guard the next day. There would be nothing we could do to prevent such an attack, and it was foolish to be seen anywhere near these men should there be spies about – as surely existed anywhere John went.

Another group further on stood in a circle, arms around each other, praying together for guidance. "... to help our brother, John. We beseech you to give us a sign: is he the savior of whom we have been taught, your prophet, or one sent of darkness to confuse us?"

And still others said: "He *is* the one, I know it! I can feel it in my heart."

"Yes, but what is he telling us? Are we to fight the oppressors? Will he lead us? He has not said he will do this, and we must be sure ...."

And so it went. He inspired, but also confused.

"It is said one will come before the Messiah, to light his way. We do not know of any who has come before John," I said to the small group who'd come with us. "And though he has not made claim to any title, in my heart I know *Jesus* is the light of whom the prophecies speak.*" I had never given voice to my belief before this, and my heart beat wildly at the sound of my own words echoing back to me in the night. In that moment belief had turned to certainty. But I noticed the others kept their silence.

"I have always known Jesus to be a great and inspired teacher. I've seen him heal those who should have died," said Thaddeus. "And I have wondered if he might be the one for whom we have waited. But if he is, why doesn't he speak against our oppressors, offering hope we might one day govern ourselves? Why not speak directly to the people in the marketplace instead of hovering with us behind closed doors or in isolated valleys and hills where it is safe, speaking to a chosen few? Hearing John now, I think he must be that one, and not Jesus."

"No, I agree with Veronica," said Naomi. "John *is* inspired, speaking the words of the Holy Spirit. But listen closely, and you will hear him hint at another to come. He claims nothing for himself."

"He is a wild man," Mary interjected. I think she was Thaddeus' cousin, who had joined our party only the day before. "He frightens me. Surely our savior would not be so angry as this one. Mother said the soldiers plot against him and as soon as the crowds disperse, will take him during the night to prison … or worse."

"Then we must warn him," said Thaddeus, jumping to his feet.

"Sit down, brother," said James, pulling on his sleeve. "Of one thing we can be sure. John knows what he is about, and no warning would prevent him from speaking. He is indeed inspired, and we know he has Jesus' blessing."

"Do we? How do we know that?" asked Marta. "They separated after Egypt, even before Jesus returned to us. How do we know they have not taken separate paths?"

"No, they have not," I said. Since his return Jesus told us that John has his role to play, while he has another. Each of them is working toward the same goal. He says John is his other half in this work, and together they offer a single message. For myself, I see John as a raging sea, and I confess he makes me uneasy. He has come before Jesus to wake people up, and yes, to make us uncomfortable with our lives so we will be willing to look at things differently, to seek a new way of living."

Miriam, who had said little over the past several days, spoke up. "Both sides exist side by side within us as well. We live in the world of men with all its passions and human shortcomings. At the same time we pursue an inner life, which is more in line with the vision our Creator has of us. We are at peace within, certain of our place in the world, while chaos reigns outside. John speaks to the outer part of us and Jesus the inner."

We returned to Nazareth and went to Mary's house, hoping to find Jesus, to share with him what we had seen and heard, and to hear what we had come to expect from him: a reasoned view that brought everything into perspective.

But he was not there.

Mary's eyes were grave. "He has gone to be by himself for a time, to commune with his Father. I asked why he would not take one of you with him. He answered: 'It is a journey I alone must take. None can walk it with me.'

"Is he alright? Has something happened here?" Thinking back to the opposing forces surrounding John, I wondered if he might be in danger.

"He is well. Nothing has changed here."

"James," I said when we were in our own home, "I am afraid."

"Of what?"

"I am afraid for Jesus. Maybe for us, too."

He stared off into the darkness. "Fear is what he warned us against, our greatest enemy. As with John, nothing would deflect Jesus from his purpose. And we will be of no help to help him if we cower in fear. Sit with me, and we will ask the Holy Spirit to fill us with the same certainty of purpose. We have been born for what is to come, as well as he. And he will need friends who are unwavering in their support."

We sat across from each other in front of the altar upon which burned a single flame. Deep in meditation I saw that flame take light in the altar of our hearts.

We lost count of the days until his return. But I see now that he never fully came back to us after his time in the desert. I saw in his eyes, even before he spoke a word, that another plateau had been reached.

Mary called James and me to her the following day.

"You must prepare yourselves. The time has come for my son to leave his home for good, and he will need you with him. His is a solitary journey, but he will yet need companions."

These were strange words, saying one thing and then another, I thought. "You are sure he will abide our company?"

"Yes. You who have been with him from the beginning, will bring him comfort. Others are even now being called to his side, and the circle will grow ... and then diminish. Yet the

inner circle will never be broken."

"Won't you join us? Your children are nearly grown. Even Elizabeth and Andrew stand on the threshold of adulthood. Others can watch them now. I am sure he ...."

"Not yet. But I will join you before long. A wedding in Canaan," she trailed off.

I knew of no wedding in Canaan, but Mary was clearly finished, and asked us to return in the morning. We went straight from there to mother's house. Matthias sat outside on a bench with young John. We embraced them and went inside. Mother had a pot on the fire, though seemed to have forgotten it. Her face bore a faraway look and she did not notice our arrival.

"Mother," I said, sitting down next to her. She turned and put her arms around me, and held me to her as she had when I was a child. James went back out to sit with Matthias, leaving us alone. We swayed back and forth, the movement somehow comforting us both, as if rocked in the arms of angels. I remember her saying that as she rocked my sister Elizabeth in her cradle, and it's probably what she said to me when I was small as well.

Sighing, we moved apart. "Daughter, it is now your time. You are ready, no matter how you feel at the moment. You and James, Miriam and the others are ready. Stay close to him; surround him in the circle of your love. Do not fear, but seek only the joy that is found in walking the lighted way. When you falter, do not indulge in self-pity or self-judgment. Drawing upon all you have been taught, the way will be shown and answers given. Remember who you are and with whom you walk. Expect nothing. Do not try to control anything. Remember to love. Let events unfold.

Mary and I will join you when we can, as will others. You will not be alone."

I wanted to return to her embrace, to cry like a child, to refuse my path. But I could not. And so I kissed her, and went out alone. James took my hand, and we walked away together.

"We will be with you soon," Matthias called after us.

"I will come too," said John. And I turned to look back at the young man, whose strength I would soon come to know. Until that moment, he had been a boy in my eyes.

The next morning we gathered at Mary's house. Jesus had not been home all night, she said, but would soon arrive. We sipped tea while we waited. No one knew what to say. When at last he appeared in the doorway, we went outside to give mother and son their time.

Once on the road, Jesus seemed to relax, and we along with him. Before long he was joking and had us all laughing. I wondered then – no, hoped that this whole thing about prophecy and destiny existed only in our imaginations. And that this, the laughter and lightheartedness would be the enduring reality. But though I fancied we were just another group of men and women on the road to some everyday event, we walked with no ordinary man. Everyone we passed sensed it, and many approached him for a healing, or a blessing. He denied no one, though now and then he called one of us to share grace, according to our ability.

He was ever the teacher, the guide, the friend to each of us, never, never placing himself above us. When I think back to him now, I realize this was probably his most profound lesson, one he repeated ceaselessly: that all are one in the Father's eyes.

Word went ahead that a great teacher and healer approached. We soon found people waiting for us on the road even before we arrived. Jesus took no thought for himself, slowing the pace of our journey so he would not leave anyone behind without a word, a touch, a smile. He could not help himself. Once the floodgate had been opened, a constant river of light flowed out from him. We arrived in twice the time it might have taken, but we were exhilarated, feeling we had at last taken up our calling.

"Master," called out a young man as we approached Capernaum. He stopped to hear him. "Master, are you or is John the Baptist *the one* of whom the scriptures speak?"

John the Baptist? For a moment I didn't know who he meant.

"Ask yourself the question, and find the answer in your own heart," he replied. "Then return to me tomorrow with what you have learned." The man looked at him, confused, but walked away.

Before we could speak, Jesus said, "Half of you stay with me and the others go on ahead. It is my cousin John of whom he speaks. You will find him at the river. Bring him my greetings, and then return to me. We will await you there." He pointed to a cluster of trees partway up a hill off the road.

Six of us continued on, soon arriving at Capernaum. We passed by the town, pressing on to the river. John had attracted a huge crowd, and we

"Repent your sins, or the doors to the Kingdom will be closed to you," he called out to the throng. "Come brothers, come sisters, enter the waters of life and be cleansed of the filth that clings to you from your narrow thoughts and selfish deeds!"

We found John thigh-high in the waters of the Jordan. In ones and twos people waded into the rushing waters, while others lined up, awaiting their turn. He placed his right hand on each one's forehead, or sometimes both hands on the temples of the one who stood before him, speaking quietly to them. Some few bent down to immerse themselves in the water, while most fell backwards, as if in a faint. John applied no force causing them to fall, nor did any seem to resist the hand of spirit.

Two strong men, whom we did not know, stood at his side, catching those who fell so they would not be swept away in the current. They righted each one, gently guiding them back to shore, where many sat bewildered.

"Surrender your fears," he continued in between baptisms.

"Repent your sins. Give them over to the Father, who is always forgiving.

"There is no wrong so heinous that it cannot be forgiven.

"Enter into the waters of life."

Long after sunset, in the faint moonlight John turned and walked away. One of the men with him shouted out to the crowd. "Return tomorrow. Come back at sunrise. The Baptist asks you to spend the night in prayer and introspection." And they were gone.

Before we left, we spoke with some of the people who had been in the river with John, asking them to tell us of their experience. "What did he say to you?" asked Mark of one of them.

"He asked what burdened me. He said that what burdens me also burdens the Father. He said the only gift I had that is worthy of the Father was to release these burdens to Him. I spoke them aloud, and when I had done so, the next thing I knew a man had lifted me out of the water and onto the shore." His face shone in the moonlight. "My heart is light, my brother," he said, putting his hands on Mark's shoulders. "I have been washed clean. Go to him tomorrow. You will see for yourself."

When we told Jesus these things, he simply nodded.

"Return to the river tomorrow," he told us. "I will again remain here."

Late in the afternoon the following day a woman shouted out to John. "Are you the Messiah, the anointed one long awaited by our people?"

The crowd hushed to hear his answer. Many had wondered, but feared to ask the question. John's hand dropped from the forehead of an old man who stood before him. His two aids stepped up to keep the man steady.

"I am not the one of whom you speak, not worthy even to fasten his sandals. But he is nearby, and will soon arrive. Prepare yourselves. Surrender your transgressions, forgive your shortcomings. Enter into the waters of life."

He turned back and touched the old man's forehead, who then collapsed into the water. Yet moments later he walked away up the hill, looking as if he had lost twenty years.

Again Jesus listened to our report, saying nothing.

The third day he sent us off to witness John's ministry, and again he was asked if he were the Messiah, the shining one who would bring light into a world of darkness.

"I have told you. I come before him, but I am not he who will lift you up out of the night. I am here to show your fears to you, to expose the sins you have so long hidden, even from yourself. I invite you into the waters to purify yourself. But he soon comes who offers you the waters of eternal life."

The following morning Jesus rose and without a word to any of us began walking toward Jordan. For the first time he seemed unaware of the many people along the road who approached to ask for healing or alms. Even so there was an obvious affect on each of those we passed. They stood straighter, involuntary smiles spreading across their faces, each blessed in his healing light.

As we approached the river, the crowd began to open before us. All eyes turned to Jesus. The silence was overwhelming, after the deafening sound of John's voice which still reverberating between the hills.

We found him standing as before in the deep water. Only his two disciples were with him. Everyone else had withdrawn to the shore. When they saw our approach, the two men backed away until they joined the others on either bank of the river.

When Jesus drew near, John pointed to him with a shout, "Behold, the lamb of God who takes away the sins of the world."

Without hesitation Jesus walked into the water until he stood face to face with his cousin. And then he did a shocking thing. He dropped down on one knee, reaching out his right hand to John's arm to steady himself in the strong current.

John's face, until then radiant as if from an inner fire, suddenly contorted.

"No, stand! It is I who must kneel before you!" he said in an anguished voice, barely loud enough for any but the closest of us to hear.

"No, it has been written. I must first be washed in the rivers of life before I can carry out my Father's will. Baptize me, I ask you."

"No Master, I cannot," pleaded the bearded man. "Do not ask me to do this thing."

Jesus rose and taking both John's arms said, "It is my right to ask, and it is that for which you were born. You are the gatekeeper, and I cannot pass through the gate until you do your part. Without you, it all stops right here. I am beholden to you.

"Baptize me," he repeated.

John took a deep breath, turned his eyes to heaven, lips moving in a silent prayer. Then he nodded and Jesus dropped back down on his knee, the waters rising to his chest.

John's eyes glistened as he spoke the words of blessing. "In the name of the Father, I baptize you, His holy Son, in the One Spirit."

As the two men initiated the *great awakening*, a glorious light rose up and filled the ravine to the tops of the hills, illuminating each man and woman and child. I could not tell the source of this light, whether from the heavens, or from the one who stood below us in the rushing waters.

But he forever reminds us there is just one light, infinite and supreme, shining throughout all creation. We have only to open our eyes and hearts for the river of love to flow abundantly through our lives.

EPILOGUE

I shivered, pulling the shawl tight around my shoulders. The hot sun bore down upon us, but the sight of the two men in the river below filled me with dread.

"What is the matter, Veronica?" James had been hovering protectively around me all morning. He felt it too.

"It has begun," I whispered.

Jesus stood eye to eye with our cousin. John was nearly naked, his matted hair a thicket of brambles jutting out from his head. Jesus tucked his robe into a rope tied round his waist, and lowered himself into the swirling waters. The robe came undone, floated up and twisted about him in the strong current. A gasp rose up from the crowd. John bent down and pulled his cousin to his feet and a wave of dazzling light moved out to fill the ravine, casting itself upon the throng gathered there.

John fell to his knees as if losing consciousness and might have been washed away, had Jesus not grabbed him from the water's pull.

A sharp pain brought me back to myself.

"I am sorry dearest, but we must wait here," said James. The crowd surged into the water, and I must have tried to join them. "It is not our time." James' gentle words challenged, his tight grip on my arm.

The river, now crowded with people became a blur of color and sound behind my tears.

* * * * *

AFTERWORDS

This story's end is really only the beginning. The next book in the series starts out with the baptism, covers the years of Jesus' public ministry, his trial and crucifixion, the time spent with his disciples and others while in a body of light after his resurrection, and ends with the ascension and Pentecost. This book is called *Veronica: Eye Witness to the Ministry of Jesus*.

In this book Jacelyn continues to share memories from her incarnation as Veronica, cousin of Jesus. While the three years of public ministry are documented in the New Testament and certain other accounts, this book offers a new perspective on a narrative that continues to influence the entire Western world to this day. This is a story never before heard, revealing the secret teachings and intimate relationships with Jesus and others, offering a unique view of the crucifixion and resurrection. As in *The Lost Years* her account brings to life the power and significance of the women in Jesus' life.

A third book will trace the lives of a small cadre of disciples during the Jewish diaspora that had already begun by the time of the ascension, and which escalated dramatically when Rome invaded Jerusalem in 70 CE. Few of the followers of Jesus escaped persecution. The majority left Israel, going out into the world to share his teachings. Veronica spends time with Paul and Jesus' mother Mary in what is now Turkey, with Thomas in India, Miriam [Magdalene] in France, and the family of Joseph of Arimathea in Britannia, among others. This book will be available early 2011.

jacelyn@jacelyneckman.com

Books by Jacelyn Eckman

Veronica: The Lost Years of Jesus

Veronica: Eyewitness to the Ministry of Jesus

Veronica: Taking the Message into the World

> Veronica, cousin of Jesus of Nazareth, shares her memories of the time: the studies, travels and eventual ministry of Jesus and the parallel role of the women in his life, without whom his mission would never have come to fruition.

The Spiraling Dance of Creation: The Seasons of our Lives

> Combining the Chinese Taoist and Native American traditions, Jacelyn offers meditations and practices to help the reader become intimate with life's cycles to empower themselves personally and spiritually.

Children of the Light

Children of the Stone

Children of Prophecy

> A trilogy that begins with the final destruction of Atlantis, and follows a small group of survivors as they recover, rebuild and finally reseed human culture. The series ends in modern times as we face the same challenges that brought ruin to that once great land.

The Travel Tree

> An adventure tale involving Sheila, a girl of eleven, who discovers a gateway to other lands and times in a hollow tree near her home.

The Crystal Web

Jacelyn hitchhikes through Latin America and across the U.S. and Canada, encountering strange and wonderful beings and experiences that cannot be explained by ordinary means. It's a grand adventure tale with profound esoteric insights.

Made in the USA
San Bernardino, CA
06 June 2018